THE CRESSWELLS
OF
WINCHMORE HILL

THE CRESSWELLS

OF

WINCHMORE HILL

A Gifted Victorian Family

Peter Hodge

Tears are the showers that fertilise this world;
And memory of things precious keepeth warm
The heart that once did hold them.

Jean Ingelow

Southgate District Civic Trust
1999

To the memory of my dear parents

Published by Southgate District Civic Trust,
64 Houndsden Road, Winchmore Hill, London N21 1LY.

Text © Peter Hodge

ISBN 0 905494 07 5

Typeset in Palatino 10/12. Made and printed in Great Britain by The Local History Press Ltd, 3 Devonshire Promenade, Lenton, Nottingham NG7 2DS.

Contents

Introduction

My interest in the family of Cresswell dates from the early 1960s, when I bought a second-hand copy of the first edition of Henrietta Cresswell's *Winchmore Hill: Memories of a Lost Village* for what was, even then, the absurdly low price of three shillings. As a resident of Winchmore Hill, I was charmed by her poetic descriptions of the mid-Victorian village. Some years later, I saw the fine collection of local drawings and watercolours done by her father, John Cresswell, and now in the care of Forty Hall Museum, Enfield. I recognised that, taken together, the prose and the pictures constituted a valuable portrayal of the locality at a time when it was still no more than a village in the Middlesex countryside.

Here were two talented people who had employed their skills to create a permanent record of the community in which they lived. I began to wonder about the family to which they belonged. It was well known that John Cresswell had served the village as a medical practitioner for half a century, and that Henrietta, like her father, had earned a reputation as an accomplished amateur artist. But where had the family come from? Had any of their forebears left a distinctive mark on *their* generation? Were there similarly gifted contemporaries? What sort of life did the family lead? And what became of the survivors who forsook Winchmore Hill early in the 20th century when the village was being transformed into a suburb of London? This book is the outcome of my search for answers to these questions.

The story begins among the minor gentry of Northumberland seven centuries ago, but I have traced in some detail five generations of one line of the Cresswells from the mid-18th to the mid-20th centuries. Members of this branch of the family settled in Winchmore Hill in the early Victorian era and remained there until the opening years of the 20th century. During this period 13 members of the family lived in Winchmore Hill at one time or another, occupying seven different residences, and others stayed for holidays or were frequent visitors. The narrative is centred on the Winchmore Hill Cresswells, but they were just part of a wider family and can be fully appreciated only in that context. The story therefore extends further in time and place than the strictly local interest might dictate. It could have been written, let us say, from the perspective of the closely related Cresswells resident in Devonshire during the 19th century. Their lives were no less eventful, and deserve attention here not least because of the strong ties of kinship which they enjoyed with their relatives in Winchmore Hill.

Family history is seldom interesting to the outsider unless it assists understanding of the period to which it relates. Subject to the rather limited class boundaries within which the Cresswells moved, I have attempted to use their experiences to illustrate some characteristics of the society in which they lived. In following their fortunes, the world we shall enter is one of country clergy, London lawyers, and medical men. Church, law and medicine were the three professions which, during the late 18th and early 19th centuries, most attracted the sons of well educated, well-to-do gentlemen. Trade and commerce are also represented, though in popular estimation the mercantile class stood one or two rungs lower on the social ladder. The sons of successful professional and city men were expected to follow in their fathers' footsteps, and their daughters were expected to marry into the same occupational class. That is, if they married at all, for spinsters surviving from the Victorian age well into the 20th century, and living on property income and inherited wealth, carry the narrative to its inevitable, sad conclusion.

Creative talent in literature and art flourished through generations of Cresswells. Freed by servants from domestic responsibilities, members of the family, especially unmarried daughters, developed their skills with pen and paintbrush. Other interests, such as botany and handicrafts, were likewise employed to fill long hours of leisure. We are fortunate that some of the fruits of this activity survive.

With a few exceptions, the Cresswells emerge as a close knit family, proud of their ancestry and loyal to their inheritance. One of the very few first-hand recollections of the family that I have been able to secure from surviving contemporaries is of well regarded, benevolent, kindly folk, who nevertheless stood slightly aloof from those around them. With all their talents, abilities and charming eccentricities, it seems that, like Arthur O'Shaughnessy's Music Makers, they dwelt "a little apart from ye".

A genealogical tree of the Cresswells and related families folds out at the end of the book. This shows all those who receive a significant mention in the text, and the years between which most of them lived. For the sake of clarity, forenames and surnames are given in full in each case. This avoids confusion where surnames are used as forenames in succeeding generations. Females who married are identified by their maiden names. The tree extends from 1666 to 1965. Cresswells in direct line of descent who were born before the mid-17th century are listed in Chapter 1. The reader may find it helpful to refer to the tree as the story unfolds.

There are no surviving descendants of this branch of the Cresswell family, and there are now very few people alive who knew any of its members. I have therefore had to rely almost entirely on documentary evidence. I am acutely aware that, where this is lacking, or where I have failed to identify it, important facts may have been missed or only partly understood. For any such shortcomings I take full responsibility. However, I have attempted to pursue thoroughly all lines of enquiry open to me, and wherever I deal with matters on which my research has been inconclusive I explain the uncertainty or lack of knowledge. The problem of incomplete evidence is well expressed in some lines written by one of the last of the Cresswells:

> One of the difficulties which besets the searcher into the byways of history is that no generation explains the obvious. We do not detail to our friends or correspondents familiar facts....all that can be done is by comparison and combination of such evidence as we possess, to offer the most

> reasonable explanation within our powers of matters formerly the com-
> mon knowledge of all concerned.[*]

If the act of publication reveals hitherto undiscovered information, I shall be the first to welcome it.

My sources are indicated either in the text or in the notes to each chapter. Although there is no comprehensive family archive for the Cresswells, there are four primary sources which relate specifically to the family and on which I have drawn widely:

(i) *The Barming Manuscripts of the Reverend Mark Noble* (1802) (including his un-published *History of Barming*), containing much biographical information on his immediate family and on others, such as the Cresswells, to whom he was related. The original is held at the Centre for Kentish Studies, Maidstone; there is a slightly abridged, typescript copy at Barming Rectory.

(ii) The *Liber Cresswellii* (1906), a compilation by Henrietta Cresswell (1855–1931) of family history, stories and pedigrees gathered from many sources. The original manuscript was addressed to her brother Francis, and I have been unable to trace it; there is a transcript by Arthur Willis in the Local History Unit, Enfield Libraries.

(iii) The Cresswell Bequest, left to the Exeter City Library by Beatrix Cresswell (1862–1940), containing books, pictures, maps and manuscripts written, cre-ated or collected by Beatrix. Some of the material is of a biographical nature. The items are deposited in the Westcountry Studies Library, and in the Devon Record Office, both in Exeter.

(iv) The Cresswell botanical collection, comprising albums of specimens, draw-ings and notes assembled by the Reverend Richard Cresswell (1815–1882), including items contributed by other members of the family. It is held at the Royal Albert Memorial Museum, Exeter.

Unless otherwise indicated, basic biographical information has been obtained from birth, marriage and death registrations, wills and population censuses; generally, these sources are not separately identified in the notes. Parish regis-ters and records referred to are located in the parishes concerned unless the name of a repository is shown. Local newspapers have yielded much useful information. I have also made substantial use of published material written by various members of the family. Other sources are too numerous and diverse to mention here.

In describing places as they were at the time the family knew them, I have for the most part refrained from making textual comparisons with their appearance today, relegating such remarks to the notes. Wherever I have drawn attention to the present day scene, in order to emphasise change or the absence of change, the contemporary descriptions offered relate to the time of writing (1992–7). Likewise I have avoided frequent textual references to place-name changes, although these occasionally intrude to assist clarity.

---

[*] Beatrix F. Cresswell, *A Short History of the Worshipful Company of Weavers, Fullers and Shearmen of the City and County of Exeter*, 1930, p.10.

The Cresswell trail has been a fascinating one to follow. It has taken me from London to Kent, Devonshire, the East Midlands, Cumberland, Northumberland and South West Scotland. It has involved many hours of work in libraries and record offices, and has brought me in contact with numerous people who have been generous with the help they have given me. I have derived much pleasure from my discovery of the Cresswells; if any of that pleasure is shared by my readers through the narrative that follows I shall be more than content.

I acknowledge the help received from many archivists, librarians, curators and their staff, and from the clergy who have afforded access to parish records. In addition, I would like to express my gratitude to the following people who have provided information or photographs, or who have invited me to visit properties formerly occupied by members of the Cresswell family: John Schmolle of Barnes; Roger Chappell, Dr. John Earl and Vivienne Everett of Barrow-upon-Soar; Mrs. D. Farley of Clapham; Tricia Whiteaway of Dawlish; Gordon Little of Dumfries; Peter Faulkner of Exeter; Elizabeth Milewicz of Hobart, Tasmania; Jennifer Leatham of Ipswich; Roger Willson of Loughborough; Hugh Ellison, Jeremy Godwin and Jean Robinson of Penrith; John Grange and John Reed of Teignmouth; Thomas Coulthard, Mary Craig, Mrs. H. Eccles and Elizabeth Walton of Watermillock; David Hicks, James Thomson, Peter West and Gillian Western of Winchmore Hill. My thanks are due also to Stanley Smith of Winchmore Hill for reading through my text and offering many helpful suggestions for improvement.

Permission to reproduce illustrations or maps is acknowledged to the following: Alan Godfrey Maps, p.102; All Saints Church, Watermillock, p.229; British Library, pp.62, 67, 121; Centre for Kentish Studies, Maidstone, pp.19, 27; Enfield Libraries, pp.72, 74, 78, 111, 138, 154; Forty Hall Museum, Enfield, pp.60, 97, 98, 143, front and back covers; Guildhall Library, Corporation of London, pp.18, 31, 32, 33, 107; Jennifer Leatham, pp.172, 238; Leicestershire Museums, Arts and Records Service, pp.14, 196; London Metropolitan Archives, pp.40, 66, 123; Royal Albert Memorial Museum, Exeter, pp.76, 113; St. John the Baptist's Church, Holland Road, Kensington, pp.169, 208; St. Margaret's Church, Barming, p.20; St. Paul's School, Winchmore Hill, pp.70, 188; Southgate District Civic Trust, pp.61, 101; Westcountry Studies Library (Devon Library Service), Exeter, pp.12, 22, 83, 84, 159. In addition, acknowledgment is made to the Ordnance Survey for the maps reproduced on pp.61, 102 and 215. All other illustrations are from photographs taken by the author or in the author's collection.

Publication of this book has been dependent on the support of Southgate District Civic Trust, most particularly in the form of financial assistance from the bequest of the late Hilda Bocock, a member of the Trust and resident of Winchmore Hill who loved the district and the study of its history.

PETER HODGE

Winchmore Hill, London
April 1999

CHAPTER 1

Cresswell of Cresswell

My Love dwelt in a Northern land.
A gray tower in a forest green
Was hers, and far on either hand
The long wash of the waves was seen,
And leagues and leagues of yellow sand,
The woven forest boughs between.

Andrew Lang

Ancestral Home

Overlooking the broad sweep of Druridge Bay, on the Northumberland coast, stands a grey, stone, battlemented tower. It is sheltered on three sides by weather-beaten trees, whose seaward branches have been stripped bare in North Sea gales. Tower and trees are enclosed within an ivy-capped boundary wall, inter-rupted at one point by a pedimented doorway. From the trees, rooks fly up and circle over the battlements, their raucous cries mingling with the sound of wind and waves.

This sturdy pele tower is the ancient home of the Cresswells of Cresswell, a Northumberland family whose ancestry can be traced back at least as far as the reign of King John (1199–1216). The tower, dating from the late 13th century, is a fine example of a fortified mansion house. From a vaulted byre on the ground floor, a circular stone staircase gives access to two upper rooms. Within a turret at the north east corner there is said to be a rough inscription reading "William Cresswell, brave hero".[1]

It is no surprise that this sombre ruin should have attached to it the legend of a ghostly apparition — the White Lady of Cresswell. The daughter of one of the medieval barons of Cresswell planned to marry a Danish prince, but her three brothers hated him for his foreign blood. One day, as the prince rode towards the tower to visit his lover, her brothers attacked him with swords and spears, inflicting mortal wounds. The young girl witnessed this event from the top of the tower, was driven instantly mad, and threw herself from the tower to her death. On the anniversary of this tragedy, a lady dressed in white is said to appear on the roof of the tower, pacing to and fro and shading her eyes as she looks out for the prince's arrival. Below, the sound of a horse's hooves is heard approaching, followed by an agonised cry of despair.[2] In due course the reader will discover that, centuries later, a descendant of the Cresswells of Cresswell was to meet her death in a similar fashion.

Cresswell Nothumberland. 1809.

Cresswell, Northumberland, in 1809, from a watercolour in an album belonging to Henrietta Noble, daughter of the Reverend Mark Noble. The 13th century pele tower of the Cresswells is on the left; adjoining it is their late 17th century residence, of which only the pedimented doorway survives. The tower is now sheltered on three sides by trees, but the view across Druridge Bay remains broad and open.

Adjacent to the pele tower is the village of Cresswell, separated from the sea by a ridge of grass-covered sand dunes, and neatly disposed around a wide expanse of green. Trim, stone-built cottages, erected for estate workers, still overlook the green, but their inhabitants no longer serve the family whose name their village perpetuates. The church of St. Bartholomew, consecrated in 1836, was built for the owners and employees of the Cresswell estate. The neo-Norman building contains two stained-glass windows showing the family coat of arms including corn sheaves and squirrels. A squirrel, worked in stone, also appears on some of the estate buildings in the village.

The doorway in the wall surrounding the pele tower is now blocked. At one time it was the entrance to a house which superseded the tower as the family seat in the late 17th century. Writing in about 1800, the Reverend Mark Noble said: "the present residence built near the old Tower....is not very desirable — yet his Highness the Duke of Gloucester some few years ago asked for the use of it for a little time, and returned thanks to the present owner of it".[3] In the early 1820s the house was replaced by a fine sandstone mansion, built a short distance inland. This was to be the last Cresswell Hall. Its impressive interior was richly decorated, and furnished with tapestries, Classical ornaments and other *objets d'art*. A large conservatory housed exotic plants including tree-ferns. The grounds, planted with magnificent avenues of evergreen shrubs, contained the enormous vertebrae of a whale stranded at Lynemouth in 1822, and specimens of fossil tree trunks recovered from the shore nearby.[4]

The only surviving fragment of the last Cresswell Hall — a massive sandstone stable block — stands today in dense woodland about half a mile inland. Trees and undergrowth reach to the very walls; bushes and saplings push up through the floors of the gutted interior, now open to the sky. A once imposing clock tower, clockless now but for a few numerals on one face, rises above the ruined walls. A soaring, arched entrance, spanned by rusting iron gates, leads to nowhere. No stable yard, no horses, no carriages driving past to the great house; for the great house has gone, and this sad relic, built to impress but now overwhelmed by nature, moulders away in the encroaching wood.

The Pedigree

The Cresswells of Cresswell were minor gentry but of ancient descent. The first recorded name is that of Robert de Cresswell in the early 13th century. The Reverend Mark Noble lists the male heirs through whom the estate passed during the 13th and 14th centuries — Robert, Simon, Roger, Robert, Alexander and John — and records that John's son, John de Cresswell, owned the castle during the reign of Henry V (1413–1422).[5] His son George is the first name on the earliest official Cresswell pedigree, at the College of Arms, though no dates are given.[6] However, *Burke* states that he was on the Commission of Peace for Tynemouth in 1509.[7] His heir, Robert Cresswell, married Elizabeth, daughter of Sir Thomas Lumley, of Lumley Castle, Chester-le-Street. Her mother was Elizabeth Plantagenet, illegitimate daughter of King Edward IV. So the Cresswells could claim illegitimate descent from the royal house of Plantagenet, "if it can be accounted an honour".[8]

After Robert Cresswell, the male line continued through Oswin (died 1569), John (1562–1599), John (1588–1673), William (1635–1698) and William (1666–1750).[9] This latter William heads the genealogical tree at the end of the book. He married Dorothy Stafford, the daughter of a clergyman,[10] and there were 11 children of the marriage.[11] The first son, Robert, was an adherent to the Jacobite cause in the 1745 rebellion, for which he was attainted of high treason and forfeited his estate.[12] The second son, William, inherited the estate, and through him the inheritance has continued to the present.[13] The third son, Henry, was born *c.*1700, and it is with his descendants that the remainder of this narrative will chiefly be concerned. The eight other children were daughters.[14]

"Our hardy ancestors faced the north east winds at the gateway of the ancient keep", wrote Henrietta Cresswell in 1905; "it is hardly possible to imagine a bleaker situation".[15] Still today the visitor may stand on the lonely, windswept shore below the Cresswell Tower, and, as sea, sky and flat coastline merge in a grey mist, experience a sense of timelessness which seems to bring closer the ancient Cresswells, their legends and their inheritance.

CHAPTER 2

Town and Country

London Lawyers

It is now time to introduce the family of Cheslyn, of Langley Hall, near Diseworth, Leicestershire. Richard Cheslyn (1634–1717), a London metal-founder, bought the property in 1686, and it remained in the family until 1847.[1] Richard was married four times. His first two wives died without issue, his third had three sons, and his fourth two sons. The Langley inheritance passed through one of the latter. The second son of the third marriage was Richard, who married Elizabeth Rock. Their first son was also christened Richard, and it is he who appears at the head of the genealogical tree.[2]

This Richard Cheslyn (*c*.1700–1761) entered the legal profession. In 1727 he became a proctor in the Court of Arches, an ecclesiastical court of the Archbishop of Canterbury at Doctors' Commons in London.[3] He married Mary Courtney, and they had four sons and three daughters. The third daughter was

Langley Hall, Leicestershire, home of the Cheslyn family, who were linked by marriage with the Cresswells in the mid-18th century. This engraving, c.1795, is reproduced from J. Nichols, History and Antiquities of the County of Leicester. *The house still stands.*

christened Sarah. Her marriage to Henry Cresswell (*c*.1700–1775) created the link with the Leicestershire Cheslyns which was to be a source of pride to later generations of Cresswells.

Richard Cheslyn resided at Doctors' Commons, but also had a house at Hackney.[4] He died in April 1761 and is buried in the churchyard of All Hallows, Tottenham, "much esteemed for his honesty [and] friendly disposition". Buried with him are his eldest daughter Charlotte, his second daughter Mary (who predeceased him by 11 days), his grandfather Thomas Rock (also a proctor in the Court of Arches), and his mother Elizabeth.[5]

Richard's son-in-law Henry Cresswell, third and youngest son of William Cresswell of Cresswell, had left his family home on the bleak Northumberland coast and had moved south to pursue a career in law. He resided at different times at Staples Inn, Holborn, at Marsham Street, Westminster, and at Doctors' Commons, near St. Paul's. He became an attorney, and undertook the defence of 21 of Prince Charles Edward's followers in 1745, a cause espoused by his elder brother Robert. Seventeen of these men were acquitted, and as an expression of their gratitude presented Henry with a diamond cluster ring. This was handed down through the family, and came to be known as the "rebel ring". The last Cresswell to own it was a great-great-great-grand-daughter of Henry.[6]

According to the Bigland pedigree, dated 1731, Henry Cresswell was first married to Rebecca, daughter of John Beeson of Surrey. No children of the marriage are shown.[7] By the time he married Sarah Cheslyn he would have been well into middle age, possibly over 50, as their only son Richard Cheslyn Cresswell was born *c*.1754. (They also had a daughter Charlotte, who did not marry.) Sarah was some 20 years younger than Henry, who was about the same age as her father. Her husband and her father both practised law, and both at one time lived at Doctors' Commons. So it is probable that Henry met Sarah through professional contact with her father.

Henry also had a country estate at Windsor. After the accession of King George III in 1760, part of this estate was required for the lengthening of the Long Walk at Windsor Castle. Henry could have obtained an inflated price for the land, but he took pride in asking no more than its market value, not wishing to drive a hard bargain with his sovereign.[8]

In 1761, following Richard Cheslyn's death a few days after that of his daughter Mary, Henry and Sarah Cresswell began litigation against Sarah's brothers Richard and Edward over the terms of their father's will. Since the will had not been altered after Mary's death, Henry and Sarah claimed an interest in Mary's portion of the estate which Richard and Edward, as executors, had denied them. Henry and Sarah took their case to the High Court of Chancery, and the Lord High Chancellor decreed in their favour in March 1762. An appeal against the decree was dismissed in February 1763.[9]

Henry Cresswell died in March 1775, Sarah in September 1782. Mark Noble records that they were both buried in a vault at Tottenham; this may have been the Cheslyn family vault, although the inscription does not mention them.[10]

Henry's son, Richard Cheslyn Cresswell, also became a lawyer. In Septem-

ber 1768, at the tender age of 14, he entered the office of his uncle, Edward
Cheslyn, who had been one of the respondents in the disputed will case five
years earlier. Edward was a proctor in the Court of Arches at Doctors' Commons, and the young Richard served as his clerk for seven years. In April 1775
(a month after his father's death) he was created a public notary, and in October
of the same year, at the age of 21, was himself admitted as a proctor in the Court
of Arches.[11] About six years later he married Mary Whitfield, daughter of the
Reverend Henry Whitfield (1731–1819). The Whitfields were a clerical family
who had held the living of Bradwell, Gloucestershire, for several generations.
At the time of his daughter's marriage, Henry Whitfield was Rector of Rushall,
Wiltshire, and Vicar of Bedfont, Middlesex.[12] Richard Cheslyn Cresswell earned
a reputation as a knowledgeable and fair-minded lawyer, who "was thought to
understand the practice of the Courts better than any other man of his time
and....was always willing to give information in a polite and satisfactory manner".[13]

Doctors' Commons, in which the Cresswells were now becoming established,
had evolved from a society of ecclesiastical lawyers who had organised themselves in a collegiate manner on similar lines to the medieval college of priests
known as Jesus Commons in the City of London. The lawyers were doctors of
law, and their common hall or dining table was known as "commons", so the
term Doctors' Commons came to be used by their society. The date of its foundation is uncertain, but it probably originated in the early 16th century. In time
the name was also applied collectively to the courts in which the doctors practised, and eventually was used to describe the area to the south of St. Paul's
Churchyard in which the courts and their associated offices and residences were
situated.[14]

The courts which sat in Doctors' Commons were chiefly concerned with those
disparate branches of law later referred to as "probate, divorce and admiralty".
Testamentary, matrimonial and family matters, as well as church affairs, had
from the middle ages been the concern of ecclesiastical courts, whose practice
was greatly influenced by Roman (or "civil") law. The ecclesiastical courts which
eventually were brought together at Doctors' Commons were the Court of Arches
(the Provincial Court of the Archbishop of Canterbury), the Consistory Court of
the Bishop of London, the Prerogative Court of Canterbury (which heard testamentary cases), the Court of Delegates (which heard appeals in ecclesiastical
causes), and the Court of Faculties (which granted faculties, licences and dis-
pensations). To these was added the Court of Admiralty, created in the 14th
century to try maritime cases, and also deriving much of its practice from Roman law. It was this dependence on the rules of civil law which united the diverse elements, creating a breed of lawyers known as "civilians" who gained a
monopoly of aspects of the law in which they had expertise. This specialisation
was in time concentrated in the society of lawyers at Doctors' Commons and in
the courts which sat there.[15]

The lawyers who practised in these courts were proctors and advocates. The
proctors were more numerous, performing duties in the ecclesiastical and mari-

time courts similar to those undertaken by attornies and solicitors in the courts of common law and equity. When appearing in the Court of Arches they wore black gowns and fur-lined hoods, or academical hoods if they were graduates. As well as preparing cases for litigation, they handled a substantial amount of probate business which was a valuable source of income.

The functions of advocates were comparable with those of barristers in the common law courts. They were retained as counsel or pleaders, and cases were decided on the basis of pleadings and proofs offered by the advocates, as there was no jury. They were required to take the degree of Doctor of Civil Law (DCL) at Oxford or Cambridge, and were obliged to refrain from practising in the courts for one year from the date of their admission (the "silent year"). They were allocated a seat in court to the right or left of the judge. In the Court of Arches they wore wigs and scarlet robes, with hoods lined with taffety (if from Oxford) or white miniver fur (if from Cambridge). In the other courts they wore black gowns. Both proctors and advocates were admitted by petition made to the Archbishop of Canterbury and on receipt of his fiat. The petition would state the experience and qualifications of the petitioner and the grounds on which he sought admission.[16]

The society of lawyers at Doctors' Commons was open only to the doctors of law. This position was formalised in June 1768 (just three months before the young Richard Cheslyn Cresswell started work in his uncle's office), when the society was legally incorporated by Royal Charter as "The College of Doctors of Law exercent in the Ecclesiastical and Admiralty Courts". This formally limited membership of the College to those who had taken their DCL and had been admitted as advocates of the Court of Arches.[17]

The association between the Cresswells and Doctors' Commons, begun during the second half of the 18th century, was to be maintained by a younger generation of the family well into the 19th century. The first of this generation was Richard Henry Cresswell, eldest son of Richard Cheslyn Cresswell. He was born in 1782 into the enclosed world of ecclesiastical lawyers in the shadow of St. Paul's Cathedral, and it was natural that he should follow his father into the profession. He had the advantage of a first-class education, entering Trinity College, Oxford from Winchester College in 1799. Two years later, whilst still at Oxford, he was admitted to Lincoln's Inn. In 1806 he became Bachelor of Civil Law, was called to the Bar in the following year, and became a Doctor of Civil Law in 1810.[18] With these qualifications he was able to proceed to admission as an advocate in the Court of Arches, and this took place, on completion of his DCL, in July 1810.[19] In the same year he was admitted to the College of Advocates at Doctors' Commons, having reached a higher rank in the profession than his father.[20] His success was clouded only by the death of his mother, Mary Cresswell, in April 1809.

During his first "year of silence" as an advocate, Richard Henry Cresswell would have found it difficult to earn a living. In common with most other newly admitted members of the college, he would at first have relied on his father to support him financially. It is not surprising, therefore, that the majority of advo-

DOCTORS COMMONS.

The common hall and court room of Doctors' Commons, London, by Thomas Rowlandson and Auguste Pugin, 1808, from Rudolph Ackermann, The Microcosm of London. *The advocates are seated on the upper bench, beside the judge; the proctors, in their fur hoods, sit below. The coats of arms of the advocates are displayed on the side wall.*

cates at this time came from wealthy families, many of them landed gentry entitled to bear arms. The young Richard enjoyed this privilege, as he was descended from the Northumberland Cresswells through the male line. Each advocate was permitted to have his arms displayed in the common hall of Doctors' Commons, and Richard exercised this privilege. His arms were painted on 9th July 1810, just eight days after his admission, by Thomas Sharp, herald painter.[21] The coats of arms are clearly visible in an engraving of the common hall by Thomas Rowlandson and Auguste Pugin, but as this was published in 1808 they would not then have included Richard Henry Cresswell's. The engraving also shows clearly the advocates sitting to the right and left of the judge, and the proctors in their fur hoods below. Whether Richard Cheslyn Cresswell is amongst the proctors shown here we shall never know.[22]

It followed from the position of their families in the social order that many of the advocates were the sons of professional gentlemen — if not lawyers then probably clergymen. Only a few were the sons of tradesmen, who would most likely have been influential men of business in the City. As fees payable by the advocates increased with the rank of their father, a few did not admit to being the sons of gentlemen, describing themselves as "plebeian".[23] For Richard Henry Cresswell, born into the profession and proud of his inheritance, such dissimulation would have been neither possible nor acceptable.

During term time, the advocates resided in London, and dined together at Doctors' Commons whenever the Court of Arches was sitting. Outside law terms they might retire to a country home to be with their families.[24] For Richard Henry Cresswell, this meant a journey of some 35 miles to the rich, agricultural countryside of the Medway Valley near Maidstone.

The Fruitful Valley

In the early 19th century, the environs of Maidstone were home to several families whose names occur in the Cresswell genealogy. They appear at one time or another in the villages of Barming, East Farleigh, Loose, Boughton Monchelsea and West (or Town) Malling. Today the names of these people would be unfamiliar in the green and fertile country of the Medway Valley — with one possible exception. The Reverend Mark Noble, Rector of Barming from 1786 to 1827, has earned a small place in history through the collection of biographical and genealogical works which he wrote during his 40 years as a country clergyman.

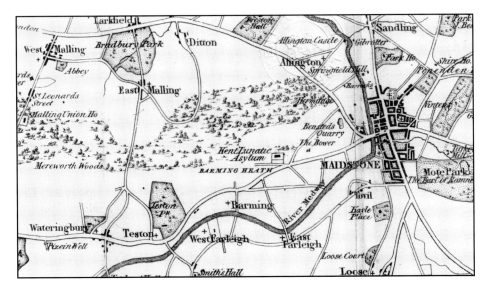

"Cresswell Country" — Maidstone and the Medway Valley in the early 19th century. Barming, East Farleigh, Loose and West Malling were all homes to the Cresswells during this period. From Topography of Maidstone and its Environs, *pub. J. Smith, Maidstone, 1839.*

The Reverend Mark Noble (1754–1827) as a young man. Reproduced from a copy of a portrait found with the typescript of Mark Noble's Barming Manuscripts *at Barming Rectory. This is not the portrait by Sherwin referred to in the text.*

Mark Noble was the fifth son of William Heatley Noble, a Birmingham tradesman "handsome in his person and a man of strict integrity".[25] Mark, born in 1754, was one of at least 20 children of the same marriage, only seven of whom survived infancy. He was a delicate child, and was once left for dead in his cradle. For two years of his childhood he lived with his grandfather at Solihull, and was later sent away to boarding school. He returned to live with his mother on the death of his father in 1767, then attended a grammar school at Sutton Coldfield. A year and a half later he transferred to a private tutor who taught only writing and arithmetic. Mark was so reluctant to enter commerce that he refused to learn arithmetic, and in later life relied on others to do any but the simplest calculations for him.

Mark had no university education, but instead learnt the basic skills required in a solicitor's office. At the age of 17 he was articled to a solicitor with a large practice in Birmingham, but "sowed his wild oats and spent his time alternately in study and dissipation". At length he became engaged to Sarah Pratchett, descended from an old Shropshire family, and married her in 1776. He had not then completed his articles, and the couple continued to live in Birmingham. As time went by he grew to dislike the legal profession, and made up his mind to study for Holy Orders.

He received tuition from the Reverend John Grant, second master of King Edward VI Free Grammar School in Birmingham. He had already developed an interest in the study of literature and history, and was elected a Fellow of the Society of Antiquaries on 1st March 1781. On 23rd December of the same year he was ordained deacon by the Bishop of Gloucester in the Chapel Royal at St. James's. Through the influence of a friend he had been offered curacies at Baddesley Clinton and Packwood, Warwickshire, and commenced his ministry on Christmas Day 1781. Less than three months later the rector of these parishes died — an event not altogether unexpected — and Mark Noble was presented to the livings. He was ordained priest by the Bishop of Hereford in Hereford Cathedral on 2nd April 1782, after little more than three months in deacon's orders. Both his parishes were actually in the Diocese of Lichfield, and he was their first resident priest. Although he came from a modest background and had limited education, his early preferment illustrates what could be achieved with influential friends.

At this time, Noble and his wife lived in a large old country house at nearby Knowle, which they were able to maintain on the income from the two parishes. Later they were given, rent free, a more modern house in Packwood parish on the road between Birmingham and Warwick. Whilst living here, Noble wrote his earliest and most ambitious historical work — *Memoirs of the Protectorate-House of Cromwell*, published in 1784. This book introduced him to Lord Sandwich, who was a great admirer of it.

Noble cultivated his connections with the nobility. He was appointed domestic chaplain to Lord Leicester, and on his recommendation and that of Lord Sandwich was offered the valuable living of Barming. He became rector in March 1786, but did not reside in the parish until the autumn of that year. For the first two years he lived in a small house in the village, as the parsonage was uninhabitable.[26] Although he could have retained the Warwickshire livings after taking Barming, he decided to resign them, and the Bishop of Lichfield and Coventry "by letter expressed his concern for parting with so respectable a clergyman from his diocese".[27]

When he came to Barming, Noble was faced with a parish in physical and spiritual decline:

> Nothing could have a more melancholy appearance than Barming at my taking possession of it. Half the inhabitants never came within the church. The clerical character at the lowest ebb. The Parsonage house reduced to one degree above the poorest residence of the village hind. The land ill cultivated. The church and chancel out of repair, and the cemetery fences on two sides down.

The new rector set about the task of restoration with vigour. He had the chancel repaired, gave an altar piece, table and rails, a press for the surplice, and a pulpit cloth and cushion. The pulpit and reading desk were painted. Later the tower was partitioned from the church, and the seats were repaired, lined and painted. "The pleasure I have had in making the sacred edifice a fit house of prayer and procuring the parish to second my efforts is more than a little." When further repairs were undertaken in 1815, a flight of steps leading to the former rood loft was uncovered, but "being ill with gout I unfortunately could not go to examine the Discovery".

His work on the parsonage was yet more extensive. When he arrived he found "a mean dwelling hid in a profusion of rubbish, trees and brambles....the ruin of the old part of the house was heaped so high that the trees growing upon it reached to the top of the roofing of that which was standing....it defies all suitable words". He tried to obtain leave from the Lord High Chancellor, Crown patron of the living, to secure money available under act of parliament to rebuild clerical residences, but this was refused owing to the value of the living. Nonetheless, within a few years he had rebuilt the house according to his own design and had relaid the gardens:

Barming Parsonage, 1813, as restored by the Reverend Mark Noble. Reproduced from a watercolour in the album of Henrietta Noble.

> No spot has been more changed; no part of the house nor of the land near
> it is the same as I found it....in fine from 1788 to 1800 from the trees grow-
> ing up, the house completed, the place is become from a cottage in a wil-
> derness to a most desirable residence.[28]

In the *Barming Manuscripts* there is a drawing of the parsonage made by Mark
Noble's eldest son after his father's restoration. It shows clearly the addition
made by the rector, its Georgian doorway and sash windows contrasting with
the diamond-paned casements of the older part. According to the caption, these
were later replaced with sashes to match.

Mark and Sarah Noble had 11 children over a period of 20 years. After the
birth of their last child in 1796, the rector conveniently entered all their names
and places of baptism in the parish register, believing that there should be a
record in one place of children baptised in several different parishes. There were
four boys and seven girls. Two children died in infancy, and four more did not
survive their father. The last four to be born, all girls, were baptised at Barming,
private baptism at home being followed some time later by a public ceremony
in church. This custom was usually followed when infants were delicate at birth.
Two of Mark Noble's children privately baptised at Barming — Henrietta and
Christiana — did in fact live to old age, and they are the only two who have any

further place in the Cresswell story.[29] Henrietta, known as Henri to her brothers and sisters, was born in 1790; Christiana, known as Kitty, was born six years later "to rule all her elders with a rod of iron".[30]

In 1803 Mark Noble completed his *History of Barming*, which remained unpublished after his death owing to its many indiscreet references to people then living. This work, executed in the author's neat handwriting, is a curious blend of factual description, personal reminiscence, comment and anecdote, and displays all too clearly his imperfect command of English grammar, syntax and spelling.[31]

It opens with a preface, dated 14th March 1802. In it the author indicates that publication was not intended, at least during his lifetime: "I write....not for the public perusal, but my own satisfaction; committing to paper what would soon be forgotten, or imperfectly remembered". He acknowledges that Barming can boast few illustrious families or great events, but claims that even the most trivial particulars are of interest to local residents. The preface concludes with this exhortation:

> Oh! Barming, strewed by nature's lavish hand with innumerable flowers,
> yet thy wicked neighbours have thrown into the clerical path many a thorn,
> I love thee passionately. Mayst thou flourish when I am gone. May thy
> land yield her full increase. May thy inhabitants be respectable for their
> united piety and virtue!

The work continues with a description and general history of the parish of Barming. At times the writing is florid:

> In the valley the Medway winds his silent, deep, and silvery stream: the
> trickling rills, bursting from their rocky beds, glide into and swell the
> river as it passes; the luxuriant meadows, bespangled with many a beau-
> tiful flower fringing its banks, the fine hanging woods of spreading oaks
> or lofty elms, terminating in the whitened church, and elegantly tapered
> spire....the beautiful village, the handsome residences of its gentry, the
> good houses of the farmers, and the neat dwellings of the cottagers, render
> it the most charming spot of this enchanting valley, no wonder that they
> boast that as Kent is the garden of England, so Barming is that of Kent.

Noble mentions an eight-fold increase in the acreage of hops in the area over the previous 50 years, and the growing of ash, chestnut and willow as the most durable wood for hop poles. He refers to a sudden thaw of the Medway after the snowfall of January 1795, the flooding of houses to first-floor level, and the appearance of boats in the streets of Maidstone.

Then comes a section on Barming Church: "nothing can be more beautiful than the appearance of this structure in so charming a country, surrounded on three sides by elms". The building is described as Gothic, of Kentish ragstone, with irregularly spaced windows and a handsome tower surmounted by a shingled spire. Noble refers to the three bells in the tower, a feature common to other churches in the neighbourhood which had earned it the name "Three-bell-vale".

The author then gives short biographies of the rectors of Barming, concluding with his own which he modestly prefaces with the words "I feel it embarrassing to make myself the subject of my own pen. My life has been eventful". This section includes the account of how he rebuilt the parsonage.

The remainder of the work describes the estates in Barming, their owners and their occupants, lists some of the inhabitants, their houses and their cottages, and contains an abundance of information on parish offices, parish and county ratings, and other local detail. The author's own preoccupations intrude from time to time: in 1792, for example, he records that "the road to the Parsonage was impassable for carriages without danger, and the Rector could not without coming to extremities get it mended".

The manuscript includes a number of illustrations, some drawn by Noble himself. The frontispiece is a portrait of the author as a young man in clerical attire, engraved by J.K. Sherwin. The church, the parsonage, and other local buildings are depicted, and there is a plan of the parish. Some pages are decorated with ornamental flourishes in the style of the period, and beneath his preface the author has drawn a two-wheeled conveyance pulled by a bird and guided by a grasshopper, with the legend "Great Attempts Deserve Great Designs". Genealogies of local families (including the Cresswells) are bound into the volume.

The personal allusions to local residents which caused Noble's executors to withhold publication say as much about the character of the author as about the frailties and misdemeanours of those he reproved. Although he did not intend the manuscript to be published, it is clear from the preface that he was untroubled by the possibility that the contents of the work might be revealed after his passing:

> In whosoever hands this may fall, when I am numbered with dead, will be shocked at the vices of many persons I have mentioned, but if men will commit sin, they must expect that others will notice it. I have ever written my genuine sentiments, neither flattering nor vilifying any one. Most who are noticed were to me perfect strangers, many lived before I knew the place. I could gain nothing by praising or blaming them. Those who survive me can neither serve, nor injure me for what they can never know until I am beyond all human reach.

Noble's comments on some of his parishioners may have been influenced by their lack of respect for him as an incomer, unaccustomed to country ways:

> The people in an underhand manner were taught to insult me openly, though I had given them not the least provocation....the neighbouring clergy were totally unacquainted with every kind of business. So I could derive no knowledge. I had eyes and I used them; my ears too were open.

> I soon learnt all that it was necessary to know, that I was every way im-
> posed upon.

It quickly became clear to him that the source of much of this opposition was
the Amhurst family, who owned land in and around the village.[32] The brothers
John and Stephen Amhurst were "vowing persecution against the new rector be
he whomsoever he would. A total stranger to the country, its customs,
unacquainted with agriculture, having never had more than would keep my
riding horses and two cows in Warwickshire, judge of my perplexity". John
Amhurst "wished to drive me from the parish and then prosecute me for non-
residence....once he said that the clergy were the greatest pests of society".
Noble regarded him as "a gloomy disagreeable man. Rude when unprovoked
even to women". Although he was on slightly better terms with Stephen, he had
little time for either of them:

> Their whole conduct was artifice....the farmers and labourers were their
> tools. They were so illiterate that neither of them could write a sentence
> grammatically or spell the words properly. Their deficiency this way is
> scarcely credible. Such were the petty tyrants of this fruitful valley.

Noble confesses that he was "hurt but not daunted". In time he was able to
show, through the improvements undertaken at Barming, that he was equal to
the task with which he had been confronted:

> The living from being an inferior one is become inferior to few in Kent. So
> little did the Amhursts think me capable of such exertions that they told
> me that *I was not a man of business*. They have been cruelly disappointed,
> having rendered myself and my successors independent.

Mark Noble's opinions of some of the humbler residents were no less censo-
rious. His judgment on one of them will serve as an example:

> Mrs. Stede pretended to be of good descent, but I suggest it was only
> pretence. She was an abandoned vixen. Besides her Lordly Paramour, who
> had intrigued with several others.

Comments such as this are not confined to the *History of Barming*. In the 18th
century it was quite usual for clergy to enter in burial registers some remarks
upon the character of the deceased. They could do so in the knowledge that
these were unlikely to be read, especially in rural parishes where many of the
people were illiterate. Noble followed this custom with enthusiasm, and his
remarks about some of the late parishioners of Barming would have caused
great offence if seen and understood by their families.

Take John Goodinge, gentleman, for example, who died in 1791 at the age of 36:

> Vexations of various kinds and a most immoderate use of spirituous liq-
> uors, with most violent gusts of passion threw him into a decline, and he
> died neglected and almost totally abandoned by his wife, an object of filth
> and nastiness almost devoured with that kind of vermin that is the con-
> stant attendant upon poverty and wretchedness.

The entry continues with a reference to the weakness of the poor man's mental
condition, but acknowledges that he had been "good natured, fond of his children, kind to his domestics and benevolent to the poor".

The death of a penitent sinner after a long illness was considered worthy of
particular comment. Of William Bridgeland, aged 80, the rector wrote in 1795:

> As he had been a publican so he was also a sinner. Few have been so
> wicked; he was blasphemous, lewd, drunken, dishonest, a cruel husband,
> and a severe parent....but it pleased God in his mercy to give him a long
> and most severe visitation, the Bible then was his only solace and he seemed
> sincerely penitent for his abandoned life. May it have sealed his peace!

Richard Day died in 1799 at the age of 72. He had been a churchwarden and
tenant of the glebe lands of Barming under Mark Noble, "to whom he returned
evil for good, at the expense of his honesty". But he gave "undeniable proofs of
knowing better, by the open avowal of his belief in the Christian religion".

Virtue and clean living were sometimes rewarded with wholly complimentary remarks. Alexander Selby, 23-year-old son of a Barming resident, and a
tradesman in Southwark at the time of his death in 1791, "shewed himself sober,
industrious, and every way deserving commendation". Joseph Farleigh, who
died in the same year aged 79, was employed by a neighbouring landowner
"and superintended all his farming concerns in this parish with punctuality and
skill, and though he could neither write nor read yet no one kept a more faithful
account". He relied on a neighbour to write out the monthly accounts for his
master.

Although the entries in the register include expressions such as "the profli-
gacy of the lower orders", praise and blame are apportioned regardless of social
status. Indeed, it is clear from his *History of Barming* that Mark Noble could be
as uncompromising in his criticism of the landed gentry of the parish as of the
humblest villager. The certainty that God's dreadful judgment would be visited
on the unrepentant sinner, rich or poor, is always present.

In March 1811, John Baker, a 16-year-old footman to Richard Cheslyn
Cresswell of Barming, was buried by permission of coroner's warrant, "having
died very suddenly, and as it appeared, by the visitation of God....a warning
this to the young and strong not to trust to what may in a moment disappoint".[33]

Richard Cheslyn Cresswell and his wife Mary came to Barming in about
1807. By this time they had seven children. In addition to Richard Henry, whose
early career we have already noted, there were William, Frances Mary, Harriet,
Henry Whitfield, Robert Nathaniel and Maria. Two others, Charlotte and John

The Seal of M & F Mary Cresswell & now 1808 the Residence of her Father Richard Cheslyn Cresswell

The Cresswells' home on Barming Heath, 1808, drawn by Richard Henry Cresswell (1782–1818). Reproduced from the Reverend Mark Noble's unpublished History of Barming.

Scott, had not survived infancy, and James had died at the age of 10 in 1803. The Cresswell family home on Barming Heath, to the north of the village, was known to Mark Noble as Steed's House. Samuel Steed, the first owner, had died in 1761. It was a "pretty neat modern house" with two and a half acres of land on the west side of the heath, and was left to Richard Cresswell's daughter Frances Mary, together with other property in the area, by her uncle Robert Whitfield, who died suddenly of a fit in 1806.[34]

Richard Cheslyn Cresswell made several improvements to Steed's House: "he obtained leave to enclose a small piece of land by it, part of Barming Heath, which with some other alterations judiciously made, has made it a very elegant small residence". The out-houses were rebuilt, and a new garden and wall added on three sides "at very considerable expense".[35] A drawing of the house made in 1808 by his son Richard Henry, and included in the *Barming Manuscripts*, shows a two-storey, double-fronted house of three bays with pitched roof and dormer windows, well shaded by mature trees.

Other pictures of Barming and its surroundings at this time are preserved in an album of paintings and sketches compiled by Mark Noble's daughter Henrietta. They include charming views of Barming Church and Parsonage, and a windmill on Barming Heath. They are unsigned, but display considerable artistic skill, and may well have been by Henrietta herself. The album was destined, in later years, to contain work by the Cresswell family also, and we shall return to it in due course.[36]

Shortly after the Cresswells' arrival at Barming, Mark Noble wrote to Henrietta, then staying with her cousin in Essex: "as for the Cresswells, the new people who have come to the 'Heath', you may fall down and worship them if you like and not break the Second Commandment as they are like nothing in heaven or earth or the water under the earth". Henrietta may have acted on her father's suggestion, for when she returned home a friendship developed between the two families, and in due course she became engaged to Richard Henry Cresswell. They were married by the bride's father in St. Margaret's Church, Barming, on 9th March 1815. At first Richard Cheslyn Cresswell disapproved of the match, but later he was on good terms with his daughter-in-law.[37] From this marriage there came a son who was to carry the Cresswell story into the Middlesex village of Winchmore Hill.

CHAPTER 3

A New Generation

The Wind of Change

Following her marriage to Richard Henry Cresswell, Mark Noble's daughter Henrietta had to exchange the peaceful atmosphere of a country rectory for the noisier and less spacious surroundings of a London house. Initially the couple lived in Great Coram Street, Bloomsbury, later moving to Doctors' Commons.[1] Within the confines of Doctors' Commons, the pace of life was unhurried, governed as it was by legal practices and procedures which had remained substantially unchanged for centuries.

Even during the 17th century, the functions of the ecclesiastical courts were diminishing, and by the late 18th century much of their surviving business had become routine and unremarkable — disputed wills, matrimonial causes, defamation, rowdy behaviour and such like.[2] Proceedings were often lengthy, sometimes tedious, and profitable only to the lawyers who conducted them. Few cases attracted public notice unless some unusual circumstance or point of law emerged.

A testamentary case heard in the Prerogative Court in 1816 was considered worthy of report under "Remarkable Trials and Law Cases" in *The Annual Register*. The proceeding concerned the will of Thomas Slack, Freeman of the City of London, who had died in a fire at his house in Kentish Town. His will had been burnt with him, but its contents were propounded by the guardians of his six children, and opposed by his widow "merely for the purpose of obtaining the decision of the Court". Advocates for the children submitted that the contents of the will must be pronounced for as the last will of the deceased. Advocates for the widow, one of whom was Richard Henry Cresswell, "admitted the principle of law contended for on the other side, but remarked upon some few points as to which the evidence might be deemed insufficient. With those observations they left the case to the candid consideration of the Court". The court pronounced for the contents of the will as propounded by the guardians — an outcome which was evidently satisfactory to both parties. Not a case, one assumes, that would have severely tested Richard Henry Cresswell's skills of advocacy.[3]

Richard Henry Cresswell's three brothers all became lawyers, and one of his sisters married a lawyer. William Cresswell was articled to his father Richard Cheslyn Cresswell as proctor's clerk for seven years from 1801, and was admitted as a proctor in 1808.[4] Henry Whitfield Cresswell, who took his mother's maiden name, was also articled to his father, the seven-year term beginning in 1812. He was admitted as a proctor in 1819.[5] His younger brother, Robert

Nathaniel Cresswell, became a barrister, with chambers in the Temple and later at Doctors' Commons. He was subsequently appointed secretary to Sir Cresswell Cresswell (1794–1863), a distinguished lawyer descended from the same Northumberland family. Robert Nathaniel's sister Harriet married into a family of lawyers. Her husband, Edward Dubois, was a barrister in the Temple; two of their sons, Edward Francis Hill and Theodore Judkin, became barristers at Lincoln's Inn.[6]

Richard Henry Cresswell and Henrietta soon started a family. Their first child, Richard, was born on 1st December 1815, and baptised at St. Benet's, Paul's Wharf, on 5th January 1816. As this was the parish church for Doctors' Commons, it is probable that the Cresswells had moved there by this time.[7] The second child, Sarah, was born a little over a year later, on 29th January 1817, and baptised at St. Benet's on 26th February. Sadly, Richard Henry Cresswell did not live to see the birth of his third child, John, for he died of consumption just six days beforehand, on 5th September 1818, and was buried a week later in a vault under the vestry of St. Benet's Church. A promising career in law was cut short at the early age of 36. John was born on 11th September 1818, the day before his father's burial, and was baptised on 14th October, also at St. Benet's.[8] Surely he must have brought comfort to Henrietta in her bereavement, after just three and a half years of married life.

St. Benet's, Paul's Wharf, situated at the south eastern extremity of Doctors' Commons on the corner of Upper Thames Street and Bennets Hill, was a church of ancient foundation, destroyed in the Great Fire and rebuilt between 1677 and 1683 by Sir Christopher Wren in a Dutch style with red and blue bricks and stone dressings. In time it assumed the role of college chapel for Doctors' Commons, as it did for the College of Arms on the opposite side of Bennets Hill. There was a gallery in the north aisle for the use of the doctors of law, and members of the College of Advocates attended the church robed, as a corporate body. Wives sat apart from their husbands in the same gallery. Memorial tablets to former members of the college lined the walls behind the gallery. Some members of the college were benefactors of the church, giving the altar, bells, pulpit and various ornaments. The college also contributed to general church expenses.[9] The old vestry, beneath which Richard Henry Cresswell was buried, stood at the north west corner of the church. It was removed, together with the adjoining graveyard, when Queen Victoria Street was made in 1867. No trace of the Cresswell vault survives.

When Richard Henry Cresswell died, his family were living on the south side of Great Carter Lane, in rooms spanning an archway between Dean's Court and Doctors' Commons.[10] From here the Cresswells could look out across Great Carter Lane towards St. Paul's Churchyard, or inwards over the maze of buildings, squares and alleys that made up Doctors' Commons.

The principal entrance to this complex was in Great Knightrider Street, to the south, with two side entrances in Bennets Hill. The main frontage was a late 17th century brick building, behind which the common hall, library, refectory and advocates' dwellings were disposed around two quadrangles and a gar-

Etched by J.W. White from a Drawing by W. Pearson.

S.T. BENNET *(ie S.T BENEDICT)* PAULS WHARF.

We have no account when this Church which is dedicated to S.t Benedict, founder of the Order of Bene-

dictine Monks, was first built, but being unhappily destroyed by the Fire of 1666 the present edi-

fice was erected and finished in 1683. The Parish is united to S.t Peters, near Pauls Wharf.

The Rector is the Rev.d Archibald Owen M.A.

The church of St. Benet, Paul's Wharf, London, from an engraving published in 1810. In 1818 Richard Henry Cresswell was buried in a vault under the vestry building shown on the extreme right; this was demolished in 1867, and no trace of the vault remains. His three children, Richard, Sarah and John, were baptised in this church.

Dean's Court, from St. Paul's Churchyard, London. The Deanery is on the right. The archway in the distance was on the south side of Great Carter Lane. Richard Henry Cresswell and his family occupied rooms over the archway, and John Cresswell was born here in 1818. Beyond lay the maze of streets and courtyards known as Doctors' Commons.

den.[11] Nearby were offices and apartments associated with the functions of the courts, including the Prerogative Office (where wills were kept), the Faculty Office (which issued marriage licences, among other things), and the private offices of the proctors. The courts, their offices, and accommodation for judges, advocates and proctors were all concentrated in this one small area between St. Paul's and Upper Thames Street, making it "a labyrinth....pervaded by an atmosphere of ecclesiastical jurisprudence".[12]

Opposite: City of London: St. Paul's and Doctors' Commons. The College of Advocates, including the common hall, lay in the complex of buildings to the south of St. Paul's Churchyard bounded by Great Knightrider Street, Bennets Hill, Upper Thames Street and Addle Hill. The courtyards and buildings between Great Knightrider Street and Great Carter Lane were also associated with "The Commons". St. Benet's, Paul's Wharf, stood at the corner of Upper Thames Street and Bennets Hill. From Richard Horwood's plan of London, 1799.

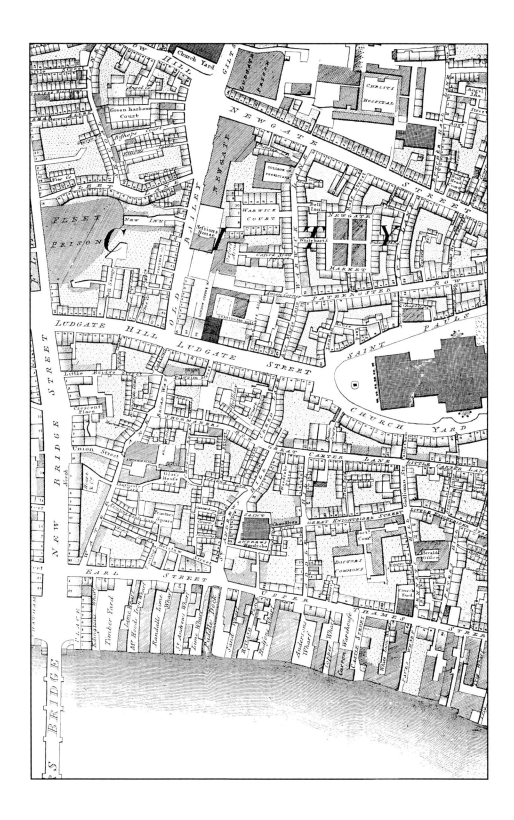

Within this enclosed community the lawyers conducted their business and lived out their lives, largely undisturbed by the noise and bustle of the city around them. To the south, wharves and warehouses sandwiched between Upper Thames Street and the river were busy with an ever-increasing maritime trade. To the north, horse-drawn traffic jostled for position in the crowded streets around St. Paul's Cathedral. In the quadrangles, courtyards and passages of Doctors' Commons, only quiet conversation and the sound of footsteps on the paving interrupted the calm.

Some 10 years after the death of Richard Henry Cresswell, but at a time when other members of his family remained there, the unchanging world of Doctors' Commons provided employment for a young man by the name of Charles Dickens. While still in his late teenage years he became a reporter in the Consistory Court, and a copy of a case in his own handwriting, transcribed from the shorthand notes he made in November 1830, has survived. He occupied an office at 5 Bell Yard, off Great Carter Lane, close to where the Cresswells had lived. The *Law List* shows him as a shorthand writer here from 1831 to 1836, though he may not have been there that long.[13]

His experiences in court, and his acquaintance with Doctors' Commons, provided Dickens with ample material, which he later used to good effect in his writing. In *Sketches by Boz* (1836) he satirises the proceedings of the Court of Arches and the activities of the Prerogative Office. Among his novels, *David Copperfield* (1849–50) offers a vivid picture of the courts, their business, and the people who practised in them. Although written some years later, his descriptions of Doctors' Commons convey with realism an institution and way of life familiar to the Cresswells.

David Copperfield spent several years as an articled clerk in the proctor's office of Spenlow and Jorkins. On his first visit to the office, with his aunt, David enters Doctors' Commons through a low archway from St. Paul's Churchyard, whence "the noise of the city seemed to melt, as if by magic, into a softened distance". The office is reached through dull courtyards and narrow ways, and Mr. Spenlow the proctor is sent for from the Court of Arches. David notices the old-fashioned and dusty furnishings of the room, the bundles of papers marked with the names of the various courts, and the massive bound volumes of evidence given in each case. "All this looked tolerably expensive, I thought, and gave me an agreeable notion of a proctor's business." Mr. Spenlow appears in a black gown trimmed with white fur, and a stiff white cravat and shirt-collar. David is accepted for a month's probation at a premium of a thousand pounds, and is immediately taken in to see the court.

He is conducted through a paved courtyard past the advocates' dwellings and into the court room. He sees the doctors — "sundry gentlemen in red gowns and grey wigs" — sitting on the raised platform either side of the judge. Below them he sees the proctors — "sundry other gentlemen of Mr. Spenlow's rank" — sitting at a long green table. Two members of the public are warming themselves over a stove in the centre of the room:

The languid stillness of the place was only broken by the chirping of this fire and by the voice of one of the Doctors, who was wandering slowly through a perfect library of evidence, and stopping to put up, from time to time, at little roadside inns of argument on the journey. Altogether, I have never, on any occasion, made one at such a cosey, dosey, old-fashioned, time-forgotten, sleepy-headed little family-party in all my life....[14]

This was the face of Doctors' Commons as seen by a spectator. Descriptively, the image was accurate, but as Sir William Holdsworth has pointed out, it failed to recognise the very considerable intellectual ability of the participants: "though the small number of the advocates, and their collegiate life in Doctors' Commons, helped to give their meetings the characteristics of a little family party, let us not forget it was a talented little family....some of its members, as judges or as advocates, have left a permanent mark upon all those various branches of law which once made up the sphere of the civilians' practice".[15] Richard Henry Cresswell would surely have agreed with that.

The snug seclusion of "The Commons", so aptly portrayed by Dickens, overlapped with the intimacy of its near neighbour, the cathedral precinct, and the Cresswells had a part in both. The lawyers of Doctors' Commons and their families lived close to, and often met with, the staff of the cathedral and their associates — the "cathedral clique". This included not only clerics but also poets, novelists and humorists — some of them well known names. Among those known to the Cresswells of Richard Henry's generation in Doctors' Commons were Sydney Smith, Richard Barham, Theodore Hook and Thomas Hood.[16]

Sydney Smith had wanted to become a barrister, but was obliged for financial reasons to abandon that idea, and instead took Holy Orders. He settled in London in 1803 and attracted a circle of friends consisting mainly of rising lawyers and men of letters, but was required to move to York in 1809 to attend to the living of Foston-le-Clay, which he had held as a non-resident parson for three years. His experience here echoes that of Mark Noble at Barming, as he built a new parsonage house to replace the "hovel" which he had found on taking up residence. In 1829 he exchanged the living of Foston for that of Combe Florey, Somerset, where he again rebuilt the parsonage. In 1831 he became a canon-residentiary at St. Paul's Cathedral, and had to reside in London for three months of the year. This he greatly preferred to the country: "I look forward anxiously to the return of bad weather, coal fires, and good society in a crowded city".[17] When in London he was able to rejoin the social circle which he had cultivated in earlier years. In 1837, publication of his first *Letter to Archdeacon Singleton*, in which he challenged the power of the Ecclesiastical Commission, exposed a dispute which he had entered with the Bishop of London over church incomes.[18] One aspect of this was the stipend of the minister at the new Winchmore Hill chapel in the parish of Edmonton — a matter to which we shall return.

It was through his election as a canon at St. Paul's Cathedral that Sydney Smith came to know Richard Harris Barham, author of *The Ingoldsby Legends*, who himself had been made a canon 10 years earlier. Barham had also intended to become a barrister, but, like Sydney Smith, took Holy Orders. He exchanged the living of Snargate, on Romney Marsh, for his canonship at St. Paul's, and attracted a circle of intellectual friends in London. He took up residence at 4 St. Paul's Churchyard, on the corner of the entrance to Dean's Court, and remained there until 1839.[19] His "inexhaustible faculty of grotesque rhyming" was employed not only in his published works but also in letters to friends.[20] In a rhyming letter to Edward Dubois, husband of Harriet Cresswell and brother-in-law of Richard Henry Cresswell, Barham wrote:

> My dear Dubois, tell me ubi's
> Cresswell's office, where they robe at?
> Not the Doctor's, but the Proctor's,
> As I want to get a probate.

In four short lines, Barham parodies legal Latin, alludes to the dress worn in court, observes the distinction between the advocates or doctors of law and the lesser breed of proctors, and indicates the principal business of a proctor's office. The two Cresswells to whom he refers were presumably Richard Henry Cresswell, DCL, and his father Richard Cheslyn Cresswell, the proctor. Richard Henry's sister Maria had a parrot, whose epitaph was written by Barham:

> Poor Poll was old, and never very good;
> And when she died, all said 'twas time she should.[21]

Barham was a lifelong friend of Theodore Edward Hook, writer and humorist. An incurable practical joker, he was the perpetrator, in 1809, of the celebrated Berners Street hoax, in which numerous workmen, tradespeople, professionals, dignitaries and others were summoned on the same day to call at the London home of an unfortunate lady who had incurred Hook's displeasure.[22] His infectious humour must have enlivened the meetings of the "cathedral clique".

Hook numbered among his friends the poet Thomas Hood, who referred to their friendship as "Hook and Eye". Hood was a family friend of the Cresswells in Doctors' Commons, and no doubt introduced them to other members of the "clique".[23] His successful literary career burgeoned after 1820, on his return to London from Scotland. In 1829 he moved to Winchmore Hill, where he occupied a charming house called Rose Cottage which would later become a Cresswell family home. His three years at Winchmore Hill were among the happiest of his life. His daughter, Frances Freeling Hood, was born there in 1830, and in the same year he began the *Comic Annual*, which was favourably received. In January 1832, whilst still at Winchmore Hill, he wrote at his publisher's request a fourth preface to a new edition of his successful *Whims and Oddities*, concluding it with characteristic humour: "come what may, this little book will now leave four imprints behind it, — and a horse could do no more". Later in the same year he left Winchmore Hill, owing to a disagreement with his landlord over repairs, and afterwards came to regret it.[24]

The world into which John Cresswell and his brother and sister were born was changing — both for the family and for the branches of law in which its members practised. John's grandfather, Richard Cheslyn Cresswell, died in 1824, and was buried in a vault in St. George's, Bloomsbury. The memorial tablet, placed high up on a wall near the back of the church, records that he was one of the deputy registrars of the Prerogative Court of Canterbury, and that he had resided in Queen Square, Bloomsbury, as well as at Doctors' Commons. He died in his 70th year. His wife Mary, who had died in 1809, is buried in the same vault. In 1828, their third son, Henry Whitfield Cresswell, died at the age of 35, and he is also buried there. With the deaths of William, Richard Henry, and Henry Whitfield, only Robert Nathaniel remained to represent the Cresswells of his generation in the legal profession.

The name of Cresswell survived in Doctors' Commons almost up to the demise of that institution. The proctor's office of Richard Cheslyn Cresswell, which had existed at least since 1800 as the partnership of Cresswell and Addams, remained at 8 Godliman Street (at the corner of Little Knightrider Street) up to the time of his death in 1824. Thereafter the practice continued under the name Addams and Cresswell at least until 1851. By 1856 the office had become Addams and Dubois, still at the same address. The new partner was Douglas Dubois, who had been admitted as a proctor in 1847 — a member of the family into which Richard Cheslyn Cresswell's daughter Harriet had married. Her husband, Edward Dubois, had died in 1850, and she died in 1853. The partnership remained at 8 Godliman Street until 1858, whereafter the firm became Richard Addams, proctor and solicitor, and continued there until 1860. At the time of the 1861 census the premises were being rebuilt, and by 1864 they had become James Jackson's dining and wine rooms.

The 1841 census shows Robert Nathaniel Cresswell, the barrister, living in Godliman Street with his sister Maria and two female servants. An 1842 directory confirms that this was at No.8, and they are still there in the 1851 census. Robert Nathaniel last appears at this address in 1859; he died on 5th January 1860, and was buried in the West London and Westminster Cemetery at Brompton. Evidently, the house at the corner of Godliman Street and Little Knightrider Street, close to one of the entrances to Doctors' Commons in Bennets Hill, served as an office and a residence for one or other of the related families of Cresswell and Dubois for at least 60 years.[25]

The last generation of Cresswells in Doctors' Commons witnessed the decline of an institution which in many ways had already outlived its usefulness. During the first half of the 19th century its business was becoming increasingly remote from public life, and opinion turned against the age-old practices, sinecures and even abuses which Dickens ridiculed. After 1830 the wind of change began to blow: in 1833 the Court of Delegates was abolished; in 1857 probate, matrimonial and admiralty business was transferred to newly constituted courts elsewhere; in 1859 advocates and proctors were merged with barristers and

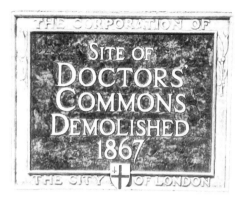

solicitors respectively. The civilian branch of the profession as exercised at Doctors' Commons had come to an end. Only church causes remained with the ecclesiastical courts, which moved from the Commons. Over the next few years the doctors surrendered their charter, dissolved their college, and disposed of their property. In 1867 the buildings were demolished to make way for Queen Victoria Street.[26] The home of Dickens's "cosey, dosey little family-party" had become but a memory.

Plaque in Queen Victoria Street, London, marking the site of Doctors' Commons. Photographed in 1992.

A City Merchant

We now turn to Richard Henry Cresswell's sister Frances Mary, the inheritor of Steed's House on Barming Heath. She was born on 15th December 1788, and spent most of her youth in or near London. Many years later she recalled childhood visits in the family coach to see her grandfather, Henry Whitfield, when he was Vicar of Bedfont. Driving across Hounslow Heath she saw corpses of highwaymen hanging on a gibbet, observing on each visit their progressive disintegration. Untroubled by this macabre memory, Frances and her younger sisters Harriet and Maria grew into fashionable young ladies, favouring narrow, short-waisted dresses, and under-garments of soft muslin sprinkled with water so that they would cling more closely to the figure. This was at a time when the young daughters of Mark Noble (later to become their sisters-in-law) were forbidden to leave the house without stout flannel petticoats beneath their dresses. Frances Mary was by all accounts a lively young lady. On one occasion she entertained guests at a dinner party at her father's house by dancing a hornpipe on the table among the wine glasses. She had red hair and was of diminutive stature, earning her the nickname "Pocket Venus".[27]

In the spring of 1812, Frances accompanied her sister, Harriet Dubois, and her brother William, on a visit to Sidmouth. It was felt that the mild, South Devon air might help to restore William's failing health. They had with them a companion, Mr. Diederich Willink, a friend of the family. Four unsigned watercolours, preserved in Henrietta Noble's album, are a reminder of this visit. Sadly, William's health did not improve, and he died at Sidmouth on 6th April, aged 26. He was buried at nearby Salcombe Regis, and a tablet to his memory was erected in the church there. Little did the family realise that, some 30 years later, a new link would be forged with that parish.[28]

Diederich Willink was a rich London merchant of Dutch extraction. At first he was no more than a friend to Frances Cresswell, but in 1815, after a broken engagement to another man, she married him — reputedly to spite her former fiancé. It reflected no credit on her father Richard Cheslyn Cresswell that the wedding breakfast was paid for by the bridegroom. This may have been a sign of disapproval that Frances was marrying into the socially inferior mercantile class, though it will be recalled that her father also disapproved of his son's marriage to a clergyman's daughter in the same year.[29]

The Willinks were Dutch farmers in the 17th century, though some of the family later settled in Altona, adjacent to Hamburg. They also had an estate at Raguth in Mecklenburg. Diederich Willink was born in Altona in 1780, the son of Maria and Dirk (the Dutch form of the name Diederich). He became a merchant, and settled in London early in the 19th century.[30]

Britain's overseas trade expanded greatly during the 18th century, as ships grew in size and number to develop links with other continents. London was the focus of this expansion, but its cargo handling capacity had become inadequate to meet the needs of a major seaport by the end of the century. The creation of the London dock system from the early 1800s enabled the capital to retain its pre-eminence as the country's chief port. With the docks came the inevitable growth of mercantile activity within and close to the City.

Much of this was concentrated in the area between Fenchurch Street and the Tower of London, adjacent to the extensive warehouses of the East India Dock Company. It was here, at 16 London Street, that Diederich Willink had his business premises and, above them, his home. London Street was a narrow thoroughfare linking Fenchurch Street with Crutched Friars. Opposite its southern end was the medieval church of St. Olave. Richard Horwood's map of 1799 shows approximately 30 numbered premises lining both sides of the street; No.16 appears on the west side close to the Fenchurch Street end. This map identifies it as New London Street, the name later applied only to the southern portion.[31]

There is no record of the original appearance of 16 London Street or adjoining premises, and most were altered or rebuilt during the 19th century. However, an early 20th century drawing of some old properties in New London Street shows part of a terrace of three-storey houses with tall, round-headed, ground-floor windows and shallower square-headed windows on the upper floors in a brick façade. Some of the ground-floor windows, behind which there would have been offices, are fitted with angled exterior mirrors to reflect light into the rooms, a common feature of narrow streets in the City during the 19th century. There are hinged trap doors in the pavement giving access to cellarage. The premises occupied by Diederich Willink would probably have been similar.[32] Their location is shown on the map reproduced on page 107.

Diederich and Frances made their home at 16 London Street, and in time real affection developed within a marriage which Frances had entered *faute de mieux*. The accommodation in which they lived must have seemed dark and confined, the surroundings noisy and overcrowded, but before the advent of railways it was not easy for men of business to travel daily into the City, and many lived over their work. London Street was well populated with merchants, agents and

VIEW of the NEW TRINITY HOUSE on TOWER HILL.   SAMUEL WYATT ESQ ARCHITECT.

The new Trinity House, and Trinity Square, London, in 1799. The square was a playground for the Willink children, whose home was in nearby London Street. Frances Sophia Willink, born in 1819, used to bowl her hoop in the garden of Trinity Square.

brokers: by 1825 there were at least 15 occupying premises in the street. As well as general merchants like Diederich, there were dealers in wines and spirits, corn and meal, and tea. There were also anchor smiths, and custom house and shipping agents. Diederich shared the premises at No.16 with the firm of Pinto, Urquhart and Company, general merchants.[33]

It was a cosmopolitan community in which the Willinks lived, and Diederich was remembered years later as "very foreign" in his manner. He also suffered from a nervous stammer, and the story of his attempt to buy ipecacuanha loz-enges for his wife was a source of entertainment in the family for many years afterwards. Their first child, Maria, was born in 1817, their second, Frances Sophia, in 1819, and their third and last, also christened Diederich, in 1824. The children's lives must have been dull: they were kept unnaturally quiet whilst at home to avoid disturbing their father at his work. Frances Sophia recalled in later life that her only childhood amusement was bowling a wooden hoop in a quiet and ladylike manner in the garden of nearby Trinity Square. She became a sedentary young lady, with an aversion to physical exercise and youthful high spirits.[34]

On a few occasions, the children were taken on a visit to their grandmother

Maria Willink on the family estate in Mecklenburg. They sailed from London to Hamburg, then went by carriage to Raguth. One return voyage, made in fog, proved to be so hazardous that the young Diederich, then two years old, was brought up on deck and rolled in a blanket so that he could be thrown to safety if the vessel grounded. Luckily this did not happen, but the incident made a lasting impression on Frances Sophia, then aged six.[35] These voyages must indeed have brought adventure to the otherwise uneventful lives of the Willink children.

Their father was for many years a prominent member of the Dutch Reformed Church at Austin Friars, near the junction of Throgmorton Street and Broad Street. He had been made a deacon of the church in 1808, and became an elder in 1832. By this time his business was suffering heavy financial losses. His health broke down under the strain, and he died on 30th December 1832. He was buried at the Dutch Church. Soon afterwards, Frances Mary moved with her family to 39 Cumming Street, Pentonville.[36] The offices at 16 London Street were taken over by the firm of Wildeboer and Kuck.[37]

The district of Pentonville had been created during the late 18th century, taking its name from the landowner Henry Penton, MP for Winchester. Wide streets were laid out on a regular grid pattern, and the houses were "for the most part of a very respectable class". Cumming Street, named after John Cumming, one of the building speculators, extended north from Clarence Place (later New Road), and from about 1780 was lined with three-storey brick terraces. No.39 was on the east side, north of the intersection with Collier Street. At the south east corner of the street, fronting onto the New Road, was the chapel of St. James, Pentonville, designed by Aaron Henry Hurst and built in 1787–8. Near the south west corner, and also facing the New Road, was the London Female Penitentiary, established in 1807.[38]

In 1836, four years after the family moved to Cumming Street, Frances Mary Willink's eldest child Maria died. Her second child, Frances Sophia, was then 16, and her youngest, Diederich, was 12. A few years later, Harriot Dubois, sister of Edward Dubois (who had married Harriet Cresswell, Frances Mary's sister), came to live at 39 Cumming Street. She was there in 1841, aged 70, and remained there until her death in 1859 at the age of 88. There were also two young female servants living in the house; they appear in both the 1841 and 1851 censuses. The young Diederich Willink does not appear at this address in either census — possibly he was staying away from home on both occasions. During the early 1850s the family's neighbour at 38 Cumming Street was the poet and novelist Jean Ingelow (1820–1897). She had great admiration for Frances Sophia, whom she would watch from her window as she walked in the garden. The poet did not know her real name, but called her "Grace". This would have been no later than the early summer of 1852, for in June of that year Frances Sophia left Cumming Street to marry her childhood sweetheart, an event to which we shall return. By the middle of 1859 the family had broken their last connections with Cumming Street, and its surviving members had taken their place among the Cresswells of Winchmore Hill.[39]

Return to Kent

After the death of Richard Henry Cresswell in 1818, his widow Henrietta returned to Barming with her three children to live at the parsonage with her
parents. She is reputed to have been a strict mother, especially with her sons,
whom she trained "with a word and a blow", the blow coming first. Even her
cat required permission before entering or leaving the room! She was left with a
burden of debt due to her late husband's college at Oxford which she insisted
on paying in full — an action regarded as misplaced idealism by members of the
Cresswell family unaccustomed to the values of a country rector's daughter
"who had learnt rigid economy and self denial from her infancy". When her
father-in-law, Richard Cheslyn Cresswell, died in 1824, she derived no benefit
from his will, as this was subject to a marriage settlement which divided the
estate between his surviving children. For some years afterwards, Henrietta had
to live in straitened circumstances.[40]

On 23rd December 1826, Henrietta's mother, Sarah Noble, collapsed and died
while walking in the garden of Barming Parsonage.[41] She was 73. Mark Noble
survived her by only five months, dying at the parsonage on 26th May 1827,
aged 72. Both are buried in Barming churchyard, and are commemorated by a
tablet on the north wall of the chancel of St. Margaret's Church. The same tablet
records the burial in the churchyard of two of their daughters and one grand-
daughter.

An obituary of Mark Noble was published in *The Gentleman's Magazine* in
September 1827, concentrating on his literary output:

> Residing in a country village, he creditably employed his leisure hours in
> genealogical and literary researches; and his works have procured for him
> the reputation of industry and application, if not of perspicuity and cor-
> rectness.

The writer draws attention to the numerous errors in Noble's *Memoirs of the
Protectorate-House of Cromwell*, a work "to which he was certainly unequal":

> That so little reliance can be placed on a work of which the design is so
> good, and in which so vast a collection of materials is assembled, is truly
> lamentable.[42]

Mark Noble receives an entry of a page and a half in the *Dictionary of National Biography*. The contributor is harsh in his judgment:

> Noble's writings are those of an imperfectly educated, vulgar-minded man.
> His ignorance of English grammar and composition renders his books
> hard to read and occasionally unintelligible, while the moral reflections
> with which they abound are puerile.

The allusion to Noble's poor learning calls to mind his own strictures on the literacy of his enemies the Amhursts.

The *Dictionary of National Biography* lists eight published works by Noble. These include genealogical histories of royal houses of Europe, and a history of the College of Arms. He also left a large number of manuscripts, mostly of a biographical nature, which were dispersed to various buyers when his library was sold in December 1827. Other manuscripts, including the *History of Barming* and *A History of the Family of Noble from 1590*, were retained by his descendants. (For a note on what happened later to the *History of Barming*, see Appendix A.)

It would be unfair to judge Mark Noble solely on his literary record. His success in rescuing the living at Barming from physical and financial decay was noteworthy. A carefully worded tribute published in 1839 suggests that he was also remembered for his contribution to the spiritual well-being of the parish:

> The name he has left for generosity and the true spirit of Christian piety as far exceeds that of his literary fame as the dignity of the Christian does that of any honor the world can confer.[43]

When Mark Noble died, his curate, Francis Buttanshaw, who had been appointed three years earlier, took charge of the parish. He became tutor to the young Richard and John Cresswell, offering them free tuition "and many a caning". Richard recalled many years later how strongly he disliked him. In 1832, when Francis took the living of nearby West Peckham, the boys became scholars with him there, lodging in his house for a nominal sum.[44] On 3rd September 1827, while still at Barming, he married Christiana Noble, the youngest child of Mark Noble. The marriage took place in St. Margaret's Church, Barming, and was performed by the Reverend Henry Jones, Vicar of West Peckham. Christiana's niece Sarah and her nephews Richard and John were among those who signed the register; their signatures are now the earliest we have of these members of the Cresswell family.[45] The first child of the marriage, born in 1828, was also christened Francis. Through his family, a direct link would later be created by marriage between the Buttanshaws and the Cresswells.

After the rector's death, and before Christiana's wedding, Henrietta and her three children moved to East Farleigh, to lodge at the house of Mark Noble's farm bailiff, Joseph Matthews. Christiana was also living there at the time of her marriage. East Farleigh was then a small but relatively populous agricultural parish, facing Barming across the Medway. A few years later the Cresswells moved to an attractive house in the nearby village of Loose. The dwelling stood on a hillside and was approached from the road by some 40 steps leading to a rustic verandah.[46] Henrietta and her daughter Sarah were still living there in 1841, together with a young female servant and an agricultural labourer, though Richard and John had left home. Prettily situated on the Loose Stream, with an abundance of fresh springs, the village supported a population of about 1,500 at this time. Many of the inhabitants were employed in paper mills worked by the stream, whilst hops, fruit trees and corn were grown on its fertile soil.[47]

From Loose, Henrietta and Sarah moved to a small house at Town Malling, six miles west of Maidstone. Here they lived somewhat frugally, Sarah occupying her time with needlework, at which she had become skilled. Years earlier, at the age of seven, she had made for her grandfather a set of fine linen shirts with hemmed cambric ruffles. Her sampler, worked at the same age, was still owned by her niece more than 80 years later. Sarah's mother was remembered as "a woman of strong intellect and marvellous memory".[48] Later she lived among the Cresswells of Winchmore Hill, and survived there to a great age.

It is understandable that neither Richard nor John Cresswell should have chosen to follow their father into the legal profession. That branch of the law which had sustained three generations of Cresswells before them was about to change greatly. Necessary as it was, the change was accompanied by uncertainty. The transition was beginning just when the two brothers were deciding on their future careers. Moreover, their father's early death exposed them to childhood influences which were less favourable to a career in law. Turning their backs on family tradition, they looked to other "gentlemanly" professions to provide them with opportunity.

Richard Cresswell's early years were spent among the family and friends of a country rector, far from the world of London lawyers which he had left as a small child. Although Richard's grandfather, Mark Noble, had died when the boy was only 12, his aunt's marriage to the curate a few months later maintained a clerical presence in the family during his formative years. His home background, and the tuition which he received from his uncle, no doubt had much to do with his choice of a career in the church.

At the age of 20, Richard obtained a Bible Clerkship at St. John's College, Oxford, which he entered in 1835.[49] This was a time of great religious ferment at the university. New ideas were circulating which would have a profound effect on the Church of England, and an undergraduate preparing for Holy Orders could scarcely avoid being influenced by contemporary thought and action. The circumstances that shaped Richard Cresswell's theological outlook cannot be fully understood without reference to the situation at Oxford at the time of his admission.

In the early 19th century, Oxford was still a strongly collegiate institution, each college being governed by a Head and a body of Fellows. The Fellows were mostly ordained clergymen, and might remain in college for life provided they did not marry. Only a few of them taught undergraduates. The university had become inbred and introspective, increasingly out of touch with society. A stronghold of the established church, its inertia and self-indulgence mirrored the spiritual impoverishment with which the wider church was then afflicted. Into this enclosed world came four outstanding men whose Christian conviction, intellect and determination were destined to transform the church. They were John Keble, John Henry Newman, Richard Hurrell Froude and Edward Bouverie Pusey. All four became Fellows of Oriel College, the first to open its fellowships to competitive examination. Together with like-minded Christians, they created what came to be known as the Oxford Movement.[50]

Keble preached his defining sermon on "National Apostasy" at St. Mary's, Oxford, in July 1833, two years before Richard Cresswell's arrival at the university. By 1835, the principles advanced by this group of theologians were being disseminated in the *Tracts for the Times*, earning them the epithet Tractarian. The Tractarians regarded the church, its priesthood and sacraments as the only true means of grace and salvation. Their faith rested on scripture as understood and interpreted by the historic church. Sacred authority was derived unbroken from the Apostles, and the English church was, by inheritance and tradition, a part of the church of Christ. On a personal level, obedience to the teachings of the church demanded a life of self-discipline and holiness.[51]

Edward Pusey was elected Fellow of Oriel College in 1823, and it was he with whom Richard Cresswell became acquainted and under whose influence he fell. Pusey was a man of great learning: in 1828 he became Regius Professor of Hebrew and a canon of Christ Church, Oxford, and in 1835 published a treatise on baptism which was a work of profound scholarship. He was not an accomplished orator, but the earnestness and sincerity of his sermons left a lasting impression on all who heard them. In his dealings with undergraduates he was gentle and understanding; Richard Cresswell later spoke of the kindness and encouragement which he had received from him.[52]

By the time Richard Cresswell was awarded his BA and ordained deacon in 1839 he had become a disciple of the Oxford Tractarians and a supporter of the Catholic revival in the Church of England — a position which he would continue to hold throughout his life and which would, in due course, be taken by the next generation of his family. His first curacy was at Boughton Monchelsea, not far from the family home in Kent. "To the lover of picturesque scenery", said a contemporary guidebook, "this village and its interesting localities will afford unusual gratification".[53] The neighbourhood evidently afforded other pleasures to Richard Cresswell, for family tradition asserts that at this time he courted no fewer than four young ladies simultaneously. Their homes lay in different directions, so when he came to the crossroads "he twirled his stick and according to the way it fell decided which lady he should honour with a visit".[54]

It is from this period in his life that we have the earliest evidence of another interest of Richard Cresswell's which would flourish in later years and serve as a lasting memorial to him. There survives an album of fine, hand-coloured drawings of wild flowers, together with handwritten botanical descriptions, executed by Richard Cresswell between July 1839 and March 1840. The 30 illustrations were made near his home in Kent — at West Peckham, Barming, East Farleigh, Loose, Tovil, Hucking and Boughton Monchelsea. They reveal not only an intelligent appreciation of the flora of the district, but also a considerable artistic talent.[55]

In 1840 Richard was ordained priest.[56] His next curacy was at Hawkhurst, an extensive and populous parish in the lower Weald of Kent. Here he met and became engaged to Miss Frances Creighton, who lived with her mother and sister nearby. Frances, six years younger than Richard, had been born in India into a wealthy English family settled in Hooghli, a town in the Ganges delta in

Western Bengal. Her father had been a judge in India, where he died of yellow fever in the 1830s. After moving to England her mother had been imbued with strong Protestant principles by an uncle, a strict Evangelical clergyman, and Frances had acquired from her an uncompromising belief in eternal damnation for the disobedient which was not mitigated by her marriage to a High Church-man. Richard was attracted less by her theological outlook than by her pretty looks, lively temperament, light-brown hair and beautiful complexion.[57]

The couple were married in Hawkhurst Church on 14th December 1843. Richard had already obtained the curacy of Salcombe Regis in Devon, so immediately after the wedding the pair travelled up to London, continuing their journey to the West Country by rail the following day. The line had not then reached Exeter, so they spent a further night at Taunton, travelling thence by post chaise to their new home on the South Devon coast.[58] Though separated by distance from their kinsfolk in the south east, the Devonshire Cresswells were to maintain strong family ties with their Winchmore Hill counterparts throughout the remainder of the 19th century.

John Cresswell's choice of career is less easily explained than that of his brother Richard. No other member of his family had entered the medical profession. However, in 1833 his tutor and uncle, Francis Buttanshaw, became chaplain to the newly opened Kent County Lunatic Asylum on Barming Heath. This establishment, occupying 14 acres of land enclosed by walls and another 20 acres of farmland worked by the patients, had accommodation for 168 souls.[59] Francis Buttanshaw's chaplaincy would undoubtedly have brought him into contact with the medical fraternity of Maidstone, forming connections which would facilitate John's assignment in 1834 as apprentice to a surgeon in the county town.

Medical Training

Of the "gentlemanly" professions, medicine was probably the least prestigious in the early 19th century. As a rule, medical men did not come from the upper reaches of society, and aristocratic connections of any kind were unusual. Families who could claim descent from the nobility or landed gentry would tend to discourage their first-born sons from practising medicine, though younger sons might do so and rely on their gentle birth as an antidote to the inferior status of their chosen occupation.[60] These were important considerations for young men contemplating a career in medicine, especially where it would involve the practice of surgery. Zachary Cope, in his history of the Royal College of Surgeons of England (1959), says that in the early 19th century "surgery was not an occupation for persons of very refined taste, for the performance of operations without the aid of anaesthesia needed a strong and somewhat insensitive personality".

At this time, the training of a surgeon began with an apprenticeship, during which the student would learn the skills of diagnosis, surgical techniques, and the prescribing and preparation of drugs. Apprenticeships could cost up to £500, but many were offered at nominal fees or none at all in return for favours, such as the education of the master's children by the father of the apprentice. The one-to-one relationship of apprentice and master was supplemented by formal education and practical observation at a teaching hospital. Courses of lectures by hospital staff became formalised during the early part of the century, and were incorporated into the curricula of medical schools attached to the hospitals. Apprenticeships normally lasted five years, with lecture courses and hospital practice running concurrently for up to two years during the period of apprenticeship. This allowed the student ample time to work in his master's private practice. During the 1830s, the range of subjects covered by lecture courses was expanded: by 1835 courses in morbid anatomy, physiology, chemistry, botany, midwifery and forensic medicine had become part of the standard curriculum.[61]

John Cresswell was apprenticed to Edward Sanders, apothecary and surgeon of Maidstone, from 22nd September 1834. John was just past his 16th birthday, and still living with his mother at East Farleigh.[62] Maidstone, a flourishing county town on the banks of the Medway, with a population of over 15,000, was growing as a commercial centre. A new corn market had been built, and a new market place laid out, in the early 1820s, whilst street paving had been improved and gas lighting installed. There was substantial riverborne trade with London along the Medway and the Thames. The expanding population found employment in a variety of commercial and retail activities, or in nearby corn and paper mills.[63]

The town's principal streets were lined with shops which "in every respect rival those of the capital, and supply the inhabitants with almost every article which even luxury can demand". There was an abundance of inns, taverns and public houses. The broad High Street ran uphill eastward from the river, continuing as King Street towards the Ashford Road. Intersecting at right angles were the main thoroughfares running north to south — Week Street, Gabriel's Hill and Stone Street.[64]

Contemporary directories list about 10 practising surgeons in the town, most of them located in the principal streets just mentioned. Edward Sanders occupied a house in Stone Street, to the south of the town centre, and it was here that John Cresswell began his apprenticeship. Although his home was less than three miles away, he would almost certainly have lodged in the surgeon's house.

There is a vivid account of the life of a medical apprentice of this period in the memoirs of Sir James Paget, who later became a renowned surgeon at St. Bartholomew's Hospital, London. He was apprenticed in 1830 to Charles Costerton, a surgeon in Yarmouth, and from his description we can gain some impression of the experience that the young John Cresswell would have had. James was also just 16 when he began his five-year apprenticeship, for which a premium of 100 guineas was paid. He had to attend the surgery from nine o'clock in the morning until five or six in the evening, with a break of an hour or so at lunch time. "The necessary daily work was dull, and at times tedious and apparently useless." The time was occupied chiefly in dispensing, seeing out-patients, receiving messages, making appointments and keeping accounts. When the master came in, the names of patients visited, the facts of the visit and the medicines required had to be recorded, and the medicines made up and sent. James quickly learnt to do all these routine tasks himself.

Beyond this, the young apprentice had the opportunity to study anatomy, both through reading and through observing operations performed by various surgeons in the town: "I was generally invited to them, and some were well done and some very ill done, and my master, who had good operative skill, taught me all he could in his criticisms of them". The apprenticeship was not all laborious, neither was life altogether dull, unsocial and pleasureless.

In retrospect, Paget valued the experience gained during the apprenticeship, though he felt that the five years required by the Society of Apothecaries was too long. At the age of 21 he had a thorough knowledge of making and dispensing medicines, account keeping and other business practices, and had learnt the importance of care, neatness and cleanliness in minor surgery. He had a good grounding in anatomy and physiology, natural history, and other branches of science, "with an unusual disposition for scientific pursuits, and an unusually educated power of observing".[65]

Four and a half years after commencing his apprenticeship, Paget began his medical training at St. Bartholomew's Hospital. In fact he entered the hospital just days after John Cresswell started *his* apprenticeship in Maidstone. By this time, London had become the focus of medical education and practice in the country. The profession was divided into three distinct status groups — physicians, surgeons and apothecaries — each with its own duties, privileges and social position. Physicians, who normally took a degree at Oxford or Cambridge, formed an élite with a monopoly of the practice of internal medicine. Surgeons, who learnt their skills by apprenticeship, were regarded as craftsmen whose work demanded speed, dexterity and physical strength. Apothecaries, originally responsible for the supply, compounding and sale of drugs, began to practise medicine during the 18th century, but were treated historically as tradesmen. Few surgeons could make a living from surgery alone, so increasingly they prescribed and dispensed drugs as well, forming a status group of surgeon-apothecaries which became numerous during the early 19th century. It was this group which John Cresswell aspired to join.The professional institutions regulating all these groups, and many of the establishments providing the education needed to satisfy their entry requirements, were located in London. It was therefore inevitable that new entrants to the profession should favour the capital as a place in which to embark on their careers.[66]

When James Paget entered St. Bartholomew's as a medical student in October 1834, the medical school was being expanded to cater for a growing demand for formal medical education to supplement the practical training available in the hospital. The school, which had evolved out of less formal courses of instruction, owed its reputation to John Abernethy, who was a surgeon at Bart's from 1815 to 1827. In 1835 the teaching facilities were greatly improved by the opening of a new medical theatre, anatomical theatre, library and pathological theatre, and in the same year the lecture course was extended to cover a period of 10 months.[67]

John Cresswell entered Bart's as a student in October 1838, just four years behind Paget. He still had a year of his apprenticeship to serve, but by this time he would have been well acquainted with the practice of the surgery.[68] The choice of medical school for an apprentice might depend on his master's connections with it or on family ties; Edward Sanders was probably the influence in John's case. Whilst at the school, the student would need to find his own lodgings; a residential college where students could live, dine and study was not established at Bart's until 1843.[69] For John, finding convenient accommodation would not have been a problem, as he had relatives living in Godliman Street, Doctors' Commons, and Cumming Street, Pentonville.

John spent 18 months at Bart's, during which time he "walked the wards" and attended lectures and practical demonstrations on subjects prescribed by the professional bodies. His demonstrator in morbid anatomy was none other than James Paget, who, after completing his own medical training

Gatehouse at the main entrance to St. Bartholomew's Hospital, Smithfield, London, photographed in 1992. Constructed in 1702, it remained in place when the rest of the hospital was rebuilt later in the 18th century. John Cresswell undertook medical training at Bart's between 1838 and 1840.

in 1836, had returned to the hospital to teach.[70] It is to Paget's memoirs that we turn again for an insight into the kind of education that John Cresswell would have received.

When Paget entered Bart's, a fee of about £100 had to be paid to attend a course of lectures and practical demonstrations. A special admission ticket was issued for each course subject. Attendance at lectures and demonstrations did not offer a structured and supervised education: "for the great majority of students....work at that time had to be self-determined and nearly all self-guided: it was very little helped by either the teachers or the means of study". Paget learnt less from the teachers than from reading and from work in the dissecting room, dead-house and out-patient room. "There was very little active practical teaching in the wards or by clinical lectures: it was customary to think it sufficient to give opportunities for learning to those who could learn by looking-on and by....talking about the cases." However, during their apprenticeships, the great majority of students "had become familiar with the language and habits and apparatus of practice".

Paget states that at the time of his pupilage "the school was not in good working order. There was constant dissension and mischievous rivalry among the teachers". Whilst standards may have been improving, most of the physicians and surgeons on whose teaching performance Paget comments so revealingly in his memoirs were still lecturing and demonstrating when John Cresswell undertook his course four years later.

Of those who taught John Cresswell, Peter Mere Latham had been at Bart's the longest, having been appointed lecturer on the principles and practice of medicine in 1824. Paget remembered him as a man of great intellect, but as one who disliked "common school-work". His teaching was admirable, and despite poor health he would arrive at eight in the morning, "would make those who went round with him examine for themselves, and would tell and show them how to....his style was clear, strong and impressive; his words apt and as if freely selected from a large classic knowledge". However, he was at times laughably pompous, and his early hours and precision "were too much for the great majority of students".

The sessions on anatomy and physiology were given by Edward Stanley. Paget claims that he was "the only one who worked hard for the school". The anatomy he taught was very elementary, "but he lectured so carefully and clearly, he was so deliberate and simple, so grave and earnest....that I believe there was not in London a more instructive teacher than he was". He was however timid and easily ridiculed, such that "men with half his good qualities and twice as many faults could appear better and have more influence than he".

John Cresswell learnt his *materia medica* from George Leith Roupell. He was amiable, painstaking and helpful, but not a good lecturer. He had traced the origins of the cholera epidemic which reached London in 1832, and became a victim of the disease when it recurred in the capital in 1854. The lecturer in botany was a younger man named Frederick John Farre. He was, according to Paget, a good teacher; his formal and somewhat unapproachable manner was only to be expected of an eminent Victorian physician. George Burrows, who shared the lecturing on principles and practice of medicine with Peter Latham, was of a similar age to Farre and also an excellent lecturer. He later became physician to Queen Victoria, and earned a reputation as one of the outstanding lecturers in the medical school.

Of all the lecturers who taught both James Paget and John Cresswell at Bart's, Thomas Wormald was the most popular. He was demonstrator in anatomy, examined his class weekly on the subjects of his demonstrations, and was responsible for banishing beer and tobacco from the dissecting room. He was selective with his subject matter, but what he did teach he taught well, in plain English, and with good illustrations. "He was a shrewd hard-headed Yorkshireman, muscular, hearty, with plenty of rough wit and plenty of good stories; he had no taste for anything that could be called science, but abundant common-sense and sharpness, and good mechanical skill."

John Cresswell's remaining tutors were appointed after Paget had completed his training — among them Paget himself. He became demonstrator in morbid anatomy in 1839 at the age of 25, the year after John Cresswell began his course. Paget's demonstrations were so popular that, in November 1839, many of the students signed a letter to the medical officers urging that he should be appointed lecturer in morbid anatomy, but this did not occur until June 1840, after John Cresswell had finished his training.[71]

From 1839, Paget kept a record of the students who attended his demonstrations, and later his lectures. His original notebook survives, and against the names of some students are brief but often telling comments on their character and performance. One student (who was later hanged for murder) was "idle, dissolute, extravagant, vulgar and stupid"; another was "one of the most laborious, clear-headed, and capacious students I ever knew....so beautiful a mind, surely never occupied so grotesque and strange a body: and this inferior part of him died after his second year of study". One of his pupils married a prostitute during his training, another was convicted of indecent assault on a female patient. On John Cresswell he remains silent — an indication perhaps of satisfactory rather than exceptionally good or bad performance. Paget continued these notes until 1859, by which time over 1,200 students had passed through his hands. He became an outstanding surgeon of great influence, was elected President of the Royal College of Surgeons, and was appointed surgeon-extraordinary to Queen Victoria. He died in 1899.[72]

John Cresswell was privileged to be taught by men who became eminent in their respective fields of medicine. The teaching may have been unstructured and its quality variable, but it was a good preparation for the qualifications needed to pursue a successful career in general practice.

In March 1839, six months after he commenced his training at Bart's, John Cresswell's apprenticeship was transferred to Richard Wedd, another Maidstone surgeon. The apprenticeship had a further six months to run.[73] Richard Wedd's premises were also in Stone Street, though John would not have spent much time there while he was attending Bart's. His new master was evidently a person of some standing in the community: he was senior surgeon to the West Kent Infirmary and Dispensary, opened in Maidstone in 1833 to accommodate 24 in-patients. He was also a councillor for Stone Street Ward, and a member of the Watch Committee and General Purposes Committee.[74]

John Cresswell completed his apprenticeship in September 1839, and his hospital training the following April. It was around this time that he became engaged to his cousin Frances Sophia Willink, then still living at 39 Cumming Street. The two cousins had evidently been close since childhood, and "were virtually engaged in their cradles". The engagement was to be a long one, as John was not in a position to marry until he had become established in medical practice.[75] To this end he pursued his studies for the necessary professional examinations. The first of these was for Licentiateship of the Society of Apothecaries. The society's legal right to grant licences to practise medicine throughout England and Wales had been conferred by the Apothecaries' Act of 1815. Over

the next 30 years the society would have a profound effect in raising the standard of medical education and enhancing the respectability of general medical
practice. Licentiateship (LSA) became a necessary qualification for medical men
who wished to prescribe and dispense drugs; it was usually taken in conjunc-
tion with membership of the Royal College of Surgeons in London (MRCS). The
requirement for registration for both examinations was the provision of evidence of attendance at specified lectures, dissections and medical practice.[76]

John Cresswell took his LSA examination on 29th April 1841, just one year
after finishing at Bart's. He gave his address as Loose, to which his mother and
sister had moved by this time. The examinations were held several times a year
at Apothecaries' Hall, an elegant 17th century building in Water Lane (now Black
Friars Lane) in the City of London, largely unchanged to this day. Until the
1839–40 session the examination was oral only; John Cresswell was therefore
among the first to answer questions in writing, an addition to the *viva voce* which
was apparently much appreciated. Not all the candidates were well behaved.
At the examinations held on 2nd September 1841 a student "who had imbibed
more than was good for him" forced his way through the gateway, overpow-
ered the porter, and created considerable alarm to two of the examiners. In their
report on the incident, the Court of Examiners admitted "that cases of insubor-
dination on the part of candidates and their friends are by no means rare", and
requested "more efficient protection for the maintenance of due order". Whether
six months earlier John Cresswell used the occasion as an opportunity for the
release of youthful high spirits is not recorded, but he certainly passed the examination.[77]

John qualified for membership of the Royal College of Surgeons in London
by an examination held on 28th May 1841. At the time he gave his address as
Doctors' Commons.[78] Presumably he was lodging with his uncle and aunt in
Godliman Street, though he also appears at 39 Cumming Street around this time.[79]
According to Paget, who qualified MRCS five years earlier, "the examination
was very simple. The ten examiners sat at the outer side of a long curved table.
Each in turn, I think, took a candidate; and, when he had finished, others could
ask questions". The conduct of the examination had been modified by the time
John Cresswell took it, but there was still no written paper except for candidates
whose performance in the oral examination was borderline. The questions,
though confined to anatomy, physiology, surgery and pathology, did in fact
present a severe challenge to most students in one brief *viva voce*. The examination was held in the spacious but dimly lit interior of the Royal College of Surgeons building in Lincoln's Inn Fields.[80] With his apprenticeship, hospital training and professional examinations behind him, John Cresswell, at the age of 22,
was fully prepared to enter general practice.

The only evidence to hand of John's first appointment is a statement by his
daughter, over 60 years later, that he was "assistant to a general practitioner at
Belper in Derbyshire".[81] No dates are given, but the best estimate is that he was
there for about a year from the autumn of 1841. It was not unusual at the time
for newly qualified medical men to be employed as assistants to established

practitioners. Vacant assistancy posts were published in the medical press or passed on by word of mouth. Typically, assistants would be required to prepare drugs, see patients, and deputise for practitioners in their absence.[82]

By whatever means John secured his position, his first appointment took him to a flourishing market town with a population of nearly 10,000 some 130 miles from London. The opening of a station on the North Midland Railway in 1840 had greatly improved communication. Belper's prosperity depended on silk and cotton mills, which employed a substantial number of the inhabitants. Its attractive situation in the valley of the Derwent, together with the surrounding hills and adjacent parkland, softened the impact of the industrial buildings. There was a market place lined with shops, and livestock fairs were held twice a year.[83]

The 1841 census (taken on 6th June) lists no fewer than seven surgeons in Belper, in four separate households. John Cresswell does not appear. Only one household includes an assistant surgeon, and this was Henry Pitman, assistant to David Evans in Market Street Lane. Two other surgeons, including David Evans's son, practised at the same address, and there was also a 17-year-old medical apprentice. Altogether there were 16 people in the household. The practice seems to have been a substantial one, no doubt offering attractive prospects to a newly qualified assistant.

Henry Pitman was just eight months younger than John Cresswell. He had been apprenticed to a surgeon in Liverpool, and had attended lectures at Liverpool Infirmary and University College Hospital, London. He qualified MRCS in April 1840 and LSA in August 1840. He could therefore have been in Belper for about nine months at the time of the 1841 census. He later pursued a distinguished career as surgeon to the Bombay Army, and became a Fellow of the Royal College of Surgeons.[84] Although there is no conclusive evidence, it seems very likely that his place as assistant surgeon to David Evans of Belper was taken by John Cresswell some time during the last few months of 1841.

It may be no more than a curious coincidence, but precisely at this time work was in progress on the construction of a new workhouse for the Edmonton Poor Law Union in Middlesex. Aspects of the design were being modelled on that of the Belper Union workhouse, whose medical officer was David Evans. Within a year, John Cresswell would be negotiating the purchase of a practice in the quiet Middlesex village of Winchmore Hill from a surgeon-apothecary who held the position of medical officer to the Edmonton Union.[85]

CHAPTER 4

Trois Vase House

A Village in Middlesex

Green Lanes was, and still is, the name given to the main road from London to Winchmore Hill. In the early 19th century the name conveyed a true impression of the road as it approached Winchmore Hill. By the roadside, near the eastern extremity of the village, stood the eight-mile stone, buried in long grass by a marshy pond opposite the lane to Barrow Well Green. Though such a short distance from London, Winchmore Hill was lost in the quiet, wooded countryside of North Middlesex.

In 1819, Winchmore Hill was described as "a large and pleasant village, situated on a considerable eminence". It was long and straggling, and contained about 40 or 50 houses.[1] On the outskirts were farms and, to the west, coppiced woodland. Lanes approaching the village met in an open space at the hill top, and this became the Green. Around the Green were small weatherboarded cottages roofed with pantiles, and a few larger houses of more recent construction; within it was a pond. Some spacious gentlemen's houses stood further from the centre.

The undulating countryside to the north west was intersected by a steep-sided valley which "resembled a half-opened book with the swiftly running streamlet in the fold of the binding....there was a mineral well here, so strongly impregnated with Epsom salts that....it nearly led to Winchmore Hill becoming a fashionable Spa".[2]

An 1826 directory speaks favourably of Winchmore Hill:

> The views from this spot are highly picturesque, and the air is very salubrious. Several highly respectable families reside at this place and in the immediate neighbourhood. The only place of worship here, is a chapel for dissenters; there are also some respectable schools both boarding and day.[3]

The writer ignored the Quaker meeting, which had been held in the village since 1662, though later editions of the same directory did recognise it.

The "chapel for dissenters" was a modest wooden building at the western edge of the Green which had accommodated the Independent Old Meeting since the mid-18th century. The first recorded pastor was Henry Pawling, who was minister from 1822 to 1842. After the lease expired in 1841, the deacon, John Radford, gave land for a new chapel in nearby Hoppers Lane.[4] Radford held much land and property in the village, including a dwelling with outbuildings and gardens to the south of the Green which he leased from 1821, and a farmhouse with nine acres of gardens, orchards and pasture land extending to the Green Lanes which he acquired in 1830. Before moving to Winchmore Hill he was a resident of White Conduit Street, Pentonville.[5] We shall return to his property in Hoppers Lane, for among his tenants there were the first of the Cresswells of Winchmore Hill.

The largest private estate in the area was Southgate Grove, owned by Walker Gray. The house had been designed by John Nash and built in 1797; the landscaped park was the work of Humphry Repton. In 1826 Walker Gray conveyed free of charge a piece of land in Winchmore Hill to His Majesty's Commissioners for Building New Churches, for the site of a new chapel. The village was in the ecclesiastical parish of Edmonton, and the parish church was two miles away. The growth in population persuaded the commissioners that there should be a branch of the established church in Winchmore Hill. The land conveyed was about a quarter of an acre in extent, with a frontage to "the High Road leading from Winchmore Hill to Southgate", then known as Chase Hill. It was given on condition that no part of the land should be used at any time as a burial ground.[6]

The chapel was erected during 1827. More than three quarters of the building cost was provided by the commissioners, the remainder being raised by public subscription. The architect was Mr. J. Davies. The yellow-brick structure was in effect a large preaching hall with external Gothick detailing in stone and a wide plaster ceiling hiding a substantial queen-post roof. An architect's drawing of the exterior shows the chapel standing on a level rather than an inclined site, and contains slight differences of detail from the design executed.[7] The building was consecrated under the name of St. Paul's Chapel, Edmonton, by William Howley, Bishop of London, on 2nd June 1828. It was a chapel-of-ease to the parish church of All Saints, Edmonton, and the first minister was Thomas Bissland.[8]

The involvement of Sydney Smith, canon of St. Paul's Cathedral, in the early affairs of the Winchmore Hill Chapel has already been mentioned. In 1828, William Howley was succeeded as Bishop of London by Charles Blomfield. It was he who wished to divide the parish of Edmonton into three, and to pay a fixed stipend to incumbent ministers at the Southgate and Winchmore Hill chapels in place of the uncertain incomes which the existing ministers derived from pew rents. The bishop applied to the Dean and Chapter of St. Paul's Cathedral to effect this change, but his request was declined on the grounds that the income of the living at Edmonton, which was already falling in value, would be further reduced by division into three, thereby creating, in Sydney Smith's words, "three clerical beggars".[9]

The bishop's forthright response was expressed in a letter to Sydney Smith in 1834:

> If you are of opinion that the district of Winchmore Hill will be as well
> provided for, in respect of pastoral superintendence, by placing there a

Curate with from £40 to £100 for his stipend, arising from the precarious
source of pew rents....as by entrusting it to an incumbent minister with
£300 per annum, all I can say is, that I should be glad to have your reasons.

He went on to say that Thomas Bissland had complained of the inadequacy of
his stipend, which at the time amounted to only £40 per annum, but that he had
consented to remain in his post for a time. "That there has been no complaint of
neglect of duty proves that the clergyman has been faithful, not that he is com-
petently provided for." [10]

By the date of the bishop's letter, Thomas Bissland had in fact resigned, and
had been replaced by Edward Blackburn Warren, son of Dawson Warren, the
Vicar of Edmonton. In 1838 the bishop authorised marriages to be solemnised at
the Winchmore Hill Chapel, but St. Paul's did not secure a measure of independence until 1851, when it became a district chapelry of Edmonton.[11] By this
time, a long association had begun between St. Paul's and the Cresswells of
Winchmore Hill.

The early parish registers of St. Paul's, Winchmore Hill, betray widespread
illiteracy in the population; many signatures were made only by mark. The "respectable schools" mentioned in the 1826 directory were for the privileged few,
and the only education available to many children was what their parents could
teach them. Some pupils attended a one-roomed school in a weatherboarded
cottage near the new church, which "might have accommodated some fifty children, if they sat close together".[12] Aware of its inadequacy, Edward Warren approached the owners of the Independent Chapel on the Green in 1842 with a
view to securing the site for a new school. He withdrew, however, when he
discovered that the dissenting congregation, who were still using the chapel,
were strongly opposed to relinquishing their property to the established church:
"as they are persons of great respectability, and neighbours, I am unwilling to
enter into any competition with them".[13] The premises in Church Hill had to
suffice until a new school was provided in 1859.

The stated occupations of male residents of Winchmore Hill whose children
were baptised at St. Paul's Chapel from 1834 to 1842 portray a rural community
of farmers and agricultural labourers, supported by carpenters, sawyers, black-
smiths and carriers. Gentlemen and their male domestics constituted some 10
per cent of those listed. The professional class was represented by schoolmas-
ters and surgeons. This record cannot of course be taken as a precise indication
of employment in the community, but it is a useful guide. Of all the tradespeople in Winchmore Hill listed in an 1839 directory, almost half were tailors, shoe-
makers, drapers, milliners and dressmakers.[14]

The only practising surgeon listed in Winchmore Hill at this time was Caleb
Radford. There is no evidence available that he was related to John Radford, the
deacon of the Independent Chapel, though the surname is uncommon in the
area.[15] Caleb was born in 1813, the son of a London hosier, and was apprenticed
to an apothecary in Whitechapel at the age of 15. He trained at Guy's Hospital,

becoming a Licentiate of the Society of Apothecaries in 1834 and a Member of the Royal College of Surgeons in 1835. He was then living at Brixton, but in 1836 began practising as a surgeon in Winchmore Hill.[16] In May of that year he circulated information about the Winchmore Hill Independent Medical Club, whose object was "to enable the Labouring Classes to ensure to themselves Medical and Surgical Attendance and Medicine during sickness, independently of Parochial aid". Membership was limited to labourers and servants in agriculture, handicrafts and trades, provided their wages did not exceed specified amounts. Caleb Radford, as "the Medical Gentleman resident in the District", undertook to attend members of the club who had paid a subscription ranging from four shillings and sixpence to eleven shillings a year, depending on family size. "Habitual Drunkards, and persons notoriously addicted to profligate habits, or who are known to be idle and disorderly" were not admitted.[17]

In 1837, Caleb Radford became the first medical officer for the Edmonton District of the Edmonton Poor Law Union, established under the Poor Law Amendment Act of 1834. Each parish within the union became a medical district, with its own medical officer. Initially there were three workhouses — for children, able-bodied adults, and the old and sick — but in 1838 it was decided to build a new workhouse for all paupers in the union except children. Medical officers were appointed to attend sick paupers who were not in the workhouses; usually patients visited their surgeries, but if they were unable to do so the medical officer was expected to visit them on receipt of an order from the relieving officer appointed by the union to look after the poor outside the workhouse. At first the medical officers were employed annually by tender, but from 1842 they were appointed at a fixed salary. They were also awarded contracts to vaccinate paupers outside the workhouse. Caleb Radford carried out vaccinations at his residence in Winchmore Hill and, from time to time, at a surgery in Duck Lane, Edmonton.[18]

In December 1839 Caleb Radford married Mary Sarah Weston, daughter of an eminent London surgeon who had died in 1818. They had four children — all boys — three of whom were born before the family left Winchmore Hill in 1843.[19] It was during the previous year that Caleb sold his practice to the 24-year-old surgeon John Cresswell.

A New Medical Gentleman

By the time John Cresswell entered medical practice, the term "general practitioner" had emerged to describe men who qualified as both apothecaries and surgeons and who therefore practised both medicine and surgery. Most people continued to speak of "medical men" and "medical practitioners", however, and use of the term "doctor" in a medical context did not become widespread until the late 19th century.[20]

Setting up as a general practitioner for the first time could be made easier by purchasing an established practice, possibly with financial support from one's family. Purchasing a practice was a way of buying a place in the local community. Purchase prices varied widely, as they were based on the average annual income of a practice at the time of sale. Some vendors required full cash payment immediately, others would accept payment by instalment. The fees that could be charged depended on the income of the patients, and had to allow for the provision of drugs where these were supplied by the practitioner.[21]

It was late in 1842 when John Cresswell completed the purchase of Caleb Radford's medical practice in Winchmore Hill. More than 60 years afterwards, John's daughter Henrietta claimed that he had been cheated by Mr. Radford, as "he was led to understand that all Parish and Workhouse emoluments were included, while in reality his predecessor had received notice to quit for misconduct and the appointments were already filled up so that only a few months of the more lucrative employments remained".[22] Presumably this refers to Radford's position as medical officer to the Edmonton Union, though the circumstances in which this appointment was terminated and the extent to which John Cresswell was actually deceived are not clear. Moreover, as we shall soon discover, the appointment of Caleb Radford's successor as medical officer had not been determined when John Cresswell took over the practice in Winchmore Hill.

During the early Victorian period, there was a growth in the number of salaried positions available to medical men outside their own practices, and appointments as medical officers of Poor Law unions were among the most common. Salaries were far from generous, and once the annual appointments system replaced the tendering process in the early 1840s boards of guardians were often influenced by personal connections in their choice of medical officers.[23] Imperfect though the system was, it did provide a useful additional source of income, especially to the newly qualified practitioner establishing his practice and consolidating his place in the community. If John Cresswell had been led to expect a continuing addition to his income, its early loss would have been keenly felt.

The minutes of the Edmonton Board of Guardians remain silent on the reason for terminating Caleb Radford's appointment as medical officer, though they do indicate that, from time to time, the guardians were not wholly satisfied with his performance. In February 1838, for example, the year after his appointment, he was criticised for giving paupers whom he attended "certificates of their being in need of nourishment" without consulting the relieving officer or other responsible person. In October 1839, the board found that his report had been "defective in observations on the state of his Patients" and had lacked his signature. In July 1842 he was requested to supply proper information in the medical report books and to date them, and was informed that "the Board think it very desirable he should see the Master of the Workhouse on the occasion of his visits there". In November of the same year he was asked to "affix his signature to the Medical Order Book in the Surgery on the days of his attendance". On two occasions he submitted bills for additional payments to which he was not entitled — one for supplying trusses which apparently had not been authorised, another for certifying before magistrates the state of mind of two individuals, a duty covered by his annual salary of £110.

Shortcomings such as these can scarcely have amounted to misconduct, for in April 1842 Caleb Radford's appointment as medical officer to the Edmonton District was renewed. At this time, he requested from the board of guardians "a Testimonial expressive of the satisfaction of this Board of his Services as District Surgeon of this Union" — a request which was immediately granted. Two months later, he certified that the new Edmonton workhouse was "in a perfectly fit state to receive the Paupers".

Early in 1842, the Poor Law Commissioners sanctioned the division of Edmonton into two medical districts; this was put into effect by the creation of one district for Church Street and Fore Street, another for South Street and Bury Street. In June 1842 Henry Samuel Hammond, a surgeon of Church Street, was appointed medical officer for the Church Street and Fore Street District, at a salary of £50 per annum, and Caleb Radford appears to have continued for a time to serve the other district at a reduced salary. Some time before March 1843 he ceased to hold this appointment, and in that month the board considered "the propriety of cancelling the existing Contract with Mr. Caleb Radford for vaccinating the Poor in the Parish of Edmonton". He retained the vaccination contract until April 1843, when the guardians resolved "that a testimonial expressive of the good opinion of this Board of Mr. Radford's abilities and of his attention to his duties whilst an Officer of this Union be drawn up and signed by the Chairman". He certainly did not leave in disgrace.

If, as his daughter later recorded, John Cresswell temporarily received Caleb Radford's "Parish and Workhouse emoluments", this must have been from the time of his arrival in Winchmore Hill late in 1842 until March 1843, when new annual contracts were awarded to medical officers for the two Edmonton districts. Henry Hammond's appointment was renewed in the Church Street and Fore Street District, but as there were two candidates for South Street and Bury Street — John Cresswell and Thomas Ward — "those Gentlemen were called in and examined as to their qualifications for the Office". This took place on 15th March 1843, when the guardians voted for their chosen candidate. John Cresswell and Thomas Ward each secured eight votes. A re-election took place one week later, John Cresswell again securing eight votes and Thomas Ward receiving nine. Ward, a Southgate surgeon, was duly elected.[24]

This must have been a great disappointment to John Cresswell, even though the salary was a modest £40 per annum, and no further opportunity arose for him to secure a similar appointment for many years. What Caleb Radford may not have told him was that his appointment was subject to annual renewal and possibly election. Failure by the vendor to impart information was just one of the many risks attending the purchase of medical practices; misrepresenting the value of a practice, deliberately or inadvertently, was by no means uncommon.[25]

When he came to Winchmore Hill, John Cresswell took a lease of a property in Hoppers Lane known as 1 Trois Vase House. Hoppers Lane (later to become

Trois Vase House, Hoppers Road, the first Winchmore Hill residence of John Cresswell.
Reproduced from a watercolour which he painted in 1868, after he had lived there 26
years. His home was at No.1, the left-hand portion of the semi-detached villas. To the left
is the Independent Chapel, opened in 1844.

Hoppers Road) ran due south from the Green towards the Green Lanes. For
anyone arriving from London, it was the most direct approach to the village.
The land on which John Cresswell's home stood had in 1801 been a three-acre
field owned by John Barnes. Two semi-detached villas, known as 1 and 2 Trois
Vase House, were built on this plot early in the 19th century. They stood on the
east side of the road, about 130 yards from the junction with Compton Lane,
and about twice as far as that from the Green. They had small front gardens,
and back gardens extending some 100 feet to the boundary of Highfield Park.[26]

A watercolour painted by John Cresswell from the opposite side of Hoppers
Road after he had lived there 26 years shows Trois Vase House as two semi-
detached three-storey dwellings with narrow frontages of a single bay each and
single-storey extensions (only one of which is clearly visible in the picture) to
right and left. There are sash windows within the plain stuccoed fronts, and the
chimneys are partly concealed behind a moulded stone parapet. John Cresswell's
home, No.1, was the left-hand residence, nearer to the Green. The painting, reproduced on this page and on the front cover, is the only known illustration of
the property.[27]

The house was sometimes referred to as Trois Vase Villas. The curious name

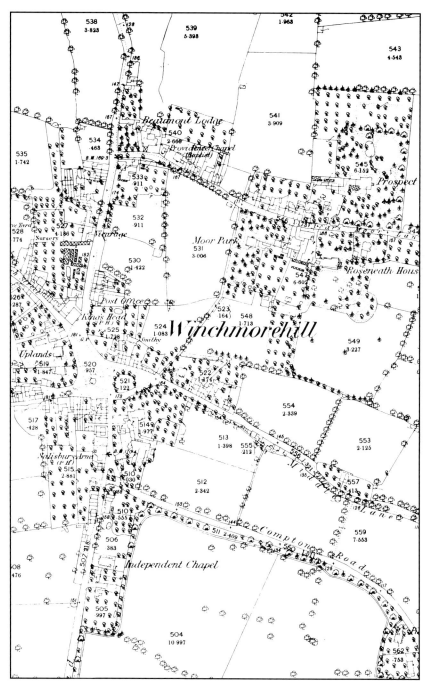

Mid-19th century Winchmore Hill. The pair of villas forming Trois Vase House lies immediately to the south of the Independent Chapel near the bottom of the map. To the north, the pond on the Green is clearly marked. Compton Road and Middle Lane descend in an easterly direction towards Green Lanes. From the 25 inch to the mile Ordnance Survey plan, 1865.

The Independent Chapel, Hoppers Road, Winchmore Hill, immediately to the north of Trois Vase House (from an article in The Recorder for Palmers Green, Winchmore Hill and Southgate, *24.11.1910).*

derived from three stone vases which decorated the tops of the stables, the single-storey extension attached to each house. The vases had been removed from the stables of No.1 by the early 1840s, but they survived at No.2. The name Orleans was also applied to No.2.[28] The owner of the property was John Radford, deacon of the Independent Chapel. In the 1850 Rate Book, No.1 is described simply as "house and garden, Hoppers Lane". No.2 was at the time occupied by a Mr. Cockrane.[29]

The immediate surroundings of Trois Vase House were distinctly rural. Opposite, fields studded with trees and grazed by cattle extended to the edge of Winchmore Hill Wood. To the south, Hoppers Lane was a leafy vista bordered by pines, larches, beeches and oaks, the hedgerows decked with flowers in spring and early summer. To the north, pantiled cottages fronted the road as it climbed towards the Green. The top floor of the house commanded views across Winchmore Hill Wood in one direction and towards the Essex hills in the other.

Not long after John Cresswell came to Trois Vase House, land immediately to the north was taken for the building of the new Independent Chapel. This was the site given by John Radford. The new building, opened in 1844, was a close and somewhat dominant neighbour to Trois Vase House; "a big building, high, with pinnacles of the Gothic-run-to-seed variety. It stood some 30 feet back from the road and was of white brick faced at the angles with white freestone. It had long narrow lancet windows on both sides....there was a gravel path all round the building....".[30] A corner of the chapel appears in John Cresswell's painting of Trois Vase House. One local resident who experienced worship at the chapel in the 1840s was Henry Cox. Born in Winchmore Hill in 1839, he lived in Vicars Moor Lane for most of his childhood. In his autobiography, written when he was an old man, he compared the chapel services unfavourably with those at St. Paul's Church, which he had also attended:

> There seemed to me as much difference between the church service and the go-as-you-please performance of the Independent Chapel as there is between a pigsty with piggies capering round, and a fashionable drawing-room with the formalities of dudes and flappers.[31]

John Cresswell did not live alone at Trois Vase House. His mother Henrietta, and his sister Sarah, gave up their home at Town Malling in Kent and came to Winchmore Hill to keep house for him. With them came Ann (or Nannie) Matthews, widow of Joseph Matthews, the farm bailiff of Mark Noble, with whom Henrietta and her three children had lodged at East Farleigh after Mark Noble's death in 1827. Nannie Matthews had been a nurse to Mark Noble's daughter Christiana, and became a close family friend as well as a servant. She and Joseph lived with the Cresswells at Town Malling, and Joseph died there.[32]

During these early years, while he was establishing his practice, John Cresswell faced considerable financial difficulty. Although the only surgeon practising in the village at this time, he had to work hard to retain his patients and attract new ones. The expense of running his surgery at Trois Vase House, and of purchasing, making up and dispensing medicines, would have been substantial. At a time when the appearance, style and speech of a general practitioner were as important to patients as his qualifications, he needed to cultivate a manner and approach that would win the confidence of local people. The reputation of a medical man depended more on social attributes than on the effectiveness of medical treatment, much of which was of questionable value. To build a reputation and extend his contacts, a practitioner needed to integrate well into the community by joining local clubs and societies, whilst avoiding controversy in politics and religion for fear of alienating some patients.[33]

A drawing of John Cresswell made two years after he came to Winchmore Hill depicts a well groomed, tidily dressed young man with a pleasing countenance. Although in later years he became less particular about his appearance, he never lost his reputation as a man of sincerity and good humour. He established himself quickly as a competent surgeon, and his dedication to the work is perhaps illustrated by the fact that "he only slept away from home twice or thrice for a single night in more than forty years".[34]

An example of John Cresswell's participation in the community was his membership of the Southgate Reading Society. This was a form of subscription li-

A crayon drawing of John Cresswell at the age of 26, two years after he came to Winchmore Hill.

brary, affording members the opportunity to borrow and read the growing selection of popular literature which was meeting the demand for self-improvement and effective use of leisure in the early Victorian period. A surviving catalogue of the Southgate Reading Society, printed in 1844, and signed by John Cresswell on 29th March 1848, indicates the wide range of material available. Its 16 pages list no fewer than 323 titles belonging to the society, and to these John has added another 64 in his own hand. Among the diverse offerings were *Siege and Destruction of Jerusalem*, *Mental and Moral Dignity of Woman*, *Miscellany by Factory Girls*, and *Campbell's Pleasures of Hope*. A later issue of the catalogue, printed in 1849 and signed by John Cresswell in 1855, shows that by then the collection had expanded to 611 works.[35]

Slowly, Winchmore Hill was beginning to grow and change. John Cresswell remembered the lower part of Church Hill when it was no more than a grass road. Henry Cox tells us that the village "was divided into fields of about ten acres each, but there were only a few of them that had gentlemen's houses on....some three or four wealthy London merchants had two or more of these fields. They went to town each day, and a confidential man was left in charge". These were recollections of the early 1840s. By 1847, the village consisted "principally of villa residences occupied by wealthy mercantile men from the metropolis". Small though the place still was, the seeds of its transformation into a residential suburb of London had been sown.[36]

By this time, John Cresswell's sister Sarah had become engaged to the Reverend Henry Combs, a college friend of Richard, her elder brother. Henry, a similar age to Sarah, had entered St. John's College, Oxford, in 1834, the year before Richard; he had been awarded his BA in 1838 and his MA in 1842. A Fellow of the college, he was well known to Edward Pusey, and, like Richard, was a follower of his Tractarian principles. Sarah had great admiration for Dr. Pusey, and in 1847 employed her skill as a needlewoman to make him an embroidered stole.[37] His letter of thanks, posted to Sarah in Winchmore Hill from Oxford on 15th September 1847, has been preserved. It begins:

> I thank you kindly for the great pains you have taken in making me what
> is very beautiful. I do hope it may, by God's mercy, do me good to see its
> beautiful white cross. You will not think your labour misemployed if I say

> I dare not use [it] in the pulpit; for whatever I do may be, more or less, the subject of cavil....the souls of men must be my one object, to win them to Christ.[38]

Pusey refers here to the controversy already being engendered by some Tractarians over their eagerness to wear priestly vestments. His own preference was for simplicity in clerical attire, which he regarded as a symbol of inward humility. In 1837 he had been required to explain to the Bishop of Oxford the wearing of an embroidered stole by one of his young, ordained, assistant lecturers at the university; he based his defence on the Ornaments Rubric of the Book of Common Prayer, adding that "it seemed a very safe way for the exuberance of youth to vent itself in".[39] No doubt this exchange was still in his mind when he received Sarah's gift.

In 1843 Pusey had faced a more serious charge, following a sermon preached at Oxford on 14th May. His subject was "The Holy Eucharist a Comfort to the Penitent". Although his words were doctrinally impeccable, he used certain expressions concerning the nature of the Eucharist which were considered heretical by a brother professor, and the Vice-Chancellor, without giving Pusey an opportunity to defend himself, suspended him from preaching at the university for two years. This was a cruel blow to Pusey, whose sense of injustice was widely shared.[40] A copy of his printed Protest, addressed to the Vice-Chancellor on 2nd June 1843, is enclosed with his letter to Sarah Cresswell; the letter reflects a continuing bitterness flowing from this affair, observing that "the world despises what is good, and hates not what is evil", and advising, in the words of Isaiah, that one must "set one's face like a flint".

The letter refers warmly to Sarah's fiancé — "I am always glad to see HC....remember me affectionately to H at any time" — but regrets that "his mind is too sensitive" to present troubles. It seems that, at this time, Henry Combs was facing a crisis of conscience over his faith, for he would soon relinquish his curacy of Summertown, Oxfordshire, and, following the example of John Henry Newman, would be received into the Roman Catholic Church. This caused his engagement to Sarah to be broken, a circumstance which evoked in her brother Richard a strong antipathy to Roman Catholics which he retained for the rest of his life.[41] No doubt when Sarah re-read Dr. Pusey's letter she drew some comfort from its closing words:

> You, my dear Madam, will recollect that the time is short. The world passes away, both its joys and sorrows, and One only abideth. May you for ever abide in Him, held fast by Himself, by the bond of love.

Sarah continued to live at Trois Vase House with her brother John, and her mother Henrietta. The 1851 census records five members of the household. In addition to the Cresswells there was Henrietta Noble, an unmarried cousin of John, aged 38. Her birthplace was Sandhurst, Berkshire, and she was presumably staying with the family. There was also one servant, Sarah Bryant, aged 23.

Saint James Church, Pentonville

St. James's Church, Pentonville, London, c.1860. When John Cresswell married his cousin Frances Sophia Willink here in 1852 it was a chapel-of-ease to St. James's, Clerkenwell. It became a parish church in 1854.

Nannie Matthews, the family friend and servant, does not appear. The population of the newly formed district chapelry of Winchmore Hill was then 1,705.

John Cresswell, now aged 32, had not yet married. It was characteristic of the era that female patients were reluctant to seek advice on personal problems from unmarried medical practitioners, for which reason a wife has been described as "almost a necessary part of professional equipment" for a man in general practice.[42] John practised in Winchmore Hill as a single man for 10 years, secure in the knowledge that appropriate provision had been made through his engagement, whilst still a student, to his cousin Frances Sophia Willink. The engagement lasted 12 years, and it was not until 1852, at the age of 33, that he felt sufficiently well established in his medical practice to support a wife.

Frances Sophia's home in Cumming Street, Pentonville, was but a short walk from St. James's Chapel, where, on Monday 28th June 1852, she took John Cresswell's hand in marriage. The building in which the marriage was solemnised had opened in 1788 as a dissenting chapel, but was consecrated as a chapel-of-ease to the parish church of St. James, Clerkenwell, in 1791. The chapel was approached by a semi-circular gravelled carriage way from iron gates in the New Road. It was a brick structure surmounted by a stone pediment on Ionic pilasters and crowned with a cupola. The simple interior, seating 700, had galleries supported on pillars of imitation marble, and the altar was placed in a semi-circular sanctuary at the north end.[43]

The officiating minister at the marriage was John Cresswell's brother, the Reverend Richard Cresswell. The witnesses were Diederich Willink, the bride's younger brother, and Francis Buttanshaw, the bridegroom's uncle and former tutor.[44] Frances Sophia chose Coronation Day for the wedding, it is said, so that every bell in London should ring. The newly-weds drove to Winchmore Hill in a post chaise, with a pair of white horses and a postilion. When Frances saw the flowering elder bushes opposite Trois Vase House, she called them her wedding bouquets. In the boot of the post chaise was a large carpet bag containing wedding presents of old silver which were quite forgotten in the excitement of arrival. They continued with the chaise to a livery stable yard at Colney Hatch, and were rescued the following morning by John's sister Sarah, who walked three miles to collect them and three miles back.[45]

The Cottage, Vicars Moor Lane, Winchmore Hill, from a copy of a watercolour painted by Richard Cresswell c.1865 (reproduced in The Palmers Green and Southgate Gazette, *28.8.1936). In 1852 this became the home of Henrietta (mother of Richard and John Cresswell) and of her daughter Sarah.*

With the arrival of Frances Sophia at Trois Vase House, John's mother and sister moved to an old house known simply as the Cottage on the north side of Vicars Moor Lane, across the village from the Green. The pretty verandah-fronted dwelling, its rear garden dominated by a noble yew tree and planted with old English flowers, remained a family home of the Cresswells for another 17 years. Nannie Matthews also lived at the Cottage with Henrietta and Sarah Cresswell; after she died, her belongings, including a fine old oak escritoire with secret drawers, passed to the Cresswells, and stayed in the family for many years.[46]

Frances Sophia's first child, a boy, was born at Trois Vase House on Wednesday 13th April 1853. He was christened Willink, his mother's maiden name, and was baptised in St. Paul's, Winchmore Hill, on Sunday 26th June. The baptism was performed by the Reverend John Dixon Frost, who had become priest-in-charge of St. Paul's in 1844, and the first incumbent on creation of the district chapelry in 1851.[47] Sadly for Frances and John Cresswell, Willink was a sickly child from birth, though unlike many frail children of his day he did not die in infancy.

Just under two years later, on Thursday 15th February 1855, a second child was born to the Cresswells. This was Henrietta, who bore the christian name of her paternal grandmother, and who became known in the family as Etta. She was baptised in St. Paul's on Wednesday 18th April, again by John Dixon Frost.[48] It is to Henrietta that we owe so much of our knowledge of the Cresswells and of life in 19th century Winchmore Hill. Her recollections of childhood, written in her fifties after she had left Winchmore Hill, form a charming yet vivid account of the ways of a middle-class family in a quiet rural community on the brink of its transformation into a suburb of London.

Henrietta's Childhood

Henrietta's elder brother Willink receives no more than a passing reference in her family recollections. She is equally reticent about her younger sister Mary, born on 20th January 1857 and baptised in St. Paul's on 22nd February by J. Hawksworth, a visiting missionary preacher from Travancore, India. However, Henrietta was not quite four years old when, on 17th January 1859, Mary died of bronchitis and whooping-cough after an illness lasting six weeks. The child was three days short of her second birthday, and was buried on 22nd January in All Saints churchyard, Edmonton, by John Dixon Frost.[49] For Henrietta, an ailing brother, and a little sister who did not survive infancy, can have provided few happy memories.

One of Henrietta's earliest childhood memories was of a visit to her maternal grandmother, Frances Mary Willink, at Cumming Street, Pentonville, in the summer of 1857. Though less than three years old, Henrietta remembered the occasion vividly. Her father wheeled her in a perambulator to Hornsey Station, then the nearest on the Great Northern line towards London. At Palmers Green the perambulator overbalanced while John Cresswell left it unattended to quench his thirst from the New River. No harm came to the child, however, and she enjoyed the day out, sleeping all the way back from Hornsey to Winchmore Hill.[50]

Two years later, in June 1859, Frances Mary Willink moved with her unmarried son Diederich, then in his mid-thirties, from Pentonville to Winchmore Hill. They took up residence at 2 Trois Vase House, next door to the Cresswells. Diederich was of course Henrietta's uncle, but it was grandmother Willink whom she remembered with most affection. Her memories of her grandmother span more than a decade, through childhood and early teenage years.

There was a ladder on the Cresswells' side of the dividing garden wall, and a set of steps on the Willinks' side. From time to time grandmother Willink would pop up her steps with great alacrity and appear over the wall like a jack-in-the-box if she heard unruly behaviour in the neighbouring garden. However, the lady who in her youth had danced on the dinner table and followed the latest female fashions became in later years a person of dignity and a "fairy godmother". She was careful to encourage good manners and proper etiquette, and would never receive visitors to tea or dinner, even members of her own family, unless they had been invited. Henrietta tells us that her red hair kept its colour into old age:

> I remember my grandmother as a keen looking but sweet faced old lady with a large hook nose and a laughing mouth, wearing a cap trimmed with rosettes of white satin baby ribbon, a dress of black silk for best, and figured alpaca for common, and black lace mittens, who did very little in a great hurry and much commotion, believing herself to work very hard indeed.

In earlier life she had been a fine netter and a worker of exquisite satin stitch embroidery. To the young Henrietta she seemed a lady of great refinement, not least because she always added a little rosewater to the basin before washing her face, and watered her window boxes from a valuable old blue china teapot.[51]

Of the events of Henrietta's early childhood, few can have made a greater impression than the "Fancy Fair", arranged to raise money for the building of the new National Schools in Church Hill. Advertised as "A Sale of Useful and Ornamental Articles", it was held in the grounds of Grovelands (formerly Southgate Grove), by then the home of John Donnithorne Taylor, in June 1859. Henrietta was just four years old, but her recollection of the event, written some 50 years later, is as acute as if she had penned it in childhood.[52]

The weather was perfect, and local residents flocked to the beautiful park. Henrietta had the pleasure of wearing a new hat and driving in a fly to the entrance gate into the park, where frightened deer retreated in alarm among the trees. The large white tents, the flags, a band playing martial airs, carriages and horses, and crowds of people, made this the greatest festivity Henrietta had yet known. Her father had written verses for the occasion, and had illustrated note-paper with tiny pictures of the village (some examples of which survive). Her aunt Sarah had produced articles for sale in needlework and featherwork. A great variety of goods was on sale, and Henrietta became the proud owner of a "real live Jack-in-the-box". Her mother bought a pair of Ormolu candlesticks with crystal drops that gave pleasure for a long time. The event lasted two days and was remembered in the village for many years. The year 1859 remained "the year of the Fancy Fair", long after the preceding general election, and the great July hailstorm, had been forgotten.[53]

The new National Schools, next to St. Paul's Church, were opened later the same year with a grand concert. For this, the walls were decorated with ever-green wreaths and mottoes of leaves. Although only four years old, Henrietta had a busy morning sewing leaves on cardboard letters. "She longed to see the decorations, but the concert was only for grown-up people." The school build-ings were considered "palatial":

> A narrow room sixty feet long with a high timbered roof and warmed by
> two fireplaces, a large infant school with galleries, spacious classrooms,

The National Schools, Church Hill, Winchmore Hill, from an engraving reproduced on the front of the annual report of the schools during the 1870s. On the left is the north west corner of St. Paul's Church. On the right is the schoolmaster's house with its attached clock tower. To the right of that is a gate giving direct access to the church for the Taylors of Grovelands, whose estate lies beyond. There are errors of detail in the engraving, but it is the earliest known illustration showing school and church together.

and large playgrounds, undoubtedly an enormous advance on the one-roomed cottage on the side of the hill.[54]

John Cresswell became a manager of the new school from the outset. The Reverend John Dixon Frost was chairman of the board of managers. Each manager had to declare that he was "a Member of the United Church of England and Ireland as by Law established". From 1864 there was an annual government inspection of the school. The second inspection, in May 1865, found that it was a well conducted school, although "the boys are mostly small". There was a recommendation that ventilation should be improved. A year later the ventilation was still found to be defective, and government grant was made conditional on an immediate improvement, which was carried out at once. "The School is pretty fairly conducted", said the report, but "it is hoped the style of the Work will be much improved next year". John Cresswell sat on the board of managers for over 30 years, and became its longest serving member.[55]

As each year passed, Henrietta's childhood was enlivened by new experiences in the village. In 1860, when she was five, a photographer set up a mobile studio on the Green for several weeks. It was "a well-to-do vehicle painted dark brown and drawn by a strong horse". The lace-curtained window and fancy barge boards gave it the appearance of a gypsy caravan. The taking of portraits was a serious and lengthy business, the prolonged effort to look pleasant producing either a furious scowl or a fixed grin. Henrietta had her photograph taken in her best black silk frock, with saucer neck and short puffed sleeves. "She was given a rose to hold in her hand, and solemnly gazed into the camera for what seemed an unending space of time, rigidly endeavouring to hold her breath and not move a muscle till the cap was safely back upon the lens." Her father was also photographed, and the finished pictures, mounted and framed, were collected the following day. "It was certainly a new sensation in the village, and caused considerable excitement."[56]

In April the following year, 1861, the census of population was taken. The Cresswell household at 1 Trois Vase House consisted of John and Frances Sophia, the six-year-old Henrietta (described as a "scholar"), and a 21-year-old female servant. Next door, at No.2, were Frances Sophia's mother, Frances Willink, by then 72, and her son Diederich, still unmarried, and employed as a merchant's clerk. Their house was run by two female servants — a housekeeper of 70, and a parlourmaid of 30. At the Cottage in Vicars Moor Lane, the third family home in the village, the census shows only John's sister Sarah, his son Willink (then aged seven), and a 17-year-old servant. John Cresswell's mother, Henrietta, does not appear at all, though this may simply mean that she was absent from home when the census was taken. It does seem likely that, by this time, the delicate young Willink was being cared for by his aunt Sarah at his grandmother's home.

In the early hours of Saturday 11th May 1861, just over a month after the census was taken, John Cresswell's family was further enlarged with the birth of another boy, Francis. He was baptised in St. Paul's Church on his parents' wedding anniversary, Friday 28th June. The ceremony was performed by an-

Henrietta Cresswell (born 1855), daughter of John and Frances Sophia, photographed in Winchmore Hill at the age of seven.

other visiting clergyman, J.B. Hawkins of St. Edmund Hall, Oxford. In her recollections, Henrietta refers to Francis somewhat dismissively as "the Boy", never as her brother, but as he grew older "the boy with the fair curls was becoming a person to be reckoned with", and Henrietta and he played happily together. The long fair curls rested upon his shoulders.[57] He was usually called Frank by family and friends.

Living in a rural community, and having to make her own amusements, Henrietta became accustomed to solitary walks as soon as she was considered old enough to go out alone. The last story that she wrote about Winchmore Hill was a recollection of a long walk taken in the autumn twilight when she was seven years old. Published posthumously, it is a pleasing re-creation of the childish imagination at work in a natural setting:

> On an autumn afternoon when the dusk fell early she had a fine opportunity for one of those lonely walks which she loved. In the damp wood there were already mists rising, and the hedge on the right of the cart road was draped with gossamer. A maid who had come from Doctors' Commons once said they made her feel she must fetch her broom and sweep them all away.

The bracken, lichens and moss in the wood were closely observed: "it was all these things that made it so much more interesting to walk alone than with some hurrying older person".

Past the wood keeper's cottage and fields bounded with heather and wild scabious, the path emerged into Southgate Lane. A glorious sunset of red and gold greeted Henrietta as she paused by the Pound in Bourne Hill, and she glimpsed a stag drinking from the lake in Grovelands as she climbed towards Southgate. Her return along the Chase towards Winchmore Hill was made in the gathering dusk, and the story of a ghostly apparition at White Lodge, "an eerie place to pass in the gloaming of an autumn evening", was easily believed. "A newly-lit candle in an upper room....cast a long beam of light across the road, and it took very little imagination to see the body of a man hanging from a branch by the roadside."

> The autumn mist lay white in the deep valley on the left, and a pond on the brow of the hill gleamed weirdly in the twilight. The new villas and old cottages near the turn of the road were a friendly sight, and it was cheering to see the lighted doorway of the Chase Side Tavern.

When Henrietta arrived home the Green and Hoppers Road were still lit by a faint orange afterglow, and she escaped being scolded for being so late.[58]

Henrietta had no fear of being out alone, even in a big city. She was a frequent visitor to her great-aunt Maria at Doctors' Commons, and her first walk in London alone was at the age of eight to take a message from Doctors' Commons to London House Yard, between St. Paul's Churchyard and Paternoster

The 33rd Middlesex Rifle Volunteer Corps (Tottenham Company) in August 1863. John Cresswell is seated on the right behind the Scottish terrier (Charley). Sitting next to him is his brother-in-law Diederich Willink.

Row. This was no great distance, but could have been daunting for so young a child brought up in the country. However, she told her great-aunt that she was not at all afraid to go, though remembered afterwards how very small she felt as she crossed below the cathedral steps. By contrast, the same great-aunt Maria was terrified to walk unaccompanied along the reputedly haunted Hagfields footpath in Winchmore Hill.[59]

Despite the demands of his family and his medical practice, John Cresswell found time for leisure pursuits. His interest in reading has already been noted; his artistic ability will be fully recognised in a later chapter. He was also skilled in hand crafting objects, many of them for his children's benefit — a pair of scales from coconut shells, baskets from walnut shells, cribbage pegs from date stones, pop-guns from elder stems, and chestnut whistles. At one time he kept a horse, and his terrier was one of several family pets. Bee-keeping was a favourite hobby, and Henrietta's account of the hiving in late May is a delight. Her father performed the hiving bareheaded and in shirt sleeves, without protection, and afterwards relaxed with a well earned pipe. A man of considerable energy, he would think nothing of walking to London and back when he had business in the City — a round trip of nearly 20 miles.[60]

In the early 1860s, John Cresswell and his brother-in-law Diederich Willink joined the 33rd Middlesex Rifle Volunteers. The volunteer movement was revived in the mid-19th century on a wave of patriotism. The government was slow to support it, but Queen Victoria showed great personal interest, thereby guaranteeing its success. In her speech from the throne in January 1860 she said: "this manifestation of public spirit has added an important element to our system of national defence", and on 23rd June 1860 she reviewed a march past of more than 18,000 volunteers in Hyde Park, including the Middlesex corps. The six Middlesex corps were formed during 1859 and 1860; the 33rd, based at Tottenham, was the last but one to be raised, on 16th February 1860. In 1862 they combined to form the 2nd Administrative Battalion Middlesex Rifle Volunteers.

John Cresswell participated in the new movement with much enthusiasm, despite opposition from his Quaker patients. Stories of his exploits thrilled the young Henrietta, for whom he made a target to shoot at with her bows and arrows. She could hardly lift her father's rifle, but learnt her drill from him with a little old rusty fowling piece. He was one of the crack shots of the corps, and brought home prizes to prove it — an achievement which would reappear in the family two generations later. Although he was offered a commission he preferred to remain a private, fearing that his professional duties might interfere with his regimental ones. A photograph taken in August 1863 shows John Cresswell, Diederich Willink and other members of the corps in their tunics, leather cross-belts, and peaked caps with woolly pom-poms. The uniform was grey, trimmed with scarlet braid, and the pom-poms too were scarlet. Henrietta says nothing about her uncle Diederich's activities in the corps, but her father remained a member until 1869.[61]

Towards the end of 1863, sadness fell upon the Cresswell family with the death of John's sister Sarah. She had been ill for 10 months with heart disease,

Orchis mascula, *from a watercolour painted by Sarah Cresswell, c.1849. One of a set of her paintings of British orchids, preserved in the Royal Albert Memorial Museum, Exeter.*

and died on 20th November at the age of 46. Her aunt Christiana Buttanshaw, then living at Blackheath, was with her when she died at the Cottage in Vicars Moor Lane. She was buried a week later in the family grave at Edmonton by John Dixon Frost.[62] In her will, made 12 years earlier, she bequeathed to her former fiancé, the Reverend Henry Combs, a gold watch and chain, and to her brother Richard a crayon portrait of Henry. To her brother John she left her copy of the *Waverley Novels*, no doubt a treasured bequest to a keen reader. In her short and at times simple life, Sarah had proved herself a talented artist and needlewoman, as well as a devoted daughter to her ageing mother. As a lasting testimony to her artistic skill, there survives a set of beautifully executed water-colours of British orchids.[63]

Following closely on the death of Sarah came that of Henrietta's great-aunt Maria. She died a spinster on 29th December 1863, at Doctors' Commons, severing another link between the Cresswell family and that venerable but dying institution. She was buried in the cemetery at Brompton with her brother Robert Nathaniel.[64] Within little more than a month the young Henrietta had suffered the loss of an aunt and a great-aunt, both of whom were dear to her.

Henrietta was now reaching an age at which she could understand and absorb many aspects of family life, and her recollections often relate to this period of her childhood. To her keenly observant eye and retentive memory we owe a description of her father's dispensary, which occupied a part of the stable adjoining Trois Vase House:

> There was an old counter of dark mahogany, shelves of dusty bottles, and rows of drawers with mysterious glittering gold labels, Radd Quass, Cort Aurant, and Pet Nit, etc....there were gallon jars of Castor oil and Mist Sennae comp, a chest of carpenter's tools, bins of physic bottles and vials, an old-fashioned ewer and basin of white delft, and sundries of every kind, and over all and among everything the largest and thickest cobwebs ever seen.

The window was small and shrouded by a grape vine, so John Cresswell usually left the door open when he was dispensing to admit some light. Medicines were distributed around the village in a basket carried by a young boy factotum.[65]

In common with other middle-class families, the Cresswells had servants, but Frances Sophia bore some of the responsibilities of a housewife. Her kitchen had no larder, and perishables had to be stored in a cold cupboard under the front-door steps, or in a perforated meat safe hung high upon the kitchen wall. On one occasion the remains of a blackcurrant pudding which she had just put into the safe were partly devoured by William, the surgery boy, when no one was looking. John's wife was a well known figure in the village shops, especially Mrs. Binsted's in Middle Lane for cakes and confectionery, and Udall's the drapers on the Green. The latter saw little movement of stock, and Frances Sophia would point to the box containing material she had purchased two or

John Cresswell, photographed in Winchmore Hill in 1862 at the age of 43.

three years earlier in order to secure a matching length. Her taste was conservative, and she kept Henrietta in skirts below her ankles while other girls of her age wore them up to the knee.[66]

Henrietta later admitted to a childhood longing to have been a boy, which she attributed to a sense of male superiority. She was indeed disappointed when she realised "that she was condemned to wear her hated petticoats all her life, and would always be expected to 'love her needle' and 'sit still like a lady'". She was a lonely child with few playmates; her chief friends were the toads, newts and frogs which inhabited her garden. She suffered agonies of despair when she inadvertently killed a frog by placing it under glass on a hot day, and her despair turned to fear when she reflected on the hell fire and eternal damnation which were preached from the pulpit in Sunday sermons.[67]

Among Henrietta's childhood pastimes, the game of knucklebones was a favourite. The pieces were fashioned from lumps of domestic coal, and she practised her skill on the stable step. Other toys included a box of bricks, dissected maps and spillikins. A prized possession was her alphabet book, which survived until after her death. The letters of the alphabet were impressed on the reader by alliterative verses, illustrated with hand-coloured prints:

> Andrew Airpump ask'd his Aunt her Ailment:
> Did Andrew Airpump ask his Aunt her Ailment?
> If Andrew Airpump ask'd his Aunt her Ailment,
> Where was the Ailment of Andrew Airpump's Aunt?

And so on through the alphabet, only X, Y and Z making the author's "brains to crack-o, X smokes, Y snuffs, and Z chews tobacco". Henrietta had been given the book by old Captain Tills of Ford's Grove Cottage; it must have been new in about 1790.[68]

For outdoor activities, iron hoops "were loved as if they were sentient beings", and long solitary afternoons spent fishing from the New River in the grounds of Beaulieu were much enjoyed. When Henrietta's brother Francis was old enough, he helped her build a garden house known as "Crown Palace". It was erected against the garden fence of Trois Vase House, and employed in its construction clothes props, logs, boughs, carpet remnants and straw from physic-bottle crates. Henrietta made a tessellated pathway to the door with coloured fragments of crockery and broken flower pots.[69]

For many years, the estate of Highfield Park, adjoining Trois Vase House, was a free playground for the Cresswell children. Highfield House, built in 1815, had extensive grounds stretching from Hoppers Road to the Green Lanes and bordered by Compton Lane. A fine avenue of oaks led to the house from the gate in Hoppers Road. In 1841 the property was occupied by a family named Firth, who employed no fewer than nine servants. By 1851 the widow of Captain Clark of the 2nd Life Guards was in residence there with her niece and nephew and five servants, and she was still living there 10 years later. The grounds contained two large meadows, known as upper and lower ten-acre,

and were surrounded by a gravel footpath and shrubbery. The Cresswell children invented their own names for the trees — Broken Bough, Splinter, Oak
Apple Tree and Owl Tree:

> The soft "whoo-whoo" of the white owls and the hissing of the baby owls
> in the nest, the rustling of small things in the grass, the grunt of a hedge-
> hog, the nibbling of the sheep and baaing of lambs in the upper ten-acre,
> the stamp of a horse's hoof as he shook off the gnats by the pond, the
> white mist wreaths rising from the grass and hiding the trunks of the trees
> so that their tops appeared to float on a silver sea. Who would wish to go
> home and exchange all this for a closely shut up room and quiet evening
> amusements by the light of a Moderator lamp? [70]

Of all the scenes of Henrietta's childhood, none held dearer memories than
the wild expanses of Winchmore Hill Wood. Although much of the woodland
was privately owned, the children had access to it: "it was a happy hunting
ground in more senses than one, for they were often the hunted ones, and the
Demon who guarded the Enchanted Forest was the hunter". This was the
woodman — gaunt, forbidding, with piercing black eyes and a nose like an
eagle's beak. The children ran from him like hares, or practised the art of walking noiselessly over dead twigs as he passed by.

Every inch of the wood was familiar to the children, and they quickly learnt
the names of the trees, flowers and wild creatures. Henrietta's love of nature,
her knowledge of botany and her affection for wildlife were nurtured here; the
pattern of her later years, which in due course we shall trace, was woven from
threads drawn together during her wanderings in Winchmore Hill Wood:

> Those who have heard the voices of the woods, and loved their whisper-
> ings in childhood, will hear them calling for ever in the after years, calling
> them to wild places, to country sights and sounds, to the unspoilt corners
> of the land, where they can forget that crowds, and cities, and struggling
> suburbs, even exist. [71]

Henrietta became fond of flowers at an early age. As a child she admired the
pelargoniums, Chinese primroses and cinerarias grown by Braid the nurseryman near the King's Head, and on one occasion she and her brother Francis
walked to a nursery near Firs Farm, across the Green Lanes, to buy china asters
for their mother's birthday. Unable to choose between the varied colours, they
bought one of each, and staggered home with five flower pots between them:
"how the Mother valued her birthday present none but a mother could know". [72]
Henrietta's love of flowers remained with her all her life, and in due course
inspired an artistic talent to which we shall return.

Although fond of solitary walks, Henrietta did enjoy country rambles with
her father, as he too was a lover of nature and imparted his knowledge to her.
These walks were sometimes combined with visits to patients; if they had con-

tagious or infectious diseases Henrietta would wait for her father on the opposite side of the road and then walk ahead of him for some distance until he had had "a jolly good blow of fresh air". This happened when he visited a child with typhus fever in the Rookery at Highfield Row, giving Henrietta an opportunity to run on ahead to the New River. The path by the river made a pleasant walk, and John Cresswell identified for his daughter the many fish and water insects living there. Another walk took them to Ford's Grove Cottage, the home of Captain Tills, beside wide ditches inhabited by sticklebacks, frogspawn, caddisworms and water rats.[73]

In common with many children of her time, Henrietta received much of her education at the feet of her parents. Her mother taught her about the natural world while she was still an infant, and even botanical Latin names were explained. She could read by the time she was four, and was soon writing proper letters to her mother when she was away at the seaside. At the age of five she began reading Ann Pratt's Botany, published in monthly parts over several years. From the illustrations she learnt the names of plants which she would not encounter in the countryside until much later in life. *Ann Pratt* was one of the few books that Henrietta herself owned as a child, and she treasured it. When she was 10, she became a pupil of Captain Tills's daughter Charlotte, who began teaching children of the village at Ford's Grove Cottage after her father's death. Charlotte was an excellent teacher, with unlimited patience and good temper. Henrietta enjoyed the lessons, though she often arrived breathless and dirty, having crossed Highfield Park over muddy fields and mossy walls. There were other places of education in the village, including of course the National Schools, but the Cresswell children did not attend them. Henrietta did however visit a "select day school for boys and girls" on the Green for breaking-up parties and great festivities, and "learnt some wonderful facts which had been taught to the other scholars; for instance, that the climate of Central Africa is so hot that all the natives have to do to *heat their flat irons* is to stand them out in the sun".[74]

On long winter evenings, Henrietta's father entertained her with stories and folk tales. A favourite recitation was *Hingerum Jingerum*, a nonsense tale from Kent; it is easy to imagine Henrietta's childish delight as she listened at her father's knee to the absurd story unfolding:

> As I was going over Hingerum Jingerum, I saw 99 miles over the moon. I saw peat-hooks and pothooks and all them kind of things. I picked up a peat-hook and knocked the brains of a goose's eye out with it, so I gathered them up and took them home to old Father Swopleg the miller, and asked him to grind them into his best wheat flour....

Having climbed the winter's pear tree and found his lap full of young peacocks, the narrator takes them to London and sells them for eightpence a piece:

> Then I had more money than I knew what to do with, so I bought some hempseed....as I was coming home I met old Father Swopleg and asked

him when to sow it. 'Twixt Michaelmas and a new millstone, says he.
Clever answer that for an old blade, so we took to words and fell to blows,
and the worst of it was that he knocked me 99 miles over a wheatstraw
and broke my neck....

And so on through a milk white sow with a purple tail, crutches for lame ducks,
spectacles for blind spiders, and wooden legs for cockchafers.[75]

In April 1865, John Cresswell was appointed a churchwarden of St. Paul's,
Winchmore Hill. He was chosen by the incumbent, John Dixon Frost, to be his
warden; the householders (or parishioners) appointed Captain Morrison to be
theirs. John Cresswell held the post for six years, his last reappointment being in
April 1870. Church and chapel were an important part of the fabric of social life
in mid-Victorian England, and to hold a position of responsibility in the worshipping community was to earn a degree of recognition which would be of
benefit professionally and socially. As one who had been educated by a clergyman of the Church of England, and as the brother of a cleric, it was natural that
John Cresswell should look to the established church to meet his spiritual needs,
and that in due course he should assume an important role in parish life.[76]

Towards the end of 1865 John Cresswell at last became a medical officer to
the Edmonton Poor Law Union, more than 20 years after his narrow failure to
secure the appointment. Thomas Ward, who had been appointed in preference
to John Cresswell, and who had latterly served as medical officer for the
Southgate and Winchmore Hill District of the union, had recently died. In November 1865 a proposal was put before the board of guardians to divide the
district into two, and to offer John Cresswell the post of medical officer for the
Winchmore Hill District. The vice-chairman of the board, Robert Richmond,
interviewed John Cresswell, who indicated his willingness to accept the appointment. The annual salary was a mere £16 10s, the district covering Winchmore
Hill village, Firs Lane, Hoppers Road, Palmers Green as far as Hazelwood Lane,
and along Chase Side Road towards Southgate as far as Hope Cottage. The
resolution to appoint John Cresswell was passed on 6th December 1865, and he
was required to commence his duties immediately. He named as his substitute
Mr. Robert Newberry Cobbett, who was appointed at the same time as the medical officer for the newly created Southgate District. Vaccination contracts with
Messrs. Cresswell and Cobbett were concluded in January 1866.[77]

General practitioner, school manager, churchwarden, defence volunteer, Poor
Law medical officer, artist, naturalist and family man — John Cresswell had
indeed established himself as an able, energetic and gifted member of the community. Although he could claim gentlemanly descent, he did not enjoy the advantages of a university education or personal wealth. His accomplishments
were to a great extent the product of perseverance, determination, common sense
and some natural talent. He was representative of the independent, self-made
men who contributed so much to middle-class society in mid-Victorian England.

An Uncle from Devonshire

We left John Cresswell's elder brother Richard at Salcombe Regis, Devon, where he took up his duties as curate of the parish following his marriage in December 1843. He lived at the vicarage, officiating on behalf of a non-resident parson, the Reverend J.H. Cardew, who also held the livings of Gulval, Cornwall, and of Curry Mallet, Somerset, where he resided. The appointment of a clergyman to several benefices was outlawed by the Pluralities Act of 1838, and future vicars of Salcombe Regis would live in the parish. A former curate, the Reverend George Cornish, was an intimate friend of John Keble at Oxford. Keble was a frequent visitor to Salcombe Regis, and preached in the church there. He formed an attachment to George Cornish's sister Cornelia, but a proposal of marriage which he made to her in 1824 came to nothing.[78]

No doubt Richard Cresswell was aware of Keble's connection with Salcombe Regis, but he would have known it chiefly as the burial place of his younger brother William. It is claimed, however, that a curacy in South Devon was suggested to him because of uncertain health, and that the choice of Salcombe Regis was a coincidence. The situation was certainly agreeable. The village, "picturesquely seated in the Sid valley, sheltered by boldly swelling hills, which terminate in the

Salcombe Regis, Devon. The church of St. Peter and St. Mary, from the vicarage garden, reproduced from a watercolour painted by John Cresswell in 1847. His brother Richard became curate here in 1844, and lived in the vicarage.

Drawing of a pink rose by Richard Cresswell, reproduced from his watercolour of c.1844.

lofty red sandstone sea cliffs", had a population of about 500. It contained "several neat mansions, with tasteful grounds, commanding extensive views of the coast and the English Channel". The Norman church of St. Peter and St. Mary, with a 15th century tower and three bells, had undergone many repairs and alterations. A parish school, supported by subscription, was attended by about 40 day and 80 Sunday pupils. The vicarage, its lower rooms lit by Gothick-style windows, commanded a beautiful view towards the sea, with the church tower visible just beyond the garden. In 1847 Richard's brother John, on a visit from Winchmore Hill, painted the scene from the vicarage garden. This watercolour has survived along with two others of Sidbury and Sidmouth which John Cresswell painted on the same occasion.[79]

Not long after his arrival at Salcombe Regis, Richard Cresswell travelled to Curry Mallet, near Taunton, to discuss parish work with his incumbent. He found there a pleasant rectory, occupied by Mr. and Mrs. Cardew, and their children and grand-children. Richard accompanied two of the young people on a walk, and was presented with a pink rose by little Edith Cardew, a grand-daughter aged five or six. He made a painting of the flower, and gave it to the child. More than 60 years later the delicate watercolour was returned to the Cresswell family, and has been preserved as a reminder of this touching gesture.[80]

Richard Cresswell's interest in botanical studies continued once he had settled at Salcombe Regis. Another surviving album of hand-coloured plant studies contains 55 drawings done by Richard in South Devon between June 1845 and April 1847.[81] During this period he began writing papers on the flora of South Devon. One of these, *The Flowering Plants and Ferns of Sidmouth and its Vicinity*, was published by Whittaker and Company of London in 1846. It is a pocket-sized, 46-page catalogue of no fewer than 572 botanical species, arranged by class, sub-class and order, and indicating in many cases where a specimen was found. Items not gathered by the author but donated "by the kindness of several Botanical friends, on whose judgment reliance can be placed" are so identified. "It can scarcely be hoped that the following catalogue is perfect", says the introduction, "though it has been endeavoured to render it as nearly so as circumstances would permit: no Plant has been admitted on conjecture". There are no illustrations, and, apart from the initials RC at the foot of the introduction, there is no reference to authorship.

At this time, Richard Cresswell was also developing an interest in the marine and fresh water algae of the area, and it was on this work that his reputation as a botanist came chiefly to depend. The warm and sheltered coastal region of South Devon strongly favoured the growth of seaweeds, and since the early 19th century botanists had searched this coastline for new species of algae. Prominent among the collectors was Miss Catherine Cutler of Sidmouth, whose discoveries included the genus *Cutleria*. She was a friend of Richard Cresswell, and many of her specimens were later incorporated in his collection. Miss Cutler's assistant, Miss Fanny Hindom, subsequently became a friend of the Cresswells, and her specimens were in due course added to the Cresswell collection. Other collectors, many of them ladies, were undertaking similar studies elsewhere on the South Devon coast. These people, though not scientifically trained, were good outdoor botanists with ample energy and intelligence. Although there was competition among collectors to obtain the best specimens, there was also much co-operation between them. Richard Cresswell specialised in microscopic plant life in both salt and fresh water, and his friend Miss Cutler described his finds affectionately as "dirty dabs". He recorded rare species, and discovered a new one which was named *Schizothrix Cresswellii*. Although he was one of many collectors preserving marine algae at this time, his work on fresh water algae was pioneering.[82]

The collection of algae is arranged in an album dated 6th February 1847. The specimens are mounted on pieces of stiff paper. To preserve them, the paper was floated in water to make them adhere, after which they were covered in muslin, dried and pressed.[83] Many of the items were collected in South Devon, though other locations around the country are identified. Much of the collection dates from 1846–7, but additions were made right up to 1880. Precise dates are given in many cases, and botanical names are usually added. Occasionally there is other information on the find, for example: "Under the dripping of a rain water spout, Salcombe [Regis] Vicarage, August 1846"; "Growing on wet moss on the face of the cliff, Sidmouth, Sept.18 1846". Donated items, including some from Miss Catherine Cutler, are acknowledged. The album contains several letters; one, dated 9th November 1855, is from "your sincere friend C. Cutler" in Exmouth, sending Richard Cresswell two specimens and acknowledging receipt of another. Elsewhere in the collection there are drawings of seaweeds made under the microscope.

Richard's collection of specimens, and his numerous botanical drawings, have been preserved in the Royal Albert Memorial Museum, Exeter. Together they represent painstaking work extending over a period of 40 years. They are the product of a methodical and enquiring mind, and reflect the growing interest taken in the natural sciences by educated people during the 19th century.

Among the botanical drawings in the collection are two volumes of illustrations of fungi drawn from life by Richard Cresswell and others. They contain several hundred carefully executed pen and wash drawings with delicate colouring. Most are of fungi seen in South Devon, but others are from further afield. Some of the latter are drawn from specimens sent to Richard Cresswell by family and friends, whose initials or names are appended. Others he observed and drew himself on visits to various parts of the country. Scattered through the albums, which extend from the mid-1840s to the 1870s, are drawings of fungi found in Winchmore Hill Wood.

Richard was staying with his family in Winchmore Hill during late August and early September 1848. His collection includes several drawings of fungi made in Winchmore Hill Wood at this time: on 7th September, for example, he drew *Marasmius peronatus*, *Cantharellus infundibuliformis*, and *Craterellus cornucopiodes*. In summer and autumn the wood was richly endowed with colourful and distinctive fungi, observed many years later by Henrietta Cresswell:

> The golden peziza lay like the yolk of an egg among the dead leaves, and the scarlet amanita flamed on the edge of the fir forest....at the edge of the wood at the field side, where there was warmth from the southern sun, lay a narrow path, where numbers of great boletus grew, looking like unwholesome sponges, and in some places were crowds of tan coloured lactarius, that appeared to be made of saddle leather and when broken exuded milk. There were gay patches of rosy russulas and sulphur yellow agaricus....one variety was lovely to look upon, but no one who had once smelt its odour, would ever wish to meet with it again. It was phallus impudicus, the stinkhorn....the smell was a combination of gas escape and neglected drains.[84]

No doubt Henrietta owed much of her apparently extensive knowledge of fungi to her uncle Richard, who continued to visit Winchmore Hill throughout her childhood.

Richard's wife Frances was also a botanist, and her album of pressed mosses and liverworts, dated 14th September 1847, forms another part of the Cresswell Collection. It contains over 300 specimens, gathered between 1845 and 1847. Some were donated by other collectors. Among the widely dispersed locations are Hawkhurst (where Frances lived at the time of her marriage), Sevenoaks, Oxford, Dartmoor, Tadcaster, Teesdale, Edinburgh and Braemar. Frances Cresswell's album is arranged with the same care and attention to detail as her husband's.

The first child of Frances and Richard, a son, was born at Salcombe Regis Vicarage on 28th April 1846. He was christened Richard Henry after his paternal grandfather, who had died 28 years earlier. Two reminiscences of domestic life at the vicarage survive from this time. One concerns the weekly "ceremony" of baking bread, cakes and pies in an oven heated with furze faggots and plastered up with clay. The other recalls the stray tortoiseshell kitten which Richard Cresswell found crying in a ditch: when a boy called at the vicarage to claim it, the curate offered him a shilling or the kitten; the boy chose the shilling, and Kitty became the first of a long line of tortoiseshell cats to make their home with the Devonshire Cresswells.[85]

In November 1847, Richard Cresswell completed a theological work entitled

The Christian Life: Twelve Sermons. Published in 1848 by Joseph Masters of London, its intention was "to put forth a plain view of that hidden life of the Christian, which is the restoration of all that man has lost, as well as the fulfilment of the high aspirations of which he had but a glimpse, as it were, when his eyes were opened in Paradise". The author's theme is that the church, through its priesthood and sacraments, should be concerned primarily with "the exalted object of leading along the way of salvation", and not simply with "binding up the wounds we have sustained in our course".

The texts which inspire the sermons range widely over the Old and New Testaments. The subject matter includes priesthood and sacraments, the church service, education, humility, obedience, and "The Danger of Finding Mere Pleasure in Holy Things". The sermons, though somewhat verbose, reflect sound scriptural teaching, and quote extensively from texts other than those on which they are based. They are the work of a devout and learned man.

The last two sermons, on "The Actual Church" and "The Ideal Church", provide an insight into the author's view of the Church of England as it then was, and of its place in the wider Catholic church. They are included in the hope "that they may offer some comfort to many who look with more than sorrow on the infirmities of our portion of the Catholic Church". The presence of evil and discord in the church, says the author, should be no surprise to those whose Christianity "recognizes no higher connection between faith and obedience than that which may satisfy the order of society; where expediency and utility supply the want of the high standard of faith and duty". Christians should lament the shortcomings in holiness, the imperfect worship, broken-down discipline, sin within and without, mocking and scorn on the lips of many, and pride in the wisdom of the present age. Looking to the other great Christian communions, however — notably the Roman and Eastern churches — the writer sees only schism, division and sin. "Some may have a more showy exterior, though perhaps not more glorious within than that Church whose children we are; so that while we lament her short-comings, we shall be very much deceived, if we think to find in other portions of the Catholic Church that fulness which we ought to find in her."

The whole of this work is suffused with Tractarian principles. The author's view of the English church as a means of salvation and a living part of the One Holy Catholic and Apostolic Church is entirely consistent with the teachings of the Oxford Movement under whose influence he had studied. And his strictures on the Roman church reflect not only his personal feelings but also the beliefs of the early Tractarians, whose assertion of the Catholicity of the English church was made in opposition to the spread of Romanist principles following the Roman Catholic Emancipation Act of 1829.[86]

The pleasant life of the quiet country vicarage at Salcombe Regis was not to last much longer. During 1848, the fifth year of his curacy, Richard Cresswell sought from the incumbent an increase in his stipend, but this was refused. He therefore felt obliged to look for another position, and resigned the curacy. His wife was heartbroken at having to leave, feeling that it was "an expulsion from

View of Teignmouth, looking east along the Teign estuary, c.1860, about 12 years after the Cresswells moved there. The family home, Lugehay House, is hidden behind the riverside trees in the middle distance. The lattice-work bridge crosses the Teign to Shaldon, and behind it the railway hugs the shoreline. West Teignmouth parish church can be seen immediately to the left of the foremast of the nearest boat; the tower of East Teignmouth parish church rises behind the distant harbour.

Paradise", and Richard himself later came to regret it. While he was seeking another position, Frances (and her baby son) stayed with her mother Emily, who lived at Sidmouth. Richard had hoped to obtain a curacy at Dartmouth, but this was not forthcoming, and he was eventually offered the position at West Teignmouth parish church under Dr. Lawrence Gwynne, who had been appointed in 1842. This he accepted, with some reluctance, in the absence of a better alternative.[87]

Teignmouth was a market town, seaport and bathing resort built on the north side of the estuary of the River Teign. It was divided into the two parishes of East and West Teignmouth, and traversed by the South Devon Railway, opened from Exeter in 1846. The population had been growing rapidly since the beginning of the century, and had reached 5,000 by the late 1840s. Some two thirds of the inhabitants lived in West Teignmouth. The town supported a sizeable fishing industry, whilst large quantities of granite were brought down the Teign from quarries on Dartmoor for export. A new quay was constructed on the river in 1820, and a new market place laid out around the same time. The parish churches at East and West Teignmouth were both rebuilt in the early 1820s. A bridge of iron and wood, then the longest in England, was built across the estuary in 1827. An increasing number of visitors had been coming to the resort since the beginning of the century, both for the river and coastal scenery and for sea bathing, and several new hotels had been opened to accommodate them. Some town improvements were made under an act of 1836, and a supply of gas was introduced in 1840. In 1848, a new theatre and the Teignmouth and Dawlish Dispensary were added to the town's facilities.[88]

One of several mansions in the vicinity was Bitton House, standing in extensive grounds on the West Cliff, overlooking the river in West Teignmouth. Immediately opposite, also on Bitton Hill, was a more modest but nonetheless substantial property, known as Lugehay House, and it was here that Richard Cresswell and his family took up residence in 1848. Bitton Hill (or Bitton Street), which was widened under the Town Improvement Act of 1836, was one of the main thoroughfares of West Teignmouth.

Lugehay House had previously been occupied by the well known banking family of Jordan. Robert Jordan, who died in 1837, was a great benefactor of the town. The three-storey house, which still stands, is believed to have originated as a farmhouse in

The three-storey Lugehay House, standing back from the road, became the Cresswell family home in Teignmouth from 1848. The main frontage, overlooking Bitton Hill, dates from about 1800. It still stands, in what is now known as Bitton Park Road. Photographed in 1994.

the 17th century, though the main frontage was built about 1800. The lower part of the house had a rambling layout, with walls four feet thick. The unusual name is said to derive from "large hay", meaning "the large field". Until the mid-1850s the property included a substantial portion of land fronting Bitton Hill. The house stands well above the road, the level of which was altered in the widening. The Cresswells rented it from a Miss Mary Roberton of East Teignmouth. Compared with the vicarage they had left, Lugehay was not an attractive property, and they took it in the expectation of finding something better in due course. In the event, it was to remain a Cresswell family home for half a century.[89]

The parish church of West Teignmouth, at which Richard Cresswell served as curate, was situated in an elevated position about a quarter of a mile east of Lugehay House, overlooking the town and harbour. It was an architectural curiosity, the 1821 rebuilding having preserved the 13th century sandstone tower and added to it a new octagonal structure in the Gothic style with a central lantern. The vaulted roof of the octagon was supported on cast-iron pillars, and a reinstated 18th century oak pulpit spanned the entrance to the chancel. There were galleries all round, and seats for 1,500.[90]

From time to time, Richard Cresswell exercised his ministry well beyond the confines of his own parish. During his visits to his brother's home at Winchmore Hill, for example, he was sometimes invited to preach at St. Paul's Church, and the texts on which his sermons were based are recorded in the preachers' book. His name first appears there on 27th August 1848, the 10th Sunday after Trinity, then again on the following Sunday. He reappears three years later, on 20th July 1851, at the time of the Great Exhibition. Almost a year passed before his next appearance, when the family were gathered to attend John Cresswell's wedding on 28th June 1852. On the previous day, the third Sunday after Trinity, Richard Cresswell preached in St. Paul's Church on a text from the prophet Zechariah, Chapter 12, Verse 10. For John Cresswell, the closing words of the verse contained a grim prophecy: "they shall mourn for him, as one mourneth for his only son, and shall be in bitterness for him, as one that is in bitterness for his firstborn".

The baptism of Willink Cresswell in St. Paul's Church on Sunday 26th June 1853 provided another occasion for the Devonshire Cresswells to visit Winchmore Hill. Richard Cresswell's text on that day was from Psalm 98: "Let the floods clap their hands: let the hills be joyful together before the Lord....". Thereafter, five years were to elapse before his next appearance at St. Paul's. He normally preached (and probably officiated) at either Morning or Evening Prayer, and on a few occasions celebrated Holy Communion after Morning Prayer; the number of communicants, recorded in the preachers' book, never exceeded 40.[91]

The second child of Richard and Frances Cresswell was born at Lugehay House on 19th April 1849. Christened Christiana Frances Emily, she became known to her family as Chrissy. By this time, Richard was becoming increasingly dissatisfied with the Evangelical character of the services at West Teignmouth parish church, and decided to resign his curacy. His relatives in Winchmore Hill felt that he and his family should then have moved to the London area, but he chose to remain at Teignmouth and take in private pupils as a source of income. He later said that he had stayed in Devon "to put 200 miles between himself and his relations" — a sentiment prompted more by the differing lifestyles of the two branches of the family than by any loosening of kinship bonds. By 1851 Richard had given up full-time parish ministry, as the census describes him as a "clergyman without cure of souls". He had also begun residential private tuition, as the household includes, in addition to the Cresswells and their two female servants, two scholars — James Charles Barber, aged 10, and Leighton George Hayne, aged 15. Five years later, James Barber and another companion inscribed their names very neatly on the inside of a small window pane in a ground-floor room at the front of Lugehay House, and the inscriptions remained clearly visible some 140 years afterwards.[92]

On 16th August 1852 Richard Cresswell's family was further enlarged with the birth of twins, Alured Robert and Clara Anastasia. The name Alured had occurred several times on Mrs. Cresswell's side of the family, most recently with Sir Alured Clarke (1745–1832), who had had a distinguished military career in North America, South Africa and India.[93] Sadly, the twins did not survive infancy, Clara dying at the age of four weeks and Alured at five weeks. They were buried in West Teignmouth churchyard, under a simple grave slab inscribed "BAC, CAC, 1852". The incorrect initials of Alured Robert are assumed to be a stonemason's error.[94]

   Although retired from parish ministry, Richard Cresswell maintained his ecclesiastical connections, not only through preaching engagements but also by attending church functions. On Tuesday 18th October 1853, for example, he was present at the consecration of the new church of St. John the Evangelist, Luton, about four miles north west of Teignmouth. St. John's, a small and simple stone building with nave, chancel and bell turret, was founded as a daughter church of neighbouring Bishopsteignton. The consecration was performed by the Bishop of Exeter, Henry Phillpotts. Richard Cresswell recorded the occasion in his diary:

> An autumn morning, could not be more beautiful. I was up very early and got myself ready for a start at half past nine. Went to Mr. Gordon's (curate of West Teignmouth) where we were picked up by the fly; and soon to Luton through Bishopsteignton. We were all assembled some time before the Bishop arrived, when the consecration was proceeded with much after the usual manner. There were, I think, about 17 of the clergy present....after the consecration all proceeded to Vooght's farm where Mr. Comyns had provided an excellent and liberal luncheon. The Bishop had his chair and a table to himself in a corner. Of course all parties waited until he made a move to go, and then it soon broke up.

Mr. Comyns was Vicar of Bishopsteignton, and, in common with other clergy present, an intimate friend of Richard Cresswell.[95] Henry Phillpotts, who had become Bishop of Exeter in 1830, was a controversial High Churchman opposed to political and ecclesiastical reform.[96]

   The Cresswells' fifth child, Charlotte Mary Anastasia, was born at Lugehay House on 31st May 1855. No doubt her third name was chosen in memory of the baby girl who had died three years earlier; it was by this name — often shortened to Stasia — that she was known throughout her life. In the 1861 census she is described as a "scholar", together with her sister Christiana, then aged 11, and her brother Richard Henry, then 14. As in 1851, the household contained two pupils — Henry Holdsworth, aged 16, and Thomas Parkin, aged 15. There were also two female servants, making a total of nine in the household. On 14th January 1862 the sixth and last child was born at Lugehay House. Christened Beatrix Feodore Clara Augusta Grace, she was to become the best known of the Devonshire Cresswells. Within the family she was called Beatie or Bee, but in later life she complained of being overburdened with an unwieldy list of names. Beatrice and Feodora were two of the christian names of Queen Victoria's youngest daughter, born five years earlier; Clara was the first name of the infant twin who had died in 1852; Augusta was not registered, but was, she says, "added at the font". The font in question was at Bishopsteignton Church, where her baptism took place on 28th January 1862. Her godfather was her 15-year-old brother Richard Henry. Her first entry into church through a fine Norman doorway, and her baptism in a Norman font, were later seen as precursors of the deep love of ecclesiastical antiquities for which she would become well known![97]

The year 1862 saw publication of the second of Richard Cresswell's major literary efforts — a very different work from *The Christian Life* but no less erudite. This was an English translation of Aristotle's *History of Animals* from the Latin text of Johann Gottlob Schneider, published in Leipzig in 1811. It is a wide ranging descriptive work of 10 books, dealing principally with the animals of the Greek world with which Aristotle would have been familiar, and drawing on his own observations and those of his predecessors. It includes biological descriptions, comparisons with humankind, and the character and habits of the animal world. Richard Cresswell's translation runs to over 300 printed pages. In his preface he describes the text as "the most ancient and celebrated contribution to science which has come down to us....a work which has ever been admired by naturalists, and must continue to rise in their estimation the longer it is in their hands". The translation was published by Henry G. Bohn of Covent Garden, London, whose libraries of several hundred volumes were popular in Victorian England. His Classical and Antiquarian Libraries featured English translations of ancient and medieval texts — many of them the only translation available to contemporary readers.[98]

When Beatrix Cresswell was still a young child, Bitton House, the large property opposite the Cresswells' home, was bought by John Parson, chairman of the Metropolitan Railway. The Cresswells enjoyed his hospitality, and the children of the two families formed friendships, at least one of which lasted into adulthood. Many were the nursery teas taken at Bitton House under the supervision of Maria, the dictatorial head nurse. Beatrix, the youngest of her family, suffered some bullying from the older children, and really preferred her own company, playing in the old herbaceous garden at the rear of Lugehay House.

One evening, when Beatrix was about three years old, her parents had gone out with their eldest daughter Christiana, leaving Anastasia to put Beatrix to bed. Anastasia, then 10 years old, had been reading about early English woad painting, and, seeing a handy saucer of vivid blue paint which her brother had been using, decided to apply the technique to Beatrix. Stripped of her clothes, the child was decorated on her back with a large blue cross and other devices. Desperate attempts to remove the adornments with cold water in a foot bath were largely ineffective, and Beatrix carried her cross for weeks until the paint eventually faded. Whether any punishment was awarded for this misdemeanour is not recorded, but excessive naughtiness was sometimes repaid by a beating with the back of a hairbrush. On one occasion, cousin Henrietta from Winchmore Hill, who was staying at Lugehay House, joined Anastasia in the performance of "some crowning piece of mischief"; Mrs. Cresswell offered the girls the choice of writing out an "imposition" or receiving a beating: "Etta chose the imposition, and was all the afternoon over it, Stasia took the whipping soon done, and shaken off like water on a duck's back".[99]

A pleasing glimpse of Christmas Eve at Lugehay House during Beatrix's early childhood has been preserved amongst family papers. The year is 1865; the 19-year-old Richard Henry, who the previous year entered St. Mary Hall, Oxford, to read for the church, has arrived home for the Christmas vacation. The scene is set in the dining room of Lugehay House, decorated with ever-greens; firelight flickers in the grate, and the table is laid for supper:

> Two wreaths of holly have been made; a large one....is hung over a map above the mantelpiece, [but] there is no nail available for the smaller wreath, which lies on the floor. There is a stir in the hall, the brother has come down from Oxford, bringing with him an undergraduate friend. There are welcomes, greetings, and enquiries. Some of these last refer to the little wreath on the floor. The sisters explain that they have nothing to hang it on. "Brother" snatches a small knife from the supper table, thrusts it into the panels of the folding doors, and hangs up the wreath. This thrills a very small person who ought to be in bed, but has been allowed to stay up to see "brother".

Richard Henry's friend was a young American from the southern states; during the vacation he teaches Christiana to sing *Maryland*, an American folk song, to the tune of *Der Tannenbaum*.[100]

The following winter, Richard Henry's father was very ill, so the whole family stayed in Bath, at the home of a cousin, to aid Richard Cresswell's recovery. It was a miserable and uncomfortable experience, but Beatrix, at the age of four, had with her a children's book which she could read, and this, she later declared, was the beginning of her love of literature. Within a few years her reading had become "omnivorous and universal" — a pastime she shared with her sisters. Their staple fare included the novels and stories of Charlotte Mary Yonge, a High Churchwoman who had founded the Tractarian magazine *The Monthly Packet* in 1851. At the age of seven Beatrix was reading the novels of Sir Walter Scott, which her sister Anastasia was buying in sixpenny editions with her weekly pocket money.[101]

At the same age Beatrix attempted to learn French from her mother, but this was wholly unsuccessful and her father took over. At length she was taught by a French lady from Torquay. On one occasion they had a fierce argument which ended with Beatrix tearing up her essay and throwing it in Mademoiselle's face! Her mother's teaching of music was no more satisfactory; later Beatrix was sent to a music teacher in Teignmouth "who was of a sarcastic temperament and took no interest in any pupil who did not show real talent". In common with other members of her family, Beatrix had little aptitude for music; aside from literature, her strength lay in botany, geology, history, Greek and Latin, all of which she learnt from her father at an early age. Some of this knowledge she acquired by sitting in on the lessons which her father gave to his private pupils. But arithmetic she never could master. Book learning was supplemented by excursions with her father — botanical expeditions, wildlife observation and

visits to medieval churches. These outings instilled in her a love of the Devonshire countryside which she claimed no other member of her family, not even
her father, developed to the same extent. From her church visits she acquired an
interest in heraldry, which found early expression when, as a child, she designed
a coat of arms for each of her dolls. Sewing she learnt from her mother; her
ambition was to become as good an embroiderer as her aunt Sarah had been. In
later life Beatrix expressed satisfaction with the fact that she had never been to
school, as she hated competition with other children.[102]

Not unexpectedly, the children of a country clergyman received their religious education at their father's knee, and the whole family attended church on
Sundays. Although Richard had given up the curacy at West Teignmouth after
only a year or two, the Cresswells continued to worship at that church for many
years. Several wealthy local families, including the Parsons of Bitton House,
had spacious, private pews, whose doors were opened for them by their servants. To the children, the Sunday morning services seemed interminable, consisting of Matins, a long sermon, Litany and Ante-Communion; the younger
children were not really expected to pay attention, reading to themselves from
their own bibles and prayer books instead. Anastasia was confirmed in 1868, at
the age of 12, by Bishop Harper of Christchurch, New Zealand; Bishop Phillpotts
of Exeter would not go near Teignmouth because of an earlier disagreement,
and the services of a colonial bishop had to be obtained. By 1874, when Beatrix
came to be confirmed, Bishop Phillpotts had been succeeded by Frederick Temple, who had no scruples about confirming the young people of West Teignmouth.
Many years later Beatrix wrote: "half pagan though I have always been, I had an
intense desire to be confirmed".[103]

In later years, it was a source of surprise to Beatrix that her father had continued to worship at West Teignmouth Church for so long, given his dislike of
Evangelical services. In the 1860s and 1870s, however, it was still the "done
thing" in country areas to attend one's own parish church, whatever its character; to have strayed into another parish would have been frowned upon. Yet the
young Richard Henry did not feel bound by this convention; during the university vacations he refused to go to West Teignmouth Church, worshipping instead at St. Michael's, East Teignmouth, which had a Tractarian vicar named
Simpson. Richard Henry persuaded his sisters to join him there, and they were
amazed to see a surpliced choir entering the church behind a processional cross.
Such things were considered ritualistic in the Church of England then; within 20
years the growing influence of the Oxford Movement would have made them
commonplace.[104]

During the 1860s the vicar at West Teignmouth was Joseph Birch, and he had
a curate named James Twamley. Whilst continuing to attend their services, Richard Cresswell composed a rhyme at their expense:

> Twamley and Birch
> In defending the church,
> Say that old Simpson

> Smells strongly of brimstone.
> And Simpson replies
> With a leer in his eyes
> That Twamley and Birch
> Are no sons of the church.

Another West Teignmouth curate named Vale was ridiculed in verse by Richard Cresswell in 1867:

> Tho' eyes are raised, and hands are spread,
> And stilted phrase your ears assail;
> Be not afraid 'tis only noise
> That echoes feebly thro' the "Vale".

These rhymes, together with other material in the same vein, were entered in the commonplace book kept by Christiana Cresswell.[105] The opposing voices of Low Church and High Church which they represent could be those of Trollope's Mr. Slope and Mr. Arabin; they were becoming increasingly strident in the mid-Victorian Church of England.

Upheaval in the Village

In her recollections of childhood in Winchmore Hill, Henrietta Cresswell says little of the visits by her uncle, aunt and cousins from Devonshire. She does mention, however, that her uncle Richard referred to the stable block of 2 Trois Vase House as "Gallipot Cottage", because of the three stone vases that surmounted it.[106] She also provides two stories told at the expense of one of her Devonshire cousins. Though not named, this was almost certainly Anastasia, who was the same age as Henrietta. On one occasion the cousin joined some of the Winchmore Hill children in taking a nosegay to their teacher in the village school, but her bouquet, fine though it was, lacked a covering of tissue paper, "and every girl in the school was sniggering at the gaudy vulgarity of the glorious blossoms, and mentally comparing them with their own refined little button-holes". On another occasion, Henrietta's cousin, "who came from a West of England watering-place, and had never in her life been out walking for herself", was sent from Trois Vase House to pay the butcher's bill, but came back without having seen that it was properly receipted: "poor child, she knew nothing whatever about such things". She was nine years old at the time, which dates the incident to 1864–5.[107] There is an inference that Henrietta looked down on her country cousins as not being well practised in the ways of the world!

It was in 1865 that coming events cast their shadow over Winchmore Hill with the passage of a bill in parliament enabling the Great Northern Railway to construct a line from Wood Green to Enfield and Hertford. Soon enough,

Winchmore Hill residents would discover that the line was intended to pass through the heart of their village, requiring the excavation of a cutting, the demolition of a number of buildings, and the loss of gardens and trees. In the following year, the Great Northern Railway served notice on property owners in the village that land would be required for the new line. This included the site of the Independent Chapel and Trois Vase House in Hoppers Road, where a cutting would be dug to carry the line under the road at an acute angle. It is recorded that the railway company paid £2,750 for the chapel and the land on which it stood, but the amount given for Trois Vase House is not known.[108]

Neither is it recorded when the Cresswells became aware that they would have to move, though the arrival of the railway contractors in the summer of 1869 appears to have taken the village by surprise. The first sod was turned in a field near Vicars Moor Lane, and within a few days rows of wooden huts had been built for the navvies. The excavations revealed bright cobalt blue clay, which changed with exposure to orange. To these colours were added black and white flints, yellow gravel and red heaps of burnt ballast.[109]

The havoc caused by the building of the line can well be imagined:

> The pretty row of cottages where the Grandmother lived were pulled down,
> the great ash arbour ruthlessly destroyed, and the garden devastated: the
> holly hedge, dense as a wall, was grubbed up, scarcely anything remained
> but the tall yew and a golden-knob apple tree.[110]

The Cresswells and the Willinks were hard hit by the construction of the railway. John Cresswell and his family were forced to move from 1 Trois Vase House, his mother-in-law Frances Willink and her son from No.2 next door, and his mother Henrietta from the Cottage in Vicars Moor Lane. This was the "Grandmother" referred to by the younger Henrietta, and her cottage was the easternmost of three which stood on the north side of Vicars Moor Lane where the railway bridge was built. She had to leave the house during 1869, and moved to Rose Cottage, a short distance away on the other side of Vicars Moor Lane, and formerly the home of Tom Hood.[111]

The railway contractors took possession of Trois Vase House on New Year's Day, 1870, after a heavy snowfall. Frances Willink, at No.2, had dreaded the coming of the railway, and was much disturbed at having to move.[112] The Cresswells, next door, appear to have taken it in their stride. Henrietta Cresswell, in her recollections, expresses no sadness at leaving the house in which she had spent her childhood. At the age of 14, her feeling may have been one of excitement at all that was going on around her and the prospect of starting life in a new home.

CHAPTER 5

Grove Lodge

A New Home

Middle Lane, formerly Grove Lane, descended gently from Winchmore Hill village to the Green Lanes and the hamlet of Ford's Grove. A watercolour painted by John Cresswell in 1858 from the eastern end of the Green shows Middle Lane as a narrow thoroughfare bordered by cottages and mature trees, and, to the south, by the boundary wall of Roseville. The 1865 Ordnance Survey plan reveals that, some 200 yards beyond the village, the lane curved gently to the right and continued through fields and farmland to reach the Green Lanes.

In 1869, the railway cutting sliced through the upper part of Middle Lane, and the scene depicted in John Cresswell's painting was transformed by the building of a bridge to carry the railway under the road. Cottages, gardens and hedgerows on the north side of the road gave way to a double-fronted railway

Middle Lane, Winchmore Hill, looking east, from a watercolour painted by John Cresswell in 1858. The railway station was built on the left-hand side in 1870; opposite is part of the boundary wall of Roseville.

Looking across the railway cutting towards Grove Lodge, Winchmore Hill, from a watercolour painted by John Cresswell's daughter Henrietta in 1873. On the extreme right is a corner of the railway station.

station in stock brick, its twin gables fitted with decorated barge boards and wooden finials. A shallow forecourt gave access to a canopied entrance and booking hall built over the tracks.

Immediately to the west of the station was a tall, spacious house known as Grove Lodge, taking the earlier name of the road in which it stood. It was built a few years before the coming of the railway by Mr. Henry Morgan of Vicars Moor Lane for his son Charles on the occasion of his marriage. Henry Morgan was a wealthy papermaker and keeper of greyhounds. He owned land between Vicars Moor Lane and Middle Lane which, together with Grove Lodge, was bought by the Great Northern Railway before construction of the line. Charles Morgan moved to Hazelwood House, on the corner of Green Lanes and Hedge Lane, Palmers Green, and the tenancy of Grove Lodge was offered by the railway company to the Cresswells and the Willinks in replacement for Trois Vase House.[1]

Grove Lodge was a bleak and somewhat forbidding house of stock brick with stone dressings. It consisted of a cellar, two full-height storeys, and an attic storey lit by dormers projecting through a deep cornice into the roof. The front door, facing Middle Lane, and a tradesmen's entrance on the west side, were approached up short flights of stone steps. The sash windows had deep sills fitted with ornamental ironwork. A rear two-storey projection to the north, covered by a separate hipped roof, had a bay window overlooking the garden. The tall, corniced chimney stacks accentuated the height of the building. Some of the uppermost windows commanded extensive views across the Lea Valley.

The irregularly shaped garden, reduced in size by the railway construction, was enclosed within a brick wall with stone cappings. There were two gateways with brick piers and pyramidal stone caps on the Middle Lane frontage, whence the house was approached by a short, curving, gravel drive. One gateway was opposite the road skirting the south side of the Green; the other adjoined the railway station. The western boundary of the garden faced the footpath which later became part of Wilson Street. The garden was well stocked with trees and shrubs.[2]

Construction of the railway was continuing apace when the Cresswells and the Willinks moved into Grove Lodge at the end of 1869. The heavy snowfall, and the proximity of the work on the cutting, caused domestic disruption:

> It was then all deep snow, and the cutting was so close to the side of the house that the garden shrubs were constantly slipping over the edge and having to be brought back and replanted. A portion of the wall was built, but the frost got into the mortar and it fell almost immediately, so the garden became a thoroughfare for the navvies at their work.

The villagers had feared annoyance from unruly navvies brought in from Yorkshire and Lincolnshire, but on the whole these men were well behaved. Many of them brought food and tea cans to be heated on the great kitchen range at Grove Lodge, and a ganger nicknamed "Dandy" checked any bad language in the vicinity of the house.[3]

There were some injuries and a few fatalities during the construction of the line. At least two men were poisoned to death by fumes rising from the heaps of burnt ballast on which they had slept during cold nights.[4] On 26th January 1870 a serious accident occurred on the railway at Winchmore Hill to the 25-year-old Charles Tanham. He was attended by John Cresswell, who recommended that he should be admitted to the infirmary of Edmonton Workhouse. It was found necessary to amputate one of his arms, and this was performed by Charles Morris, the workhouse medical officer. There was a subsequent complaint of unnecessary delay in attending the case, made against Mr. Morris and his assistant. This resulted in John Cresswell being called before the board of guardians on 9th February to explain his actions. He reported that, having "performed such offices as circumstances required....he recommended as more convenient and better for the man his removal to the Infirmary of the Workhouse in preference to his being conveyed to the Hospital".[5]

Poor Frances Mary Willink, John Cresswell's mother-in-law, never recovered from her enforced move to Grove Lodge during the bitterly cold winter of 1869–70. The move took place barely two weeks after her 81st birthday, and she said it would kill her. By the end of February she had contracted bronchitis, and she died at Grove Lodge on Sunday 20th March, attended by John Cresswell. She was buried in the Cresswell family grave at Edmonton on 26th March. She had of course been born a Cresswell. Less than six months later, the family suffered another loss with the death of Willink Cresswell, Henrietta's elder brother. The sickly child had reached his 17th birthday in April 1870, but during the summer he caught a fever and died at Rose Cottage, Vicars Moor Lane, on 5th September. The principal cause of death was his congenital debility. He was buried a week later in the family grave, beside his sister Mary. The first year at Grove Lodge was indeed one of sadness.[6]

After some delay caused by the failure of earthworks, the railway through Winchmore Hill was opened on Saturday 1st April 1871. By this time it had become a short branch line between Wood Green and Enfield, the powers to continue to Hertford having been abandoned. Although Grove Lodge was very close to the edge of the cutting, the sparse weekday service of 16 trains to London and 15 to Enfield can scarcely have disturbed the calm of John Cresswell's household.[7] At this time, the population of St. Paul's parish (formerly the district chapelry) was still below 1,800.

The day after the railway opened was census day. Grove Lodge afforded ample accommodation for the relatively small Cresswell household, then numbering seven. John and his wife, aged 52 and 51 respectively, and their surviving children Henrietta and Francis, aged 16 and 9, shared their home with Diederich Willink, then 46, still unmarried, and employed as a banker's clerk. His christian name proved too much for the census enumerator, who recorded it as "Fredrick"! The family was supported by two female domestic servants — a housemaid aged 18 and a cook aged 20.

The other Cresswell residence, Rose Cottage in Vicars Moor Lane, was still the home of John's mother Henrietta, then aged 81. She was suffering from gout, and the census records that she was supported by her nieces and grand-daughter. The nieces must have been grandchildren of her father the Reverend Mark Noble; the grand-daughter was the 21-year-old Christiana from Teignmouth, who appears at Rose Cottage in the 1871 census. The household included two female servants, Elizabeth and Jane Cavill, members of a large family from south west Essex who had settled in Winchmore Hill as gardeners, agricultural labourers and domestic servants.

The younger Henrietta Cresswell became well acquainted with Rose Cottage after her grandmother moved there in 1869, and some 60 years later she set down her recollections of it. She states that it was little altered since Tom Hood left in 1832. It fronted northward to Vicars Moor Lane, and eastward, down the hill, to a long garden. The bay windows facing Vicars Moor Lane were characteristic of the house. The building was approached through carriage gates beneath two fine pollard elms, their greenery enhanced by clusters of close-growing ivy. There were flowering trees in the shrubbery, including "the finest double-blossomed apple I ever saw".

The front door led to a narrow hall passage, giving access to a rather gloomy dining room, a steep staircase, the kitchen, parlour, and a small sitting room. The parlour and sitting room faced east, and were reached from the garden through an old-fashioned door with two leaves: "when it stood wide to the morning sunshine the light shone into the glass-fronted china closet which held

Rose Cottage, Vicars Moor Lane, Winchmore Hill, home of Thomas Hood from 1829 to 1832. John Cresswell's mother Henrietta lived there from 1869. The house suffered bomb damage during the Second World War and was demolished.

my grandmother's best Worcester tea-sets, and many other treasures of old Nankin china and blue Delft". Henrietta continues with a description of the kitchen, wash-house and outbuildings. She then recalls the bedrooms, the best of which "was particularly bright and cheerful, with its two windows and its view towards the orchard-like garden, and the morning sun. I remember it with a carved four-post bed, with its full complement of dossal, tester, valences, and three pairs of curtains of flowered chintz". Henrietta clearly had great affection for the old house; nowhere else does she offer such a detailed description of a Cresswell family home.[8] Her cousin Beatrix also recorded memories of the house; on a visit from Devonshire in 1872, when she was 10 years old, she was reading mystery stories on the window seat of a back room in the gathering dusk "until I was so frightened I hardly knew how to stir, yet longed to rush and find human protection!".[9]

On reaching the age of 86, in 1876, Henrietta's grandmother decided that she was too old to remain at Rose Cottage, "at the mercy of her servants", so she gave up her home, divided most of her possessions between her sons Richard and John, and in January 1877 moved into Grove Lodge.[10]

By this time, Winchmore Hill was beginning to acquire some of the features of modern urban life. The electric telegraph had arrived in 1870, and mains drainage in 1873. The train service had been improved in 1875, and public gas lighting would be installed by 1880. However, there was little building develop-

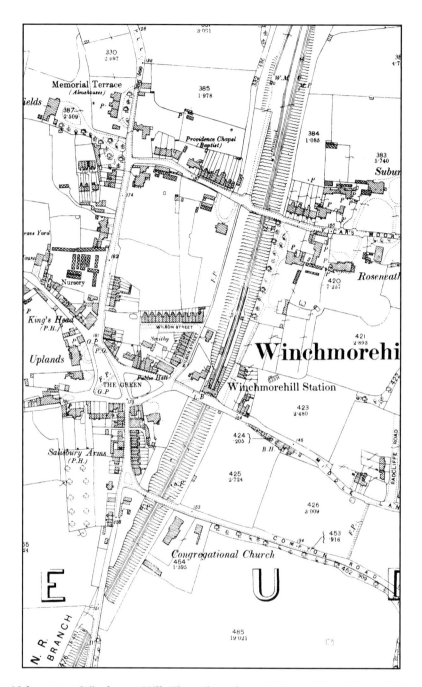

Late 19th century Winchmore Hill. The railway has cut through the village, obliterating Trois Vase House which stood where Hoppers Road crosses the line at the bottom of the map. Grove Lodge stands immediately to the west of the railway station. Rose Cottage, which became the home of John Cresswell's mother, appears just above the name "Roseneath" to the south of Vicars Moor Lane. Compare the map with its predecessor of 1865 on page 61. From the 25 inch to the mile Ordnance Survey plan, 1896.

ment in the village during the 1870s, apart from a few artisans' houses near the Green and some large gentlemen's houses such as Stone Hall, Broadfields and Vicarsmoor. At the end of their first decade at Grove Lodge, the Cresswells were still living in a predominantly rural community.[11]

Work and Leisure

John Cresswell continued his medical practice at Grove Lodge in more spacious surroundings than had been available at Trois Vase House. He maintained his position as medical officer for the Winchmore Hill District of the Edmonton Union, and appears to have performed his duties entirely to the satisfaction of the board of guardians.

From time to time he was called upon to offer medical advice to St. Paul's National Schools, of which he remained a manager. On the morning of Monday 29th October 1877 he visited the school and recommended that, as there were so many cases of measles and scarlet fever in the village, the children should be sent home for a week. The school was closed on Thursday 1st November, and remained closed until Monday 19th to enable the building to be thoroughly cleaned and whitewashed. Illness appears to have continued, however, for during the week commencing Monday 3rd December school attendances dwindled again, and three children in the village died of scarlet fever.[12]

John Cresswell, now well into middle age, was known not only for his professional competence but also for his sense of humour and unconventional appearance. Many years later, a former resident of Winchmore Hill recalled how, as a boy in the 1870s, he had received a thrashing from an older lad whom he had been fighting on the Green. The younger boy ran home to his mother complaining of a broken shoulder, and John Cresswell was called: "well, well, my lad", he said, "we must see what we can do for you; pull off your coat, waistcoat and shirt at once, and I'll attend to it". The boy quickly slipped his jacket off, and before he had finished unbuttoning his waistcoat was astonished to receive a cuff or two on his face from John Cresswell's open hand: "that's all the medicine and attention you require, my lad; if you were injured at all you couldn't slip your jacket off like that. Don't tell lies. Good day!".[13]

The same "patient" recalls how, at the time, John Cresswell always wore a high hat, carried a stick, and had three dogs with him. As the years went by he became less particular about his appearance, wearing shoulder length hair and a ragged beard; the ends of his trousers did not always meet the tops of his boots. Sometimes he rode a primitive tricycle, and dressed in a frock coat and silk hat. He suffered from poor eyesight, a disability inherited by his son Francis.[14]

The census of April 1881 records a household of 10 at Grove Lodge. The extended family consists of John and Frances Sophia, their children Henrietta and Francis, John's mother Henrietta (now aged 91), and his brother-in-law Diederich Willink, now 56 and employed as a commission merchant. This time the enumerator came a little nearer to recording Mr. Willink's christian name accurately, entering it as "Diedrick"! Jane Cavill, formerly a domestic servant at Rose Cottage, had joined the household as a lady's maid; she had been with the family more than 10 years, and still had relatives living in Winchmore Hill. The other servants, both female, were a cook and a housemaid. Also listed is John Cresswell's 25-year-old niece Anastasia from Teignmouth. Cousin and close friend of Henrietta, she stayed frequently at Winchmore Hill. Her younger sister Beatrix later said that Stasia never cared for anyone except Henrietta, and spoke disparagingly of her "scrappy" education: "I never remember her doing anything after she was about 16".[15] The Devonshire Cresswells stayed with their relatives at Winchmore Hill on many occasions during the 1870s and 1880s; we shall return to some recollections of their visits later in this chapter.

On 7th November 1881, John Cresswell's mother Henrietta passed away after a long life and 63 years of widowhood. Her son Richard, visiting from Devonshire, was present when she died at Grove Lodge. John certified the cause of death as diarrhoea and senile decay. She was buried in the family grave at Edmonton on 12th November. Born and brought up in a country rectory, she had faced alone the responsibility of raising three children after the premature death of her husband. She was certainly equal to the task, as she was said to have been "a very masterful woman" and a strong disciplinarian. She was invariably kind to her grandchildren and did not scold them, but her grand-daughter Henrietta would not have dared to disobey her: "as I look back she appears to me to have left her mark upon my own life more than any other person". Her love for her family was amply repaid, not least by her devoted daughter Sarah, who lived with her and supported her at their several homes in Kent and then at Winchmore Hill until her own death in 1863. The younger Henrietta recalls that, although her grandmother suffered greatly from gout for many years, "her mind and faculties were clear to the last, her hair still black and her eyes bright".[16]

The elderly Henrietta Cresswell had lived long enough to see her grandson Francis embark on a career in medicine. She was 89 when, on 1st October 1879, Francis followed in his father's footsteps and enrolled as a student at St. Bartholomew's Medical School.[17] Medical education and practice had changed greatly since John Cresswell began his training at Bart's 41 years earlier. Expanded course work and hospital training had replaced apprenticeship as the gateway to a medical career. The traditional distinction between physicians and surgeons was breaking down, and as fewer practitioners prepared their own medicines the apothecaries' qualification was less generally required. Medical schools were introducing cash prizes and medals for excellence in examinations, and offering scholarships for needy students.[18] In response to the increased emphasis on classroom instruction, and advances in medical knowledge, it was decided in 1876 that the Bart's Medical School should be rebuilt. A new library and museum block was opened on 3rd November 1879, a month after Francis Cresswell's admission. When the new school was completed in 1881 it "probably provided the best accommodation available to any medical students in this country".[19]

During his first year at Bart's, Francis Cresswell won a Junior Scholarship awarded to the student taking third place in examinations held at the end of the winter and summer sessions. He was evidently a most able student, for in his last year, 1883, he won two awards — the Kirkes Gold Medal and the Brackenbury Medical Scholarship. The former was established in 1865 in memory of William Senhouse Kirkes (1823–64), physician and lecturer at the hospital, and was awarded for the best performance in an examination in clinical medicine. The latter, founded in 1873, was one of two scholarships financed from the bequest of Miss Hannah Brackenbury and awarded annually to the best pupil in medicine and the best in surgery.[20]

In the same year, Francis qualified as a Licentiate of the Royal College of Physicians, and as a Member of the Royal College of Surgeons of England. At the conclusion of his training he became a house-physician at Bart's, one of four such positions offered annually to the best medical students, each of whom was provided with rooms at the hospital and a modest salary. He then entered his father's practice at Grove Lodge, first appearing there in *The Medical Directory* for 1884. In that year he contributed a paper on "Cases of Typhoid Fever" to *The Medical Times*.[21]

Francis was a member of the British Medical Association (Metropolitan Counties Branch), and in March 1886 he had an article published in *The British Medical Journal*. Entitled "A Modification of Fehling's Solution for Testing for, and Estimating Sugar in Urine", it presented the results of a technical experiment which demonstrated how the early decomposition of testing solutions could be avoided by the use of glycerine: "I hope the above will prove especially useful to country practitioners, who seldom require to test for or estimate sugar....I have had some of the above solution in an ill-stoppered bottle for between four and five years, without any signs of decomposition".[22] He must have begun the experiment when he was a student.

Francis Cresswell's uncle Diederich had also followed his father's example by choosing a career in commerce. With the growth of trade and industry during the century, class distinctions between professional and business people were becoming less pronounced, but a mercantile occupation was still rated socially inferior to a professional position, especially if it was of relatively humble status. At the time of his arrival in Winchmore Hill in 1859, the younger Diederich's position as a merchant's clerk, and later as a banker's clerk, would have placed him below his brother-in-law John Cresswell in the social hierarchy.

Some time after his mother's death in 1870, however, Diederich became a partner in a firm of City merchants. He first appears in the Post Office London Directory in 1874, the firm being Pritchard, Willink and Company, 17 London Street. The premises were next door to those formerly occupied by his father, and where he himself had lived as a small child. They were shared with five other businesses — agents, shipbuilders, wine and spirit merchants and a chronometer maker. There were many other maritime-related businesses in the street, as there had been in the days of Diederich Willink the elder.[23]

By 1876, Pritchard, Willink and Company had moved to 2 Muscovy Court, a small court off Trinity Square, near the Tower. The building was shared with a custom house and shipping agent and a firm of licensed lightermen. The enclosed court, believed to have taken its name from a nearby public house known as the Czar of Muscovy, was in an area long associated with Russian merchants. Overshadowed by the vast bonded warehouses of the East and West India Dock Company, it was a place of sparse daylight to which the winter dusk came early. The buildings surrounding the court were occupied by basket and hamper makers, corn factors and merchants, tea and wine merchants, commission merchants, a physician, an architect and a district surveyor. Beneath the offices there was cellarage for the storage of wine. Sandwiched between the high brick walls of Nos.1 and 2, in the north east angle of the court, was an elegant Classical doorway. Pritchard, Willink and Company remained at 2 Muscovy Court throughout the 1880s, becoming Pritchard, Willink and Galloway by 1888.[24]   Unlike his father, the younger Diederich had no need to live over his work; the new railway would have carried him daily between Winchmore Hill and the City in company with the growing number of merchants, bankers and clerks who were populating the developing suburbs of North London.

During the 1880s, Winchmore Hill's share of this development was modest. By 1881, the population had just exceeded 2,000, and there were some 400–500 houses by 1882. A few large villa residences began to appear; in 1882–3, for example, Park Villas were built on farmland opposite the Chase Side Tavern, and three similar houses occupied a nearby cul-de-sac known as Thalia Road (later renamed Eversley Road, now part of Houndsden Road). "We then began to talk about Winchmore Hill being ruined", wrote Horace Regnart, "and that was our cry for many years". Smaller terraced houses were erected in Wilson Street, close to the railway station, after 1882, and a new village hall was built here, on the corner of the Green, in 1887. A convalescent fever hospital was erected on land adjoining Chaseville Park in 1886. In the following year, St. Paul's Church established a mission room in Highfield Row across the Green Lanes, and at the end of 1889 St. Paul's itself was enlarged with the opening of a new chancel. By 1891 the population had reached 3,000.[25]

On 4th December 1886, Frances Sophia Cresswell died at Grove Lodge at the age of 67. She had been suffering from thrombosis of the veins for nearly two years, and this, together with a final attack of apoplexy, was the cause of death. She was attended by her son Francis in her last illness. The burial took place at Edmonton churchyard on 16th December; she was the sixth to be interred in the family grave there.[26] So ended the life of a much loved lady, who in her youth had attracted the notice of the poet Jean Ingelow by her elegance, and who had waited patiently through a 12-year engagement to marry her childhood sweetheart.

Frances Sophia's family later paid for a memorial to be placed in St. Paul's Church. This took the form of a stained-glass window depicting Martha of Bethany, and beneath it a brass tablet inscribed to Frances Sophia's memory with the words *"laborare est orare"* ("to work is to pray"). The words were appro-

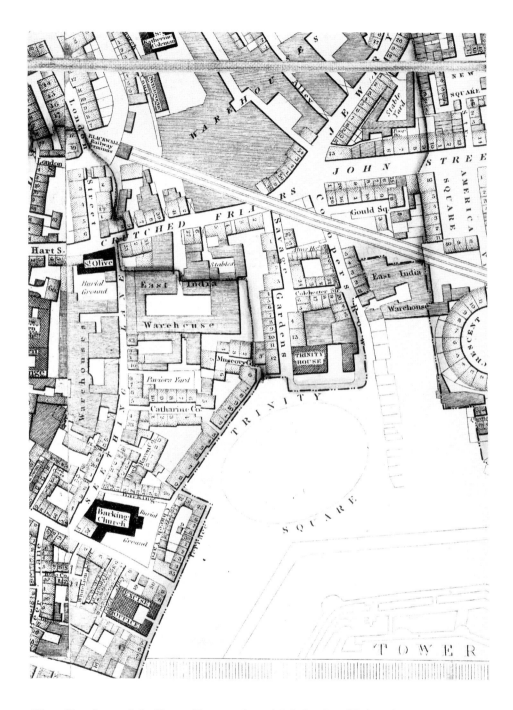

City of London and the Tower. The premises of Pritchard, Willink and Company were at 17 London Street in the top left-hand corner, adjacent to No.16 where Diederich Willink's father had lived and worked. Muscovy Court, to which the firm had moved by 1876, can be seen immediately to the north of Trinity Square. From Wyld's plan of the City of London, 1842.

priate to a lady who had given her husband and children a happy home, and who had died in the faith of Christ. The allusion to household responsibilities was made also in the figure of Martha, who is shown holding a bunch of keys and a distaff. The memorial was placed in the south chancel aisle in 1890, alongside another window and brass tablet in memory of Sarah Drought, the vicar's mother, who had died in 1888. "Both windows have been most chastely designed and well executed by Messrs. Hardman of Cockspur Street" said the parish magazine in July 1890. The south chancel aisle was created when the new chancel was completed in 1889.[27]

By this time, the Cresswells had become active members of St. Paul's Church. The earliest parish magazine dates from 1887; from this year onwards, the family's participation in church affairs is frequently recorded. On 30th October 1889, for example, at the annual tea of the Mothers' Meeting in the recently opened mission room at Highfield Row, "readings, of an amusing character, were given by Miss Cresswell, and songs were sung by the Vicar and several of the guests". At the same event in October 1891, "Miss Cresswell amused the company by the clever tricks which were performed by her dogs". Henrietta Cresswell, who had been a Sunday School teacher for some years, was amongst those "who furnished the viands" at the Sunday School Tea in January 1890, and she helped to conduct the proceedings at a special treat given for the children of Highfield Row and the mission room choir on the evening of 29th December 1890.

During 1891 Henrietta Cresswell joined Miss Annie Villiers, daughter of Mary Anne Villiers of Highfield House, in launching a project to raise money for a new baptismal font for St. Paul's. The vicar, Alfred Charles Albert Drought, complained of the existing font, which "in size and construction....is not much better than a chamber basin....I trust ere long to see a font in our Church which shall do us credit, and which shall be an ornament to the place in which it will stand". His wish was granted the following year, when a handsome new font in Devonshire marbles was erected. It was manufactured by T.H. Knight and Sons of Teignmouth, still the home of the Devonshire Cresswells.[28]

The family were generous in their giving to good causes supported by the church. As well as making occasional gifts towards the cost of new furnishings and fittings, they were regular subscribers to general church funds, to the Highfield Row mission room, and to the annual Sunday School treat. Henrietta's Sunday School class made regular collections for the Society for the Propagation of the Gospel. One of John Cresswell's more unusual donations, made in 1890, was to an appeal on behalf of Mrs. Boyling and her daughters, following the sudden and unexpected death of Charles Boyling, leaving a widow and two daughters unprovided for.[29] Mr. Boyling, a labourer, was aged about 60, his wife Martha was 10 years younger, and his daughters Emma and Ellen were in their twenties.

On 23rd December 1889, the day before the new chancel at St. Paul's was consecrated, Diederich Willink died at Grove Lodge of emphysema, from which he had been suffering for five years. He was 65. He was buried, not with his sister in Edmonton churchyard, but in the new cemetery in Edmonton, opened in 1884.[30] John Cresswell was his executor; he and his children received bequests from the will. Henrietta's bequest included a painting of mallards done by her father and given to Diederich; we shall return to this in the next chapter. Henrietta also received her uncle's interest in an estate near Maidstone which he had inherited from his mother — one of several sources of income from property by which Henrietta was able to maintain her financial independence in later life.

Henrietta, now in her thirties, had grown into an active, capable and intelligent young lady. She was a good scholar, though her practice of following New Testament readings in St. Paul's Church in Greek did not please Alfred Drought, the vicar. Her artistic and literary accomplishments will be explored in later chapters. But she also became a skilled needlewoman, botanist, horticulturist, naturalist, amateur carpenter, small animal breeder and horsewoman. As a lady of leisure she had the opportunity to develop personal interests to an extent denied to her male contemporaries. Her childhood longing to have been a boy seems to have influenced her in at least one respect in adulthood: having worn her hair in a bun, or "granny knot", throughout the 1880s, she then chose a mannish hair style parted in the middle, and later still had her hair cut so short that she was not infrequently mistaken for a man.[31]

It was in the late 1880s that Henrietta acquired two other interests — cycling and photography. In the summer of 1888, when she was 33, she attended a cyclists' "meet" at Woodford Green:

> As far as I can remember there were few, if any, unescorted lady riders, but what attracted most attention were tandem bicycles and trailers ridden by husbands and wives, carrying baby in a basket attached to the front handlebar. There were "Otto" bicycles with the rider seated between two large wheels, and ten-years-old "Coventry" tricycles with a five-foot wheel on one side and two small "pennies" on the other.

The latter conveyance was designed for two riders back-to-back, and appears from Henrietta's description to have been similar to the first tricycle ridden by her father. Some years later Henrietta went to a cycling gymkhana in Southgate — "a wonderfully pretty show":

> Skirts in those days fell over the pedals to hide a lady's shoes, and a long loop of elastic prevented the skirts being lifted by the wind....the back wheel of a machine was curtained with a fancy cord net to protect it from the skirt. Many a bad fall was the result of the endeavour to prevent a woman showing her ankles.

Henrietta herself rode a lady's tricycle weighing 80 pounds in the 1880s.[32]

Henrietta took her first photograph in May 1889. It was a view of the King and Tinker inn, Whitewebbs Lane, Enfield, and was taken during a drive in a dogcart with her cousin Anastasia, who was again with the family at Grove Lodge. In the photograph, Anastasia can be seen sitting in the dogcart. This was

one of many drives which Henrietta took through Enfield and into the Hert-
fordshire countryside. From this time onwards she photographed the changing
scene in Winchmore Hill. Some of her photographs of Winchmore Hill Wood,
Highfield Park, Firs Lane and Ford's Grove, taken in 1890, were published in
local newspapers many years afterwards.[33]

No doubt Henrietta sensed that great changes would soon occur in the village, but at the close of the 1880s she was still able to draw an effective contrast
between the densely populated suburbs of North London and the "breezy
healthful country" in which she lived. Her poem *A Lay of the Suburbs*, written in
the autumn of 1888, traces a journey on horseback from Tottenham to Winchmore
Hill; it is remarkable less for its content than for its rhythmic similarity to *The
Song of Hiawatha* by Longfellow, published in 1855:

> Homeward in the mellow twilight,
> Clattering hoofs across the tramlines
> Over bricks and over granite.
> Past the laden market waggons
> Journeying slowly to the City
> From the fields and open country.

Through nine more verses the poem gallops along by way of Whitehart Lane,
Wolves Lane, Tilekiln Lane and Green Lanes, eventually arriving at Hoppers
Road and Winchmore Hill:

> Here are houses near together,
> Here a wood and there a hay field,
> On the outskirts of the village,
> Scents of mignonette and roses,
> Floating on the breath of evening,
> Borne from many a cottage garden;
> Now we clatter through the village
> To the welcome open gateway,
> Hear the friendly words of welcome!
> Welcome! both for horse and rider;
> Welcome! in the Autumn twilight
> From our ride through town and country.[34]

The Cresswells entered their third decade at Grove Lodge as a diminished
family. In the 1891 census, John Cresswell and his son Francis are both described
simply as "Doctor" for the first time. Henrietta's occupation is recorded as "Artist,
Painter & Watercolour" [*sic*], an activity from which she derived some income,
if not full employment. Anastasia, now 35, appears here again, and there are
two female servants — Mary and Laura Stile. Among John Cresswell's patients
in 1891 was a nine-year-old girl named Antoinette Bester, who was suffering
from rheumatic fever. More than 80 years later, when she had become most

View from Grove Lodge, Winchmore Hill, looking across the front garden towards the Green in May 1889. The cherry tree to the left of the gateway is in bloom. The railings surrounding the pond on the Green are visible beyond the gate. This would have been an everyday scene for the Cresswells of Grove Lodge.

probably the last surviving former patient of John Cresswell, she recalled his kindly, bearded face and pale eyes looking down upon her — a touching memory of the man who was then approaching his 50th year as a medical practitioner in Winchmore Hill.[35]

West Country Cousins

Whilst the Winchmore Hill Cresswells were establishing themselves at Grove Lodge during the early 1870s, two of their Devonshire relatives were embarking on new careers. John's nephew Richard Henry had graduated BA from Oxford in 1867, had spent a short time as a schoolmaster at Ottery St. Mary, and was now beginning his priestly ministry.[36] His younger sister Christiana, who had been caring for her grandmother in Winchmore Hill, was seeking work in London. We shall return presently to the fortunes of these two members of the family.

Back at Lugehay House, Teignmouth, the 1871 census shows a smaller household. Only two of the children appear with their parents — the 15-year-old

Anastasia, and her nine-year-old sister Beatrix, whose four other christian names are not shown. The only other members of the household were a cook and a housemaid. By this time Richard Cresswell had ceased to take resident pupils, although some still attended daily. In earlier years there had been problems between young men staying at Lugehay House and young women in the town; with Richard's own daughters growing up, it was considered inadvisable to have teenage boys living in the house.[37]

Richard Cresswell's visits to Winchmore Hill with his family continued. During 1871 he preached at St. Paul's (usually at both morning and evening services) on eight consecutive Sundays, from the first Sunday after Easter to Trinity Sunday, presumably during the absence of the vicar, John Dixon Frost. On Trinity Sunday 1871 the evening service at St. Paul's was taken not by Richard Cresswell, but by his son Richard Henry, who earlier that year had been awarded his MA. It is doubtful whether the staid and undemonstrative Anglican worship of Winchmore Hill would have appealed to the young Richard Henry, whose clerical career was already taking him to the forefront of the Catholic revival in the Church of England. The last occasion on which either of the Devonshire Cresswells preached at St. Paul's was Sunday 13th September 1878, when the elder Richard officiated at Matins and Litany.[38]

During family visits to Winchmore Hill, Richard Cresswell continued to collect and draw items to add to his botanical collection. One of the surviving albums of fungi illustrations includes a specimen which was adhering to oak leaves in Winchmore Hill Wood in October 1871. The drawing is accompanied by a handwritten note which begins: "Anastasia sent me a few fungi from Winchmore Hill Wood in a match box, Oct.29th". This is followed by a botanical description. Below the drawing are his daughter's initials — CMAC; she was evidently staying with her uncle in Winchmore Hill at this time. The genera *Collybia* and *Agaricus* are noted on the drawing; elsewhere in the volume the specimen is listed as *Agaricus (Collybia) confluens*. In later years the item was identified by a museum curator as *Marasmius hariolorum*.[39] This example encapsulates on one page the process of collection, illustration, description and identification followed by Victorian botanists.

Further evidence of the family's visits to Winchmore Hill is found in another album of botanical drawings kept by the Devonshire Cresswells between 1873 and 1881. An unattributed sectional drawing of a double apple from Winchmore Hill is dated 12th September 1872; in June 1875 Anastasia made a pencil sketch of a sweet william found in the cutting of the Great Northern Railway there. Most of the items in this album are dated but unsigned, though many are believed to be the work of Richard Cresswell. Other locations include Exeter, Dawlish, Teignmouth and Lustleigh, with one isolated specimen "from Lincolnshire, grown in our garden".[40]

Richard Cresswell's collection of algae contains only a few specimens collected after 1870. These include an example "from the limestone steps in the garden, Teignmouth, March 1880", and a donated item found "in a stream at Kingsteignton among water cresses, May 1880". There is also an envelope con-

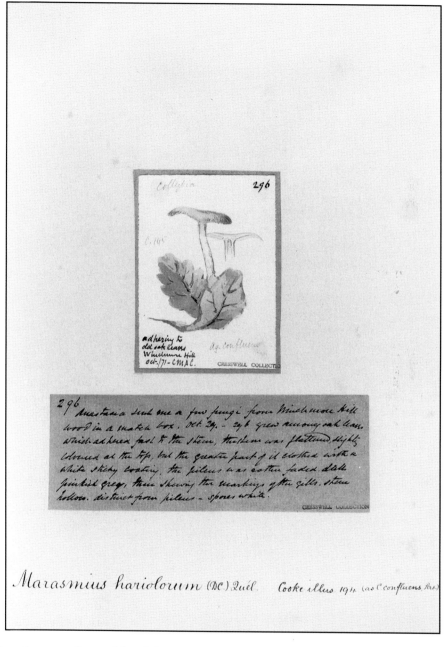

Page from an album of fungi drawings made by Richard Cresswell. This specimen was gathered in Winchmore Hill Wood by his daughter Anastasia in October 1871. Anastasia was very close to her cousin Henrietta and frequently stayed with the family in Winchmore Hill. Richard Cresswell wrote the description below the drawing. The identification at the foot of the page was added later by a museum curator, and refers to an illustration in Mordecai Cubitt Cooke's Illustrations of British Fungi *(1881–91). The album forms part of the Cresswell Collection at the Royal Albert Memorial Museum, Exeter.*

taining "Cornish seaweeds collected by Miss C.M.A. Cresswell" at Bossiney, Trebarwith and Tintagel in 1881, no doubt during a holiday taken by Anastasia.[41]

As a child, Beatrix accompanied her father when he stayed in Winchmore Hill. Many years later, she recalled visits to Grovelands in the early 1870s with her uncle, John Cresswell, whose patients included the Taylors, owners of the estate. She and her cousin Francis were given permission to go into the private part of Winchmore Hill Wood, and with a friend they would take a punt on Grovelands Lake: "we got very wet and muddy. We fished from the lake large fresh-water mussels which lived on the mud at the bottom. There were wild lilies of the valley in the wood". On one occasion Beatrix was shown round Grovelands House by the housekeeper, and remembered "one quaint room draped with a beautiful soft brown silk". She also recalled the elderly John Donnithorne Taylor in his pink hunting coat, "an old gentleman worth seeing, a survival of a generation long since passed, such as present-day young people can never imagine". This recollection was made some 60 years later, in the early 1930s.[42]

Beatrix continued to visit Winchmore Hill with her family for many more years, but she never really liked her uncle John: "he was an extraordinary contrast to my father — dark....rough, somewhat tyrannical, and fond of airing violently atheistical opinions". The comment may perhaps surprise readers who have formed an impression of John Cresswell as a kindly, benevolent gentleman and a pillar of the local church, but he certainly lacked the sophistication and learning of his Devonshire relatives, and there is more than a hint of social superiority in his niece's remarks. Her opinion may also have been coloured by what she later described as one of the most unpleasant experiences of her life — the incident of the mad mongrel of Grove Lodge. She was staying at Winchmore Hill when one of John Cresswell's dogs developed rabies, and he refused to have it put down. It ran wildly round and round the lawn of Grove Lodge, and snapped at imaginary flies in the dining room. Twice it escaped from an empty room in which it had been shut. Its presence in the house haunted Beatrix's sleep until, two or three days later, it died. This episode of canine madness tainted her memories of Grove Lodge for years afterwards.

On the other hand, Beatrix was very fond of her aunt Frances — John Cresswell's wife. Frances knew London well, and would give her niece clear directions about where to go and what to do in town. So Beatrix went shopping, visited exhibitions, and sometimes had lunch with Mrs. Cresswell's brother Diederich Willink, who, as we have seen, worked in the City. On her return to Winchmore Hill she was expected to give a detailed account of where she had been and what she had done, "but sometimes there were interludes not included in the programme nor mentioned afterwards!". Beatrix also got on very well with her cousin Francis, who was one year older. Whilst he was studying at St. Bartholomew's Hospital, other medical students and their friends would visit Grove Lodge, so there was plenty of young company in the house. Francis had a laboratory in the basement of Grove Lodge, and on one occasion he accidentally dislodged a blue glass jar from an upper shelf; it threatened to fall on Beatrix, but he caught it, steadied the shelf, and reeled back against the wall, white as a sheet: the jar contained vitriol![43]

In 1881, during a visit to Winchmore Hill in the last few weeks before her grandmother Henrietta died, Beatrix kept a diary. The few entries that survive, between late September and late October, offer further glimpses of life at Grove Lodge. The diary records several occasions on which Beatrix, then 19 years old, listened to family stories told by her aged grandmother — tales of her ancestors the Pratchetts in Kent and the Knights of Downton Hall in Herefordshire. How wise Beatrix was to write these down! The last story, an account of the ghost of Downton Hall, was entered in her diary just two weeks before her grandmother's death on 7th November.

Whilst staying at Grove Lodge on that occasion, Beatrix occupied herself with writing and needlework. On 20th October 1881 she wrote: "I have been quite inspired and have begun a musical essay which really seems quite flourishing, if ever it gets done, among my other many employments. I almost hope I shall finish that lace sprig of mine tomorrow, I am so terribly tired of it". The following day she recorded her intention of sending the essay to a magazine, and wrote with satisfaction: "I have finished my lace sprig, I am happy to say". Later the same day she accompanied her aunt Frances to Islington, "where I bought myself a new ulster with grandmama's money — I think it is a very nice one, a sort of sandy colour and fits beautifully; it cost 16 shillings and ninepence". They then went on to a show at the Agricultural Hall, and had tea at a friend's house: "I got rather tired of being there, for the children soon got so very obstreperous".

The 22nd October was a Saturday — "a horrid wet day" — and Beatrix accompanied her 26-year-old cousin Henrietta to a performance of Gilbert and Sullivan's *Patience*, which had opened at the Opéra Comique in the Strand on 23rd April that year, and had transferred to the new Savoy Theatre, also in the Strand, on 10th October. The cousins travelled by train from Winchmore Hill to Ludgate Hill, then "drove like lords" in a cab to the theatre:

> Alas when we arrived there was only standing room in the pit. I like *Patience* quite as well as *Pinafore*, and Etta thinks it much nicer than the *Pirates*. The scenery is so pretty and the dresses lovely; they are all worked by hand with such lovely patterns.

Beatrix goes on to describe one of the gowns, embroidered with peacocks, as "quite too utterly utter!!". "Etta and I both agreed in liking Archibald immensely as long as he was Aesthetic; in plain clothes he looked horrible." The opera's parody of the Aesthetic Movement, then at its height, would have amused Beatrix; her eldest sister Christiana, as we shall soon discover, was already under its influence. The girls returned from the theatre contented: "the great deed is accomplished, and Etta is not very tired after all; and we have enjoyed ourselves immensely". Sunday 23rd was also a "horrid, wet, miserable day". Beatrix took Henrietta's Sunday School class in the morning, "and all the boys were particularly good".[44]

Beatrix's impressions of her visits to Grove Lodge enable us to see the Winchmore Hill branch of the family from a different perspective; her cousin Henrietta's recollections are inevitably coloured by an emotional attachment to her close relatives. Beatrix also lacked Henrietta's affection for the Winchmore Hill countryside; in comparison with her beloved Devonshire it seemed dull, and she once likened it to a landscape of "flat ugly meadows with wooden fences between them, and scrubby trees here and there".[45]

Beatrix shared with her sister Anastasia a literary ability which flourished under the influence of a Devonshire family named Elliot with whom they had become acquainted. Mr. Elliot was a "literary dilletante", writing occasionally for magazines and newspapers. His wife's brother was George Armstrong, editor of *The Globe*. The Elliots were the first people to praise Beatrix's literary efforts:

> I had written ever since I could write. I cannot remember the time when I did not hold as my greatest ambition the desire to write and publish. I wrote innumerable poems, stories, fairy tales....there was a tacit encouragement to write as much as I pleased....but Dollie Elliot expressed more — not only admiration but surprise. She was my first "outside public" — and I for the first time realized that I possessed a gift, not given to everyone.

Anastasia, encouraged by the Elliots, started an amateur manuscript magazine for private circulation. In response to advertisements in *The Monthly Packet* and elsewhere, it attracted contributions from about 20 young ladies and won Anastasia and Beatrix some lasting friendships. The venture was a great success, and some of the contributors later earned a reputation in the literary world, though none became famous. After a few years the contributions dwindled in the face of competition from cheap newspapers, and the magazine was wound up. This pastime was not uncommon among ladies with literary ability; Anastasia's cousin Henrietta circulated a similar magazine to a selected readership in later years. Following the closure of *their* magazine, Anastasia and Beatrix went on to contribute stories and articles to *The Teignmouth Gazette*. The first writing that Beatrix was ever paid for was a ghost story for *Belgravia*; on the proceeds of two guineas she and her sister stayed at Lyme Regis and collected fossils!

Beatrix in particular acquired a reputation for learning, which she modestly tried to play down. Her godmother, who lived in Cambridge, was anxious that she should go up to Girton College, but Beatrix had no wish to do so. This was just as well, for her father said that he had had great difficulty sending his son to university, and certainly could not send a daughter. Beatrix also had a horror of examinations, and later boasted that she had never taken any kind of examination in her life. Considering her lack of formal education outside the home, her future literary and intellectual achievements would be remarkable.[46]

During the late 1870s, Beatrix's father compiled two manuscript albums recording wild flowers seen and collected over a period of several years. Only the second volume, covering the years 1878–81, survives. It is entitled *Wild Flowers: Their Names and Associations*, and is inscribed "Beatrix Cresswell, August 15th 1881, from Papa". On the title page two verses from Longfellow's poem *Flowers* are quoted, effectively linking the family interests of botany and heraldry: "Not alone in Spring's armorial bearing....". The album records observations of flowering plants, month by month, with English and Latin names, derivations, related literary references and legends, and, where appropriate, their medicinal properties. Some dried and pressed specimens of wild flowers are taped in. Observations recorded by Richard Cresswell but made by other members of the family reveal their whereabouts from time to time: "near Cinderford (Etta) Oct.1879", for example, refers to a contribution from Henrietta Cresswell on a visit to the Forest of Dean. She may also have been responsible for the *Scabiosa succisa* (Devil's Bit) collected in Winchmore Hill Wood on 28th September 1880, and the Water *persecaria* found in Peacock's Lake, Winchmore Hill, three days later. Richard Cresswell's sighting of mistletoe growing on a lime tree near King's College, Cambridge, introduces a touch of humour: "I was specially told that the plant had never been seen [in Cambridge] until Girton College was founded; a matter of much amusement to all Cambridge inhabitants".

What began as a neatly arranged, well ordered botanical album developed, through miscellaneous additions by various members of the family, into a *pot pourri* of observation, illustration, anecdote and verse. Newspaper cuttings and correspondence on botanical subjects, poems about flowers, pen and ink drawings, and nature diaries are among later additions. *An Old Love Song*, containing the repeating line "Parsley, sage, rue, rosemary and thyme" was copied from the commonplace book of Christiana, which she had kept whilst living at Teignmouth. Elsewhere there is a plea by Richard's wife Frances for the use of proper English plant names:

> But let me protest first of all against the attempt which has sometimes been made to invent English names when none exist....if the plant has no English name, so much the worse for it; if it has one, by all means use it, probably it will be much prettier, and more full of meaning than any other.

Taken as a whole, this volume forms a rich and endearing portrayal of the observations and activities of a family for whom the countryside and its flora were an endless source of fascination. Additions were made to the book right up to the late 1930s; some of these will be referred to in due course for their contribution to our knowledge of the Cresswell family in later years.[47]

In 1881, the Cresswell household at Teignmouth comprised Richard, 65, his wife Frances, 59, Anastasia, 25, and Beatrix, 19 — plus a cook and a housemaid — though Anastasia does not appear at Teignmouth in the census as she was staying at Winchmore Hill at the time. In the following year the family was shaken by the sudden death, on Easter Monday, 10th April, of Richard Cresswell. His passing was keenly felt, as Beatrix later wrote:

> The loss to us all is inexpressible. We had gone to him in our joys and sorrows, we depended on him for our pleasures. To me it was the loss of my guide, companion, mine own familiar friend.

Richard's estate passed wholly to his wife, who remained at Lugehay House with Anastasia and Beatrix. The inheritance did not include the house, as Richard had continued to rent it until his death. But in 1885 the owner sold the freehold to Anastasia, whereafter it remained in the family for another 20 years.[48]

In 1883, Anastasia and Beatrix embarked on what was then the greatest adventure of their lives — a 15-week visit to Canada to stay with a family named Stupart, distant relatives of their mother. Fred Stupart, the son of the family, had stayed with the Cresswells previously, and this visit was in response to a return invitation. A journal kept by Beatrix during the visit has survived amongst family papers.

The girls sailed from Liverpool on the S.S. *Sarmatian* on Thursday 17th May. The vessel was a barque-rigged iron steamship of 3,647 gross registered tons, built in 1871 and operated by Allan Line on their transatlantic crossing to Quebec.[49] "We had never been to Liverpool, never been on board ship before", wrote Beatrix, "no two more inexperienced young people ever set out for the far West". For the 1,200 passengers on board, the voyage was marked by sea sickness, fogs, and the monotony of sea and sky relieved only by the sighting of icebergs and whales. Ten days later the sisters disembarked at Quebec, and continued by train to Montreal, where they boarded a Pullman sleeping car train for Toronto. To these young innocents abroad, the sleeping arrangements were a novelty:

> It is very strange to English ideas, this feeling that we really were sleeping in the same place and only divided by a curtain from the nobler sex. Stasia says she couldn't sleep because she kept on thinking someone would look in.

On Tuesday 29th May they arrived at Toronto, where the Stuparts lived. Two days later Anastasia's 28th birthday was celebrated. Among her presents were ear-rings from her cousin Henrietta in Winchmore Hill. The next six weeks were occupied with visits, outings, shopping, sketching and botanical expeditions. Beatrix found a delightful shop in the city "where any amount of stuffed birds and other treasures are to be had"; here she bought a lovely fossil and the skins of a robin and night hawk — "I could have spent a great deal at that shop if I had tried". On 4th July they visited Niagara Falls by steamer and train — a highlight of the holiday which merited a long and enthusiastic description in Beatrix's journal.

On Thursday 12th July they went to stay with friends for a week in what

Beatrix describes as "an American boarding house" at Sutton, on Lake Simcoe, about 40 miles north of Toronto. Here they enjoyed the countryside greatly, and Beatrix wrote: "I shall be so sorry when the time comes to leave Canada". During the visit, a local lad presented her with the tail of a chipmunk which he had found dead in the road. This trip was followed by a few days at Collingwood on Lake Huron. Thereafter time passed slowly, and the mood of the diary changes to one of hopeful anticipation of the homeward journey. This began on 29th August with the return to Quebec, where the sisters embarked on the S.S. *Sarmatian* on Saturday 1st September. "We left with many regrets, many hopes of once more returning — hopes that may spring eternal, and bear no fruit for aught I know." Elsewhere, Beatrix said that she would not have minded settling in Canada, "but in those days no one thought of a girl of 21 earning money or finding anything to do in a colony. No doubt, had anyone known how to find it, there would have been literary work for me in Canada".[50]

Instead, Beatrix developed her talent as an author whilst still living in Teignmouth. She had an ambition to write novels, but never succeeded in getting one published and later destroyed her manuscripts: "my plots, my failures, and my secrets (for there was much of *myself* among them) no one will ever know". She was more successful with articles and short stories, several of which were published in *The Globe* and elsewhere. Charlotte M. Yonge, founder and editor of *The Monthly Packet*, took several of the stories, and one of these — *The Royal Progress of King Pepito* — was published as a children's book by the Society for Promoting Christian Knowledge in 1889. The publishers commissioned Kate Greenaway to illustrate the story. The book is a nursery tale with a religious undercurrent, combining a love and understanding of the countryside with a strong moral tone.[51]

Priced at one shilling, and extending to 48 pages, the story is of a small child ("King Pepito") who escapes from the domain of his nursery, with its army of wooden soldiers, its faithful rocking-horse, and its animals from Noah's Ark. Once in the garden, Pepito gathers flowers "with fine disregard for rank....His Majesty's taste is gaudy, a poppy or glowing *Eschscholtzia* is of more value in his eyes than all the orchids ever grown". Beatrix is evidently anxious that her young readers should sample the difficult botanical terms to which she had been exposed in her childhood. In the face of various adventures Pepito runs on through the countryside, reaching a stream along whose banks "the bitter-sweet, and blue vetch festooned the wild roses, whose broad white blossoms were spread wide to catch every ray of sun". On and on he goes, until at last, exhausted, he lies down in a leafy glade (goyle) and falls asleep, "whilst the sun travelled farther and farther round the hill, and began sinking down behind the big tors". The "goyle" and the "tors" betray the author's West Country upbringing.

At length Pepito is rescued by his parents and godfather, who is a botanist "and almost fancied that he had seen *Bartsia viscosa* in the marshy field outside". (Here Beatrix is paying tribute to her father, and drawing her readers' attention to a rare plant which in another work she identifies as a native of Teignmouth.) The little Pepito is carried back home, given strawberries and cream, and put to bed; "every one was too pleased to be angry with him". His godfather quotes a proverb: "Where the King is there is the Court; where the Master sits there is the head of the table". The following day, Pepito's mother, returning to the place where he was found, discerns in the proverb a sacred meaning: "she thought of the King who rules over the whole earth, Whose Court is in the heart of every one that loves Him, of the Master who presides over every table. Was not this beautiful green dell His Court, and had not His angels led little King Pepito here to worship Him?".

The great charm of this book lies in the 12 delicate, finely drawn, and exquisitely coloured illustrations by Kate Greenaway, one of the leading artists of the Aesthetic Movement. They were engraved and printed by Edmund Evans, the most celebrated Victorian printer of children's books in colour; it was he who popularised Kate Greenaway's drawings with the publication of *Under the Window* in 1878. During the 1880s she reached the peak of her achievement; *The Royal Progress of King Pepito* was one of a handful of books published during this period in which some of her finest illustrations for other authors appeared.[52] Because of these, *King Pepito* occupies a place in the best tradition of Victorian children's books. Beatrix Cresswell was well served by one of the foremost book illustrators of her day, a fact which, had she written nothing else, would have caused her name to be known to book collectors for generations to come. It is curious that, on the cover and title page of *King Pepito*, her first name is shown as Beatrice, a spelling which she appears not to have used again.

Beatrix Cresswell's next book, *Alexis and his Flowers*, followed in 1891. Subtitled *Flower Lore for Boys and Girls*, it was a more substantial work than *King Pepito*, running to nine chapters and over 200 pages. It was published by T. Fisher Unwin, and illustrated by Beatrix's Winchmore Hill cousin, Henrietta. The illustrations take the form of vignettes at the head of each chapter, depicting flowers with which the chapter deals. Henrietta's signature appears in tiny lettering alongside one of the flower stems in each picture. The drawings are skilfully done, reflecting the fact that by this date, as we shall observe later, Henrietta had become an accomplished flower artist. In this book, the two cousins have shared their knowledge and love of flowers to produce an attractive children's story. The text is well laid out within wide margins and a frame decorated with *fleurs-de-lys*.

The text recounts the language and lore of flowers as seen through the eyes of a small boy named Alexis. There are frequent verse quotations, many biblical references, and stories from Christian hagiology and Classical mythology; Alexis seems to be remarkably well educated in these subjects! The prose is for the most part simple and direct, and there are strong theological overtones. Several allusions to Devonshire betray the author's home background.

The story opens in the rambling garden of a rectory, where Alexis has lived since being brought there from India as a baby to live with a great uncle. Presumably the theme was suggested to Beatrix by her family background — a clerical father, and a mother born in India. Following the rector's death, Alexis moves to his grandfather's house, where he learns about the flowers, in a fanciful way, by conversing with them. Starting in winter, the tale progresses, chapter by chapter, through the seasons. In a scene reminiscent of the leafy goyle in *King Pepito*, Alexis encounters "Mother Holda" or Dame Nature, and her spring flowers. At one point there is an echo of Frances Cresswell's plea for the use of English flower names, when Alexis expresses regret at the renaming of plants by modern botany books. The author introduces her own enthusiasm for heraldry with a discussion of the heraldic use of flowers: her reference to the *Planta genista* or golden broom of the Plantagenets foreshadows a future work to which we shall return. After a lengthy discourse on iris, the boy is prompted to remark: "the amount of learned discussion they have evoked makes one's brains whirl"! The story closes with a distinctively Christian statement, as Alexis looks towards a gate beyond which lies a garden lovelier than any he had imagined: "what we shall find when we get there no one knows", explains his uncle, "only this we can well believe, it will surpass our expectations". Certain particulars of the opening and closing chapters call to mind *The Secret Garden*, written 20 years later by Frances Hodgson Burnett; the similarities may be coincidental, but they are unmistakable.

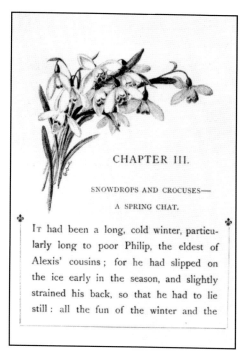

CHAPTER III.

SNOWDROPS AND CROCUSES—

A SPRING CHAT.

It had been a long, cold winter, particularly long to poor Philip, the eldest of Alexis' cousins ; for he had slipped on the ice early in the season, and slightly strained his back, so that he had to lie still : all the fun of the winter and the

Chapter heading from Alexis and his Flowers *by Beatrix Cresswell, published in 1891. The illustrations are by her cousin Henrietta of Winchmore Hill.*

With two published works to her credit, Beatrix had by 1891 embarked on a long and fruitful career as an author. Never again, however, would she write for children; her subsequent output was serious and at times learned non-fiction. We shall encounter it in later chapters. We shall also accompany her on some Continental travel which she was beginning to undertake at this time. Meanwhile, we find her, at the age of 28, still living at Lugehay House with her widowed mother, her sister Anastasia, and two servants. In the 1891 census, Beatrix's occupation is shown as "Literature, Author", her mother's as "Living on own means". Anastasia is again absent, staying in Winchmore Hill. Memories of past sadness would have been stirred when, around this time, a new choir vestry was built at West Teignmouth parish church on part of the former churchyard. This covered the grave of the infant twins of Frances Cresswell, buried in 1852. Her son Richard Henry Cresswell, now well established in his clerical career in London, requested that the mortal remains of Clara and Alured should not be disturbed. His wishes were respected, and the grave slab was removed to the vestry passage, where it remains today.[53]

Merrily on High

So far in this chapter we have followed the lives of the Cresswells at Grove Lodge, and of their relatives at Lugehay House, throughout the 1870s and 1880s. We must now return to the two Devonshire Cresswells — Richard Henry and Christiana — whose careers took them elsewhere during this period.

In 1869, two years after his graduation from Oxford, and at the age of 23, Richard Henry Cresswell was ordained deacon, and appointed curate of Christ Church, Clapham, a growing suburb of South London but still in the county of Surrey. It was a new church, serving the northern part of the old parish of Clapham, some distance from the parish church of Holy Trinity on Clapham Common. It stood in Union Grove, east of Wandsworth Road. To the north lay the Nine Elms Works of the London and South Western Railway, to the west the recently opened line of the London Chatham and Dover Railway to Battersea and Victoria. The need for the church arose from the building up of this area during the 1840s. Large houses and villas were erected in Wandsworth Road and adjacent streets to the east, whilst to the west of Wandsworth Road many streets of small dwellings were laid out to accommodate some of the poorest people in the area. In 1849 the Rector of Clapham issued an appeal for a new church to serve this part of the parish. A temporary church was erected, but by 1861 the congregation had outgrown it, and money was raised to build a permanent church in Union Grove. Benjamin Ferrey was appointed architect, and the new church was consecrated by the Bishop of Winchester in May 1862. It was built of Kentish ragstone, in early middle-pointed Gothic, with a nave and wide side aisles under separate gabled roofs. A tower was planned but never built. In 1864 the architect George Edmund Street was commissioned to furnish and adorn the interior, work which resulted in a highly ornate and richly decorated church. The adjacent red-brick vicarage, also designed by Street, was built in 1865.

The first vicar of the new church was the Reverend Bradley Abbot. Ordained from Trinity College, Dublin, he had served as curate at Holy Trinity, Brompton, and St. Mark's, Whitechapel, before becoming minister of the temporary church at Clapham in 1856. He was a supporter of the growing Catholic movement in the Church of England, and had acquired a reputation as a ritualist. He was one of a number of priests of Anglo-Catholic persuasion who identified a need for spiritual renewal among the poorest members of society, hitherto untouched by Evangelical respectability. In the early 1860s, the working class suburb of North Clapham was fertile ground for his ideas.[54]

Bradley Abbot's high churchmanship became evident whilst he was still minister of the temporary church. In 1860 he adopted the Continental practice of placing six candles on the altar instead of the two provided for in the English

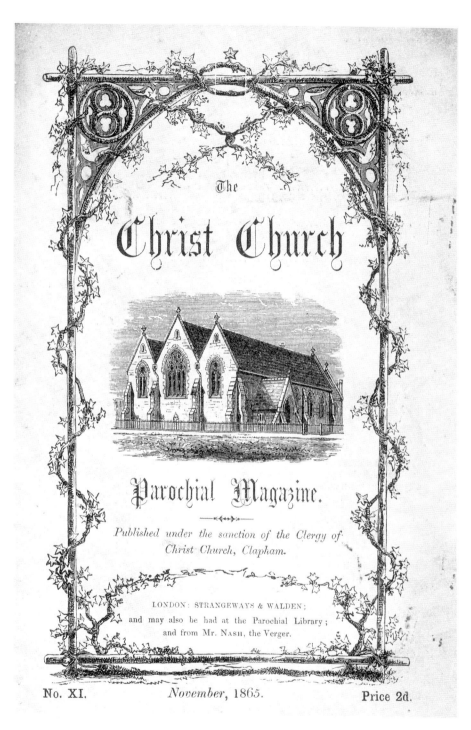

The

Christ Church

Parochial Magazine.

Published under the sanction of the Clergy of
Christ Church, Clapham.

LONDON: STRANGEWAYS & WALDEN;
and may also be had at the Parochial Library;
and from Mr. NASH, the Verger.

No. XI.   November, 1865.   Price 2d.

Cover of the Parochial Magazine of Christ Church, Clapham, November 1865. Four years later, Richard Henry Cresswell was appointed curate in this parish, under its ritualistic vicar Bradley Abbot. The church is still in being.

use. His practices attracted episcopal disapproval: three years after the new church was consecrated he reached a compromise with the Bishop of Winchester whereby only two altar lights would be used at the celebration of the Eucharist but incense would be permitted on five of the Church's festivals. In the same year, 1865, Christ Church, Clapham, became one of the first London churches to revive the use of Eucharistic vestments.[55] An inventory of vestments and ornaments belonging to the church, taken on the Feast of St. Crispin, 25th October 1865, contained no fewer than 54 entries, including a full set of Eucharistic vestments, a white metal thurible, incense boat and spoon, altar frontals and superfrontals, white linen surplices, cassocks, a brass altar cross with crystals, two copper gilt candlesticks, and a processional cross.[56]

It is clear that, despite opposition from some quarters, the congregation at Christ Church were comfortable with the ritualistic worship favoured by their vicar. In November 1865 the Parochial Magazine reported with satisfaction the harvest festivities, which "this year advanced far beyond the glories of any of our former Thanksgiving Festivals":

> We are most sincere in our wishes that the example of full ritual....may lead to the introduction of similar observances in many of the neighbouring Churches. But whatever other persons may think, we are certain that the whole of the arrangements were admirably designed as a vehicle for the devout expression of the feelings of many thankful hearts.

A London newspaper sent a correspondent to mock at the solemnities, "and, no doubt, many of those who had taken part in them were pained when they read his ignorant and profane comments".[57] All this was far removed from the liturgical simplicity favoured by Dr. Pusey, but the later followers of the Anglo-Catholic movement claimed that they were doing no more than reviving forms of worship permitted by the rubric of the Book of Common Prayer.

It was into this somewhat heady atmosphere that Richard Henry Cresswell was placed as curate in 1869. In the following year he was ordained priest by the Bishop of Winchester.[58] He performed his first baptism at Christ Church on 6th January 1870, and his first marriage on 16th December 1871.[59] He was lodging at 342 Wandsworth Road, a house on the opposite side of the road to Union Grove but a short walk from the church. It was the home of James Taberham, a builder, his wife, six children and two servants. There were two other lodgers, both shown in the 1871 census as clerks, making a household of 13 altogether. The houses were necessarily spacious. At the vicarage in Union Grove the census shows Bradley Abbot, aged 43, a niece of 29, a son of 11, and two servants. The vicar's wife does not appear.

By 1873, Richard Henry Cresswell had moved to 74 Union Grove, on the west side of the road between Albion Grove and Union Road. The houses here were a mixture of terraced and semi-detached villas, 200–300 yards from Christ Church on the opposite side of the road.[60] On Tuesday 23rd September 1873, Richard married Margaret Rosina Wolf, daughter of Frederick William Wolf, an office clerk. She was a similar age to Richard. The marriage was performed in Christ Church by Bradley Abbot at 9.30 in the morning, and was followed at 10 o'clock by Holy Communion in which we may assume the newly married couple participated. Among the witnesses to the marriage was the bridegroom's sister Christiana Frances Emily. In the register she signed her first name in the abbreviated form "Ictiana". Just under two weeks after the wedding, Richard Cresswell resumed his ministry at Christ Church.[61]

Towards the end of 1873, the first of three religious works written by Richard Henry Cresswell was published. This was *Preparation for Confirmation and First Communion*, a manual for those giving instruction to confirmation candidates. It was published by J.T. Hayes, and, not surprisingly, was strongly influenced by the Catholic tradition in the Church of England. The book contains 12 "lessons", covering doctrinal issues, the nature of the church, priesthood and the sacraments, and explanations of sin and Christian duty. An appendix deals with "the missionary character of every Catholic". Matters which have ceased to be issues for debate — such as whether separate confirmation classes should be held for boys and girls, and whether it is appropriate to receive Communion immediately after confirmation — are given some prominence. Fasting Communion is recommended — "feed your soul before your body. Let no food enter your mouth before the Body of Christ" — and monthly Communion, increasing later to weekly, is advocated. The author's views on authority and Holy Orders are uncompromising: "the Dissenting ministers are only people who dress themselves up in black, and call themselves ministers; they are no more ministers than other laymen". Persons giving instruction are enjoined to "impress again upon the candidates that they are Catholics, and that their remaining true to the Church is their only hope of salvation". The book concludes with this advice, to be imparted to confirmation candidates: "if any one speaks against the Church, let them see that you take it as a *personal insult*. Let it be known that you respect your religion, and others will learn to respect it too". The book was described by *The Church Times* as "the work of a laborious and painstaking priest".

The author's next work, *Aids to Meditation*, was published in 1874, again by J.T. Hayes. In two volumes, it offers exhortations, questions, thoughts and texts to form the basis for meditation (or "mental prayer") throughout the Christian year. The author defines meditation as "an intercourse of the mind and soul with God, by which those feelings and affections which are most pleasing to Him are aroused or strengthened within us, by the consideration of the eternal truths which He has revealed to His Church". Meditation, he argues, is necessary to the leading of a truly spiritual life. On practical considerations, he recommends meditation early in the morning if possible, certainly not immediately after a meal, and initially for not more than 15 minutes at a time. Fixing the eyes on a devotional object, such as a picture, is advised. "The most complete book we have seen to assist in Mental Prayer", said *The Church Times*, "a really valuable guide".

Richard Henry Cresswell's third religious work followed from the same publisher in 1877. *Prayers for the Laity*, sub-titled *A Selection from the Public and Pri-*

vate Devotions of the Eastern and Western Church, contains Eucharistic and penitential devotions, prayers appropriate to certain seasons and festivals, at baptism and confirmation, and for the sick and dying, together with general prayers for use on all occasions. Apart from some further advice on the practice of meditation, the prayers are printed without comment or guidance.

Richard Cresswell accommodated his writing within a pattern of daily prayer and worship at Christ Church. Matins, Holy Communion and Vespers were offered every day; on Sundays there were two or three celebrations of Holy Communion, as well as Matins, Litany and Vespers. Richard's name appears frequently in the service book, as celebrant, assistant or preacher. The texts and lengths of some of his sermons are indicated; 15 minutes was a typical duration. Attendances were consistent but not large; at the main Sunday celebration there were usually 40–50 communicants by the late 1870s.[62]

Surviving printed announcements of two services held at Christ Church in June 1879 indicate the character of worship offered on special occasions. On Monday 9th June 1879 there took place the anniversary festival service of the English Church Union, in the form of Evensong and sermon at 8 pm. The preacher was Frederick William Doxat, then canon of Bloemfontein Cathedral. The choir sang Spohr's cantata *God, Thou art Great*, and at the organ was William Stevenson Hoyte, a noted London organist and composer of church music. The English Church Union had been founded in 1860 to encourage and defend Catholic faith and practice within the Church of England, and Christ Church appears to have been the venue for its anniversary festival for a number of years. On Wednesday 18th June 1879 the choir sang John Farmer's oratorio *Christ and His Soldiers* at a special evening service to raise money for the choir fund. The preacher was the assistant priest of St. Paul's, Walworth. The oratorio, directed by the composer, was intended for young listeners; it had received its first performance in the previous year at Harrow School, where Farmer was director of music.[63]

The year 1880 was Richard Henry Cresswell's last as curate at Christ Church, Clapham. His regular ministry there ceased after the Feast of the Epiphany, 6th January 1881, though he continued to reside at 74 Union Grove and assisted at Christ Church from time to time. On 10th February 1881 he performed his penultimate baptism at Clapham; on the same day his wife gave birth to a baby girl at 74 Union Grove, and on 2nd March the infant was baptised by her father at Christ Church. Christened Clarice Mercedes, she was to be the only child of the marriage; in later years she was destined to carry the Cresswell story to its conclusion.[64] Her middle name, more generally favoured by Roman Catholics, was derived from the Spanish liturgical title *Maria de las Mercedes*, or "Mary of Mercies". The year before Clarice was born, her father had secured a position as Sunday evening preacher at the church of St. John the Baptist, Holland Road, North Kensington, another parish in the Catholic tradition. This was the beginning of a long association with this church which we shall consider in later chapters. But another 12 years were to pass before Richard resumed full-time parish ministry.[65]

In the 1881 census, the 34-year-old Richard is shown as a clergyman "without cure of souls". The household included his wife, then 36, his two-month-old daughter, a general servant and a nurse. On 20th October 1881, when Clarice was eight months, Richard had a visit from his youngest sister Beatrix, who was staying with the Cresswells at Winchmore Hill. She travelled by rail to Wandsworth Road, a journey which could be made from Winchmore Hill on a through train, or with one change at King's Cross. The journey took well over an hour; leaving Winchmore Hill about 11.30 in the morning, Beatrix reached her brother's home, a short walk from Wandsworth Road Station, in time for lunch.

This was her first sight of baby Clarice, and she recorded her impressions in a diary:

> My first feeling was dire disappointment. After having heard so much of her beauty, she was very red in the face with the wind, and she had a claret coloured dress. Added to this her face was rather screwed up, and she is so marvellously like Richard!

However, Richard and his wife Margaret made Beatrix most welcome, and after lunch she spent a long time playing with Clarice in the nursery: "she is much prettier out of her red dress....I do not know if I think her so very pretty, but she is a dear little thing and her mother adores her".

At length, Beatrix returned to Wandsworth Road Station for the journey home. The first train to North London was for stations on the Midland Railway, necessitating a change to a Great Northern train at King's Cross. There were about a dozen stations between Wandsworth Road and King's Cross; as the train rumbled on through Brixton, Loughborough Park, Camberwell and Walworth to the City Beatrix fell to daydreaming, until "I thought it worth while to look up, and saw the train gliding out of King's Cross and carrying me I knew not whither!!". The next stop was Camden Road, fortunately no more than five minutes away, and there was a train back to King's Cross in about seven minutes. On returning to Winchmore Hill, she recounted the experience to her cousin Henrietta: "Etta and I have had a fine laugh over the adventure. I think I was an awful fool!!".[66]

At Easter 1882, a month before Richard Henry Cresswell performed his last duty at Christ Church, Clapham, a further inventory was taken of the vestments and ornaments of the church. The list had grown substantially since 1865; it included a silver chalice and paten given to the church by Richard in 1878, and many items which were the personal property of Bradley Abbot.[67] The Cresswells remained at 74 Union Grove until the late 1880s, when they moved to No.66, four doors nearer the church.[68] The household remained at five in the 1891 census, though the previous servants had been replaced by a cook and a housemaid. Within a year or so the family would be moving to a new home and a new parish.

A Literary Diversion

During 1880, a three-volume novel entitled *A Modern Greek Heroine* appeared from the London publishers Hurst and Blackett. Its authorship was not revealed, and its plot need not concern us. It had a contemporary English setting, and its central character was a young Greek lady whose name was drawn from an ancient Cretan poem: "Bourbachokátzouli with the long tresses, who fought bravely though she was but a girl". A reviewer judged it to be "decidedly a very clever novel....the story may be read with interest from beginning to end"; but he added, disapprovingly: "the moral drawback to the book is that almost all the characters in the story have such very lax and confused notions of right and wrong, and that the author is so very indulgent to their *lâches* against truth and honour".

The indulgent author remained anonymous. Readers of three-volume fiction, then a popular format, may however have come across another novel, *Fair and Free*, published by Smith, Elder and Company of London in 1882. The title page simply declared it to be "by the author of *A Modern Greek Heroine*"; the reader was again left guessing as to his or her identity. The action moved between London, Kent and the West Country.

Two years later Hurst and Blackett published *Incognita*, again in three volumes "by the author of *A Modern Greek Heroine* and *Fair and Free*". In contradistinction to its title, the novel's author was this time revealed: his name was Henry Cresswell. Reviewers received the work enthusiastically, *The Spectator* welcoming it as "really a noteworthy book". Over the next 13 years no fewer than 14 more novels appeared from the same author, all but two in three volumes, and all but one published by Hurst and Blackett. Henry Cresswell's readers would have had no reason to suppose that he was an Anglican clergyman, and only his family and close friends would have recognised the many autobiographical allusions which signal these novels as the work of the Reverend Richard Henry Cresswell, lately curate of Christ Church, Clapham. A few examples will suffice.

A Modern Greek Heroine opens in the lodgings of the Reverend Frederick Sarleigh, deacon and junior curate of St. Adhelm's [*sic*] in South East London. It is a wet, windy evening in early February; the curate has just finished his tea, and is looking forward to an evening's study of a Greek text — *Saint John Chrysostom on the Priesthood*:

> The deacon was distinctly conscious of being comfortable. His little room, its homely furniture, shabby carpet, and tall book-shelves, the faded damask curtains and mahogany sideboard, looked cosy and snug in the cheerful lights and shadows made by the leaping flames....

It is most likely that we have here a picture of the author's original accommodation at Clapham, and an indication of his studious lifestyle. Moreover, it is not too fanciful to suppose that the deacon's surname was a rhyming allusion to the former home of the author's grandmother - East Farleigh in Kent.

The author's fourth novel, *The Sins of the Fathers*, appeared in 1885. Its opening evokes the mood of a warm, still, late spring afternoon in Devonshire, such as Richard would have experienced in his youth: "nestled in one of the snuggest of Devonshire valleys, the little country town of Ottery-Saint-Olave stewed contentedly in the afternoon sun....not a breath stirs in the stillness of the heavy, languorous atmosphere; the very shadows seem oppressive, and the air faint and exhausted". The place is no doubt a thinly disguised version of Ottery St. Mary, where Richard had taught briefly before taking Holy Orders. Much later in the novel we find ourselves in some run-down lodgings in Clapham, South London — a shabbily furnished chamber of uneven floors with a dreary outlook over a weed-choked garden. Perhaps the author had reflected on the contrast between the idyllic surroundings of his younger days in Devonshire and the forlorn appearance of the London suburb in which he now resided. Even in Clapham, however, the natural world could excite wonder:

> The sun had gone down. Great masses of clouds, the colour of a bruise, some of them catching on their edges the crimson of the dying day, were weirdly hustled together in the November sky; through the rents and fissures between them, lowered in the west, wild, red and saffron-coloured lights, against whose glow the leafless boughs of the trees, around the edge of the common, stood out black and eerie.

Richard Henry, in this passage of rare intensity, employs a descriptive idiom which would be used to remarkably similar effect by his daughter some 35 years later.

Of all his novels, *The Hermits of Crizebeck* (1891) affords Richard Henry the greatest opportunity to blend nostalgia for the countryside of his youth with the religious outlook of his maturity. The story concerns the restoration of an ancient monastery in Devon by a group of scholarly ecclesiastics anxious to revive the contemplative life in the Church of England. The narrative is written in the first person singular, and there are many occasions on which the author's voice can be discerned:

> In the soft, low, evening light the familiar prospects; the many-coloured, rolling hills, ending in the distant grey moors, the deep valleys, and the lush meadows threaded by erratic streams overgrown with the luxuriant Devonshire vegetation, brought me back to memories of my boyhood, recollections of summer evenings of long ago.

Elsewhere in the novel, the author's dismay at the spiritually undemanding nature of much of the contemporary church surfaces in a reflection on the attributes required of modern clergy:

> The Church of England, just at present, does not want men who study —
> she wants a good kind of journeymen, upright, presentable fellows, who
> can read like gentlemen, who will repeat from the pulpit, in the familiar
> phraseology, the truths with which the people are already familiar, who
> will execute reverently the simple functions prescribed by the Book of
> Common Prayer....

Neither the Hermits of Crizebeck, nor the Reverend Richard Henry Cresswell and
his clerical companions, were cast in this mould.

We return to *Incognita* for the final illustration of how Richard Henry's plots
seem to draw on personal or family experience. Fifteen years earlier, his uncle,
aunt and cousins in Winchmore Hill had witnessed the construction of the railway which dispossessed them of their home. The family from Devonshire had
visited Winchmore Hill while this work was in progress, and stories of the up-
heaval it caused would undoubtedly have been shared in correspondence as
well. John Cresswell personally attended to at least one injury on the line, and
the account of fatalities caused by fumes from the ballast heaps appeared in
family recollections many years afterwards. It is probable that this was the inspiration for an episode in *Incognita* concerning the widening of the London and
South Western Railway through the cutting across Wandsworth Common. The
author's narrative describes the lineside ballast heaps in the cutting, smoking
gently and giving off a pungent gas:

> The night was calm, perfectly calm. The smoke of the burning earth could
> not be seen, but it must be rising vertically. "He's got smothered up on the
> mound", said Bill; "that's what he's done. The smoke's took un, and he's
> fallen down and been smothered. And I'm darned if I remember which
> mound he said he was a-going up on". His conjecture was correct. In the
> morning they found the smothered man....

If further evidence were needed of the true authorship of these novels, a
surviving copy of *Incognita* provides it. On the dedication page of Volume 1 is
written: "Mamma, from Richard Henry, August 1884 (Bound in Reseda - New
Colour)". The printed dedication "Margaritae", below the personal message,
may be taken to refer to Richard's wife, Margaret Rosina. This, together with
the retention of all 17 novels within the Cresswell family for another half century, establishes beyond reasonable doubt that they were indeed the work of the
Reverend Richard Henry Cresswell.

Among the titles not so far mentioned, *Sliding Sands* (1890) was praised for
its exceptionally good writing and dialogue. *Fairest of Three* (1892) was felt to be
"clever, yet disappointing....the sketches of character are for the most part unfinished, and though the plot is rather elaborately constructed...the average reader
may find considerable difficulty in feeling any sort of sympathy with the principal personages". *Broken Fortunes* (1894), "whatever its imperfections, is not only
clever, but engrossing, and bears many marks of Mr. Cresswell's artistic touch".

The Wooing of Fortune (1896) "once begun....is likely to be finished, though the people are not particularly charming, nor their sentiments or mode of expression very attractive....we should never call Mr. Cresswell's a sympathetic touch".

A mixed press, certainly, and one is bound to conclude that Richard Henry Cresswell's novels rarely rise above the standard of much of the popular fiction with which the reader was presented in the late 19th century. The fact that the author continued to produce the works, at the rate of one a year for a period of 17 years, does however suggest that they sold well. He began writing in the year in which he gave up his curacy at Clapham, and maintained the flow throughout the period during which he was not employed in full-time parish ministry, and for another five years beyond. No doubt the activity was intended primarily as a source of income when his regular stipend ceased, and when he would have had spare time in which to undertake it. He cannot be blamed for the fact that his work has long since joined the vast quantity of unexceptional late Victorian fiction gathering dust on the shelves of library stockrooms.[69]

The transient nature of the project may explain why no specific reference to these works has been found in family papers. They are perhaps not something for which the Reverend Richard Henry Cresswell, MA, would wish to be remembered, and it may have been of some comfort to his family to know that the abbreviated *nom-de-plume* was enough to dissociate authorship from the name of a scholarly London clergyman. His younger sister Beatrix did however value Richard Henry's criticism of her own manuscripts at a time when he was "doing literary work in London". At the age of 18 she may also have been flattered by some few lines of dialogue in *A Modern Greek Heroine*:

> "But we cannot call you Bourbachokátzouli, it is too long."
> "Then call me Bee, unless you can make my name still shorter."
>   The girls laughed.
> "That will do very well", said Ethel, "and people will think you are called
>   Beatrix, which is a very pretty name".

The dedication of *The Sins of the Fathers* provides evidence that Richard Henry travelled to France after completing his first two novels:

> Dédié a la jeune dame qui a quêté pour les pauvres à la grand'messe à l'église de Saint Remi, Dieppe, le dimanche 9 Septembre 1883, fête du très saint nom de Marie.

Around this time, Beatrix became very friendly with Richard's wife Margaret, who took her young sister-in-law on her first Continental trip — to Brussels, Aix-la-Chapelle and Cologne. This whetted her appetite for foreign travel, and for Germany in particular.[70]

Beatrix's mother Frances numbered among her friends a Miss Lucy Gardiner of Bishopsteignton — "never to be forgotten by those who knew her remarkable, somewhat overwhelming character....a wonderfully cultivated woman".[71]

When Beatrix was still a child Miss Gardiner had been to the Passion Play at Oberammergau, and had sent back alpine plants to Beatrix's father "who tried, not very successfully, to naturalize them in the sheltered hollows of our humid west country garden". Miss Gardiner had excited Beatrix's interest in the play, and in 1890 invited Beatrix to accompany her to Oberammergau. The experience thrilled her, and her recollections of the event were published in 1900 by Simpkin, Marshall, Hamilton, Kent and Company in a 64-page booklet entitled *A Retrospect: Life at Oberammergau*. On arrival the friends received a hearty welcome from their host, Herr Schilcher, and attended Mass in the village on their first Sunday. They saw the play several times, and "never found the drama lose any of its impressiveness by frequent repetition....some captious critics have complained that the costumes are an anachronism....cannot they see that the whole *mise-en-scène* of the Passion Play is a piece of pure mediaevalism, brought down unbroken through two centuries?".

Of the people of the village, Beatrix had this to say: "taken as a whole in their everyday life, nearly all the men were good looking and the women plain....there were pretty girls, but the elder women were lamentably plain". Two young lads who accompanied her on a mountain climb were certainly to her liking: "Oscar gathered Stein Rosen and gave them to me, romantically declaring that I must keep them for ever to remind me of being on the top of the mountains with two Bayerische Knaben. I have his flowers now in my *Buch des Passions Spiel* but I expect Oscar has quite forgotten both me and our walk together". Recalling her descent of an almost perpendicular grass slope, Beatrix declares: "the boys had long since found out that there was very little I could not or dared not attempt". Hermann, the older of her two companions, was then 15.

Beatrix and Lucy had been in Oberammergau just over a week when Princess Beatrice (daughter of Queen Victoria) and her husband Prince Henry of Battenberg arrived to see the Passion Play. They had been travelling under the assumed names of Lord and Lady Carisbrooke, but when Beatrix became aware of their arrival she prepared a posy of lilies, orchids, pinks, campanulas and mountain ferns to deliver to the princess who was staying at a nearby house. She had a note of thanks from "Lady Carisbrooke" which she kept as a treasure. "I had never seen her, but having been named after her, had learnt to regard her as particularly my own Princess." After leaving Oberammergau, Beatrix and Lucy visited other places in Germany, "but nothing I saw afterwards has so vivid, so loving a hold on my memory as Oberammergau, last seen through a mist of blinding tears".

Artist and Aesthete

Whilst Richard Henry Cresswell was becoming established in parish ministry during the 1870s, his sister Christiana was seeking employment as an artist in London. She took up residence in Kensington, and mingled with the followers of the Aesthetic Movement, then gaining ground under the influence of D.G. Rossetti and W.S. Godwin. Her family considered it to be a rather "fast and shocking" venture; despite her talent for design, she did not make a great success of her attempts. By 1879 she was living with an artist friend at Coleherne Terrace, West Brompton, on the south side of what was then called Richmond Road, a westward continuation of Old Brompton Road. The terrace of shops, with rooms above, extended from Redcliffe Gardens to Coleherne Road, about 150 yards from the north east corner of the West London and Westminster Cemetery. Christiana's precise address is not recorded, but in the 1881 census only one dwelling in the terrace, No.9, was occupied by art students; although Christiana had left by then, this is probably where she was living two years earlier.[72]

In 1879 Christiana's father, and her younger sister Beatrix, stayed with her at Coleherne Terrace, Beatrix remaining in London for three weeks after her father had gone back to Devon. During that time Christiana persuaded her sister, then 17, to sit as an artists' model; Beatrix later recalled how "one of the artists asserted that I resembled 'a broken lily' — until he saw me jumping furze bushes at a picnic we had on Hampstead Heath — when he had to modify his opinion". This was followed by a studio dance, after which Beatrix and other guests had to sleep on hard mattresses on the studio floor. Christiana also took her to see Henry Irving playing Hamlet at the Lyceum Theatre, off the Strand. This was only six months after Irving had taken over management of the Lyceum, playing Hamlet to Ellen Terry's Ophelia. In three short weeks Christiana gave her younger sister a taste of London's artistic, social and theatrical life, the like of which she had never before experienced. The sisters also visited their uncle and aunt in Winchmore Hill; years later Beatrix recalled with irritation the incident that accompanied their departure:

> Uncle John slipped me half a sovereign when we said goodbye. It was the first piece of gold I had ever possessed, and the fact still rankles that Chrissy — ever impecunious — took it at the station for our tickets, and eventually only gave me very much depleted change.

In fact, Christiana was not too well liked by her kinsfolk. To Beatrix she seemed, like Anastasia, poorly educated, but worse than that she was "the family tyrant, best described by the Devonshire adage 'apples abroad and crabs at home'".[73]

Whilst living in London, Christiana became engaged to a young man named John Henry Jennings, son of Henry Rigg Jennings. The couple were married on 7th October 1880 at the church of St. Matthias, Warwick Road, Earl's Court. The officiating minister was Henry Westall, senior curate. Christiana and John resided nearby at 92 Richmond Road, in a terrace almost opposite the main gate of the cemetery at Brompton, and less than a quarter of a mile from Christiana's former lodgings. John Henry Jennings, who was then 28, appears to have been unemployed at the time, as he is described on the marriage certificate as "gentleman".[74]

The wedding took place in splendid and elaborate surroundings, for St. Matthias, built between 1869 and 1872, was firmly rooted in the tradition of high churchmanship which characterised Christ Church, Clapham, and to which this branch of the Cresswell family was becoming fully accustomed. The first Vicar of St. Matthias, Samuel Charles Haines, was, like Bradley Abbot at Clapham, a noted ritualist, and his curate Henry Westall played a key role in the spread of Anglo-Catholicism in Kensington. Haines resigned in 1878 after several accusations of ritualistic excesses, but Westall pressed ahead with the establishment of another new church in West Kensington. This was to be St. Cuthbert's, Philbeach Gardens, built between 1884 and 1887, and the grandest Anglican church in the area. Westall, who became Vicar of St. Cuthbert's, turned it into "the most flourishing stronghold of Anglo-Catholicism in west London".[75]

By 1883 John and Christiana had moved to South Holmwood in Surrey, and John had become a journalist. Holmwood, adjacent to a 600-acre common, was a semi-rural district two miles south of Dorking and some 30 miles from London, with a population of about 1,500 and a station on the London Brighton and South Coast Railway. It was here, on 21st December 1883, that the first child was born to John and Christiana. The baby girl was christened Mary.

Two years later, the Jennings family had moved back nearer London, and were living in a substantial semi-detached villa at 21 Halford Road, Richmond.[76] This was in a fashionable area between the town centre and the Vineyard, almost opposite the early 18th century Halford House. Their second child, Frances, was born here on 2nd September 1885. Her father appears at that time to have been without work again, as the birth certificate shows his occupation as "gentleman".

Almost two years passed before the Jennings family was further enlarged with the birth of twin girls, Alice and Margaret, on 22nd May 1887. Their home was still at 21 Halford Road, and John Jennings had become a clerk in the Irish Office of the Civil Service. Alice was to have a tragically short life, as she died the following January and was buried in the churchyard of St. Mary's, the old parish church of Richmond nearby.[77]

There were no more additions to the Jennings family. On his 10th wedding anniversary, 7th October 1890, John Henry Jennings died at the early age of 38 from pulmonary consumption. His death occurred in the presence of his mother, Hannah Jennings, in Cambridge Road, Barnes, and it was here that the widowed Christiana settled with her three daughters. Cambridge Road was a pleasant, unremarkable street of mid-Victorian houses between the Thames and Barnes Common. The 1891 census shows the family in residence at 2 Goodwood Villa — Christiana, 41, living on her own means, Mary, 7, Frances, 5, and Margaret, 3. There were no servants or other members of the household.

Sweetness and Sorrow

The year 1892 was to be an eventful one for the Cresswell family. While Richard Henry Cresswell prepared to move from Clapham to a new parish, his relatives in Winchmore Hill faced great changes.

At this point we must return to John Cresswell's upbringing in Kent, and to his uncle and tutor Francis Buttanshaw. It will be recalled that he became Mark Noble's curate at Barming, and later married the rector's daughter Christiana. Francis was the sixth son of John Buttanshaw, a papermaker, who had married Ann Carnell of Hadlow, a village between Tonbridge and Maidstone.[78] Francis was educated at University College, Oxford, and received his BA in 1822. In 1824 he was ordained deacon and became curate at Barming. In the following year he was awarded his MA and ordained priest.[79] He was one of several Buttanshaws who became clergymen during the 19th century. Three of them were his children.

Francis and Christiana, married in September 1827, had a large family. Their first child, also christened Francis, was born in June 1828, and was privately baptised by his father at Barming.[80] Like his father, he went up to University College, Oxford, where he read for the church. He was ordained priest in 1852, having been appointed in the previous year to the curacy of Harmondsworth and West Drayton, Middlesex. He later served in the parishes of Fobbing, Essex; Chinnor, Oxfordshire; St. Giles, Camberwell; Sunbury, Middlesex; and Smeeton Westerby, Leicestershire. In 1887 he became Vicar of Cotterstock with Glapthorn, Northamptonshire, in the Diocese of Peterborough.[81]

Of Francis and Christiana's other children, Henry, born in 1830, and George, born in 1839, also went into the church. Their clerical careers need not concern us. Their brother Mark Noble Buttanshaw, born in 1834 and christened after his maternal grandfather, became a lawyer. It was through him and his brother George that the *Barming Manuscripts* of the Reverend Mark Noble were handed down and preserved (see Appendix A). The two other children of the marriage — both girls — were Ann Maria, born in 1831, and Martha Henrietta, born in 1836.

On 13th June 1854, after his move from Harmondsworth to the parish of Fobbing, the younger Francis Buttanshaw married Eliza Emily Alexandrina Cox, then in her mid-20s, and daughter of the Reverend Frederick Cox. The wedding took place in Aylesbury parish church. The bride's brother was the Reverend Frederick Holdship Cox, who became Dean of Hobart, Tasmania, and later an honorary canon of Ely Cathedral.[82] Francis and Eliza's children included yet another Francis, born at Fobbing in 1855, another Mark Noble, born at Chinnor in 1856, and Emily Christiana, also born at Chinnor in 1862. Emily was still a child when her mother died in 1868 at the age of 39. In the following year she also lost her paternal grandmother, Christiana Buttanshaw (née Noble), and in 1872 her grandfather Francis Buttanshaw. She was still at home with her father when, on 8th February 1887, he was appointed to the living of Cotterstock.

The Northamptonshire village of Cotterstock, two miles north of Oundle on the River Nene, was united ecclesiastically with Glapthorn, to the west. It was a low-lying parish, rising gradually from the bank of the river, which formed its eastern boundary. The road from Oundle to Fotheringhay passed through the parish. On the village green stood an ancient cross, and to the south a water mill and a stone bridge over the Nene. On the west bank of the river, close to the green, was St. Andrew's Church, consisting of a 13th century tower, and 14th century nave, aisles and chancel. It had been restored as recently as 1878, when the removal of plaster from internal walls destroyed traces of medieval wall paintings. To the north of the village street stood Cotterstock Hall, a mid-17th century E-shaped house of wrought stone with gables and mullioned windows. It was the property of Viscount Melville, lord of the manor and patron of the living.[83] The nearby vicarage, a mellow, stone building, carried the date 1651 on a gable end. Living there, in the Buttanshaw household, was Frances Emily Gamble, a young servant who had joined the family in 1883 when Francis Buttanshaw was Rector of Smeeton Westerby, Leicestershire. She was born at Sileby, in that county, in 1864, and her name will reappear several times in this narrative.

Three years before Francis Buttanshaw became Vicar of Cotterstock, his eldest son Francis, who had also entered the church, died at Grahams Town, Cape Colony, South Africa, at the age of 29. As a memorial to him, his father restored an ancient churchyard cross at Cotterstock and erected it at Easter 1890 near the

The vicarage, Cotterstock, Northamptonshire, home of Emily Christiana Buttanshaw from 1887 until her marriage to Francis Cresswell on 17th May 1892. This photograph of the house (no longer a vicarage) was taken almost exactly 100 years after the wedding in nearby St. Andrew's Church.

south porch of St. Andrew's, overlooking the quiet water meadows of the River Nene. Just over two years later, on 17th May 1892, his daughter Emily Christiana brought her 31-year-old fiancé to be married at this peaceful place. He was her second cousin Francis Cresswell, son of John Cresswell of Winchmore Hill.

There had been close ties of kinship between the Cresswells and the Buttanshaws ever since Richard and John Cresswell were educated by their uncle Francis at Barming and West Peckham. The same uncle had been present at John Cresswell's wedding in 1852, and continuing contact between the families brought the younger generations together. The engagement of Francis Cresswell, now well established in medical practice, and Emily Christiana Buttanshaw, the only daughter of a country clergyman, can have been no surprise. It found public expression in Winchmore Hill with the first reading of the banns in St. Paul's Church on 24th April 1892, the Sunday after Easter.[84]

Tuesday 17th May saw the pretty village of Cotterstock *en fête* for the wedding. The weather was fine and dry. Just before 11 o'clock a large congregation assembled in St. Andrew's Church to witness the ceremony. The bride was attired in a dress of heliotrope, and carried a bouquet given by Lord Melville, the patron. She was attended by her brother, Mark Noble Buttanshaw; his children Barbara and Emily were bridesmaids, his son Mark was a page. The best man was John George Ashley, a friend of the bridegroom and eldest son of the late John Ashley, formerly goods manager of the Great Northern Railway and resident in Winchmore Hill. The path to the church was strewn with flowers by the village school children. The ceremony was performed by the bride's father, and the sermon was preached by Dean Frederick Cox (formerly Dean of Hobart), the bride's uncle. The singing was led by a surpliced choir, and the church bells were pealed at intervals during the day. John Cresswell, his daughter Henrietta, and John Ashley, were among the witnesses who signed the register. The wedding breakfast took place at the vicarage, after which the couple left for a honeymoon at Streatley-on-Thames. During the following week, entertainments were provided for the school children, choir and bellringers of Cotterstock and Glapthorn. Weddings were a rarity in the village; the marriage of the vicar's daughter must have been a delightful and memorable occasion.[85]

Francis and Emily returned from their honeymoon to live at Grove Lodge, Winchmore Hill, where Francis continued in medical practice with his father. Later that year, John Cresswell's health deteriorated. Early in October he suffered a stroke, which left him paralysed on his right side. Francis took over his medical practice, and on 5th October was authorised by the Edmonton Board of Guardians to perform his father's duties as medical officer for the Winchmore Hill District of the union.[86] The end came on Wednesday 9th November 1892, when John Cresswell, attended by his son, and in the presence of his daughter, passed away at Grove Lodge after a sudden circulatory failure. He was nearly two months past his 74th birthday.

The funeral took place the following Monday, 14th November. The cortège, which left Grove Lodge shortly before one o'clock, consisted of four mourning coaches conveying near relatives, and the private carriages of two prominent

John Cresswell, aged 71, photographed at Grove Lodge, Winchmore Hill, by his daughter Henrietta in 1890. He is sitting in the "Cherry Wood Chair", made from a cherry tree in the garden of Barming Parsonage, home of his maternal grandfather the Reverend Mark Noble.

local gentlemen — Dr. Richard Thomas Vivian of Roseville, and Mr. Clare Henry Regnart of Stone Hall. The burial, in the family grave at All Saints, Edmonton, was attended by a large number of local residents, including about 100 children from St. Paul's School, who added their own floral tribute to the many beautiful wreaths. All the shops in Winchmore Hill closed during the hour of the funeral as a mark of respect.[87]

Francis Cresswell informed the Edmonton Board of Guardians that he would continue to perform his father's duties as medical officer until a new appointment had been made. On 16th November the board agreed to advertise for a replacement. Applications were received from John William Jackson, a Winchmore Hill surgeon, and from Francis Cresswell. The two doctors attended for interview on 14th December, and John Jackson was selected. Almost 50 years after John Cresswell had failed to secure a position as medical officer to the union, history repeated itself.[88] John Cresswell had died intestate, and Francis was granted administration of his estate on 17th December 1892.

An obituary notice for John Cresswell was published in the December 1892 issue of the St. Paul's parish magazine. It observed that he was one of the original members of the National Schools Committee, "and by his death the last of those gentlemen who managed our Schools from their first establishment has passed away". The next meeting of the managers was not until 16th March 1893, when a message of condolence to Miss Henrietta Cresswell on the death of her father was proposed by Mr. William Thomas Paulin of Broadfields, and adopted. Dr. Vivian was appointed to take John Cresswell's place on the management committee.[89]

It is perhaps surprising that no permanent memorial to John Cresswell was placed in St. Paul's Church. There is little doubt, however, that he was a much loved parishioner and a well respected figure in the locality. Seen in retrospect, his passing was indeed the end of an era. He had arrived in Winchmore Hill early in the Victorian age, when the village was isolated and untouched by urban development; half a century later he had died in a late Victorian community which was already becoming a favoured residential area for those employed in the capital, and which would, within a few years, be transformed into a prosperous modern suburb.

CHAPTER 6

A Family of Artists

An Enduring Gift

The artistic abilities of the Cresswells were manifest in several generations. Of all the talents they possessed, their skill in painting, drawing and sketching was the most prevalent and enduring. It is the purpose of this chapter to bring together these achievements and comment upon them, giving due emphasis to the work of John Cresswell of Winchmore Hill.

The earliest surviving examples of the art of the Cresswells and related families are found in the album autographed by Henrietta Noble, and noted briefly in Chapter 2.[1] Dated 1814, it contains a bookplate displaying a version of the Cresswell arms, and an inscription indicating that Henrietta gave it to her son John Cresswell in 1841 whilst he was still associated with St. Bartholomew's Hospital. It would be interesting to know whether it was a reward for success in his professional examinations that year. Certainly it was a treasured family possession, and we are fortunate indeed that it has been preserved.

The 54 leaves have pasted upon them 69 paintings, ink drawings and pencil sketches by members of the family, and possibly other artists. Of those that are dated, the earliest were executed in 1806, the latest in 1847, John Cresswell having made additions after the album became his own. Many of the pictures are unidentified and unsigned, but the charming watercolours of the Barming area of Kent, some 12 in number, are most probably the work of Henrietta Noble, undertaken before her marriage to Richard Henry Cresswell. The style is bold yet precise, conveying a pleasing impression of the green, well cultivated countryside and river scenery eulogised by her father Mark Noble in his descriptions of the "fruitful valley". These pictures are dated from 1808 to 1814, corresponding closely with the period between the Cresswells' arrival at Barming and their removal to London after Henrietta's marriage. They are interspersed with paintings of other places done over the same period, including the ancestral home at Cresswell, Northumberland, in 1809. This picture, inserted near the front of the album, is indicative of the friendship which developed between the Nobles and the Cresswells some years before the families were linked by marriage.

One or two pictures in the album are marked with the initials of Richard Henry Cresswell, Henrietta's husband-to-be, and others may be his work. Two landscapes are marked "Franchie" and "Francia" — this could have been Richard Henry's sister Frances Mary. Others are initialled "MN", and are probably by Mark Noble's eldest son, who took his father's christian name. Landscapes predominate, though some human portraits and animals also occur. A handful of paintings follow the style of well known artists of the late 18th and early 19th centuries — Giovanni Cipriani (1727–85), Carl Vernet (b.1758) and Caspar David Friedrich (b.1774). The album contains a small group of watercolours done on the family visit to Sidmouth in 1812, and referred to in Chapter 3. Among the last pictures to be included are the paintings of Salcombe Regis, Sidbury and Sidmouth done by John Cresswell during a visit to his brother Richard in 1847, and noted in Chapter 4. These are the only known paintings by John Cresswell of places beyond the London area. It is to his more numerous drawings and watercolours of Winchmore Hill and its neighbourhood that we must now turn.

Leaves from a Sketch Book

John Cresswell's daughter Henrietta said of her father: "his sketch book was always in his hand and his drawing minutely accurate in detail". During his residence in Winchmore Hill he produced at least 200 paintings and drawings, chiefly of the village and its surroundings. Happily, most of these still exist; they form an attractive record of aspects of a 19th century village community in rural Middlesex.[2]

The surviving pictures by John Cresswell fall into three categories: about 40 are watercolours, 50 are "washes" (ink drawings with a thin colour wash), and just over 100 are plain drawings, mostly in pencil. Their artistic merit varies, but as a whole they are comparable with the work of other good amateur artists of the period. The watercolours, executed in subdued tones with an emphasis on brown and green tints, convey a pleasing impression of rural solitude. Typically, they depict a sparsely populated countryside of leafy, mature trees, winding lanes, thick hedgerows and weatherboarded cottages. Skies are rarely blue and cloudless; often they are diffused with the pale yellow of a watery sunlight casting long shadows across the scene. The washes are in many ways the most satisfying compositions, their grey and sepia shading and white highlighting lending subtle contrasts and pleasing tonal effects. Some of the pencil drawings are extremely detailed, their precision affording an almost photographic record.

Much of John Cresswell's drawing and painting of the Winchmore Hill area was undertaken in the course of visiting patients. Of nearly 200 surviving items, only seven are outside the district altogether — at Wood Green, Waltham Abbey, Goff's Oak, Epping Forest and Greenwich Park. Another 40 are just beyond the boundaries of Winchmore Hill — in Edmonton, Palmers Green and Southgate. That leaves about 150 views of Winchmore Hill, of which the most common subjects, amounting to nearly 100 pictures, are Hoppers Road (including Highfield Park), Middle Lane, Green Dragon Lane, Ford's Grove, Highfield Road and Barrowell Green. The remainder are well scattered around the village. It is not surprising that John Cresswell should have favoured the roads in which he lived, nor that he should have portrayed the rural fringes of the community. It is remarkable, however, that there is not a single picture of Winchmore Hill Green in the collection; perhaps this was just too commonplace and familiar a subject to command the artist's attention. Locations of all the pictures are listed in Appendix B.[3]

There is no reason to doubt Henrietta Cresswell's claim that her father's pictures are topographically accurate, but taken together they do not offer a wholly representative portrait of the area. He had an eye for the picturesque, and little interest in depicting features of modern life: the railway does not appear in his later output, for example, and new buildings, if they are shown at all, are incidental to the main subject. Some of the village scenes are populated, but there is little sign of activity on the farms or in the fields. The artist responded more to the charm of a quiet countryside than to the working life of a village community. He should not be criticised for that, however: his purpose was clearly to create pleasing images of an unchanged landscape, not to document contemporary developments.

The pictures span almost the whole period of John Cresswell's residence in Winchmore Hill. About 80 per cent of them are dated by year, though some of the datings are approximate and are not the artist's own. There is a great concentration of work during the 1860s, when he was in his forties — no fewer than 85 per cent of the dated items belong to this period. The earliest dated subject is a watercolour of Greenwich Park (c.1841), probably executed when John was visiting his family in Kent before settling in Winchmore Hill. His first dated picture of Winchmore Hill is a drawing of 1842, showing the Chase Side Tavern from Cock Hill (later Eversley Park Road). Another early subject — Chaseville Park in 1848 — exists in two versions as a watercolour and pencil drawing.

A few of the pictures have precise topicality. Among the earliest are two views of the gunpowder mills at Waltham Abbey, drawn on 13th April 1843 after a devastating explosion. Thirty years later come a watercolour and a drawing of the original Alexandra Palace as seen from Palmers Green shortly before its destruction by fire in June 1873. A handful of his drawings depict characters well known in the village: Mr. Waters, the Middle Lane grocer, and his young son; "Old Scarborough" the roadman at his work; and "Dandy" the railway navvy. After the move to Grove Lodge, John Cresswell drew and painted less; the last picture in the collection to carry a date is a drawing of the Dog and Duck Cottages, at the south end of Hoppers Road, c.1887. Not long after that his daughter began to record the local scene on her camera; photography took over as advancing years brought an end to John Cresswell's most enduring hobby.

Many of his pictures were done on small pieces of paper — either from his sketch book or on the reverse of unwanted scraps such as old notes and letters. They are usually in landscape format, the most common sizes being approximately 7"x 5" and 6"x 4", though many of the pencil drawings are as small as 5"x 3". The largest picture in the collection, a drawing of trees in Highfield Park, does not exceed 11"x 9". The artist was therefore working on a miniature scale, and the degree of detail accommodated within these limited dimensions is often remarkable.

An ink and wash drawing by John Cresswell of Winchmore Hill Wood and the keeper's cottage. It was one of a number of such drawings which he made to decorate sheets of notepaper sold at the Fancy Fair in aid of the National Schools, Church Hill, in 1859.

In some cases the reverse of the illustration can be as interesting as the face. Many carry informative captions, usually added at a later date in the process of identification and preservation. Some are in Henrietta Cresswell's handwriting. A few pictures have rough sketches of other subjects on the back, including one of "Dagmar, Mama's cat 1863". The watercolour of Middle Lane painted in 1858 and mentioned at the beginning of Chapter 5 is on the reverse of a fragment of a discarded letter (or the draft of a letter) in John Cresswell's handwriting, of which the following is decipherable: "....kindness in sending me such useful and handsome presents demands more acknowledgement than second hand messages sent through others....". This tiny painting measures no more than 5"x 3". A pencil drawing of Hoppers Road, made in about 1865, has several handwritten notes on the back: these include a recipe for claret cup, and a reference to the wife of Robert Newberry Cobbett, the surgeon whom John Cresswell nominated as his substitute when he was appointed medical officer for the Winchmore Hill District of the Edmonton Union in 1865. The endorsement "this is my Father's handwriting" has been added by Henrietta. A drawing of Pike's Fields (later Grange Park), though undated, has on the reverse a list of roses for planting in 1873. A drawing of an old cottage in Bury Street, Edmonton is backed by another of Wood's Cottage, Firs Lane, which has been crossed through and marked "do not use this it is reversed". The collection includes examples of the drawings made at the head of writing paper for sale at the Fancy Fair held in aid of the National Schools, and referred to in Chapter 4. In short, the pictures have by chance preserved an assortment of incidental details which offer fascinating glimpses of everyday life in the Cresswell household.

John Cresswell's name became known briefly in the wider art world when, in 1857, he exhibited a painting entitled *Mallards* at the Royal Academy.[4] It was the only time he is known to have exhibited at a public gallery, and the only recorded example of wildlife painting by this artist. We observed in Chapter 5 that he gave this painting to his brother-in-law Diederich Willink, who bequeathed it to Henrietta. Its subsequent history has not been traced.

The botanical art of John Cresswell's brother Richard has already been referred to in some detail — his fine hand-coloured drawings of wild flowers done in Kent, Devonshire and elsewhere over a period of more than 40 years, and his accurate depiction, with pen and pencil, of the fungi and diatoms of which he made a special study. Thanks to the recognition given to his work by other botanists, to his family's concern that it should be preserved, and to the care exercised by its more recent custodians, we are still able to examine and enjoy many of the hundreds of illustrations of plant life which he produced, and share some of the pleasure which he derived from the natural world.

Unlike his brother, and other members of his family, Richard Cresswell was not a painter of landscapes. If any of his work appears in Henrietta Noble's album it is not attributed to him. Indeed, the only pictures of places positively identified to him are four watercolours of his mother's cottage and garden in Vicars Moor Lane, Winchmore Hill, painted around 1865. One shows the front of the cottage, with its verandah, dormer windows and weatherboarded extension, standing behind a white wooden fence and five-barred gate. Another depicts the rear of the dwelling with a porch giving direct access from the drawing room into the garden. Two views of the garden show the great yew tree which continued to flourish close to the railway cutting after the line was built, and the ash arbour which was "ruthlessly destroyed" by the railway contractors. On the path by the weeping ash tree are two small figures — the young Henrietta and her baby brother Francis. The originals of these pictures have not been traced; we are aware of them only through reproductions of copies made more recently.[5] Of the other members of Richard Cresswell's family, his daughters Christiana and Anastasia, and his sister Sarah, have left a few examples of their botanical art. Sarah's fine drawings of British orchids were noted in Chapter 4. When Sarah died at Winchmore Hill in 1863, her niece Henrietta was still a child. In time she would develop into a flower painter of some distinction — but in a different idiom from that of her cousins, aunt and uncle.

Henrietta and her Flowers

Henrietta's known illustrations of Winchmore Hill are represented by a handful of watercolours and one engraving. Three of the watercolours date from 1870, when she was only 15. The earliest shows the waterfall in Green Dragon Lane near the confluence of Houndsden Gutter and Salmons Brook; the others, painted in November 1870, depict Roseville on the Green and the newly built railway bridge in Compton Road. They are the work of a careful but immature artist, and give little indication of the talent which would emerge in later years when Henrietta concentrated on her chosen subject. Another of her early paintings is of great interest, for it shows with some accuracy the front of Grove Lodge, a corner of the railway station and bridge, and a very tall post which appears to carry a semaphore signal for the railway. A portion of the station also appears in a dry-point etching which she did in about 1875 from the garden of Grove Lodge; part of the station roof and a gable finial are visible behind snow-covered conifers. Over 20 years separate this from the last known example of Henrietta's local work — an 1897 watercolour of Ford's Grove Farm.[6]

By the time Henrietta illustrated her cousin Beatrix's book *Alexis and his Flowers* in 1890, she had become an accomplished flower painter in both watercolour and oils. Her work was first shown in public in 1875, when she was 20, but it was during the late 1880s and early 1890s that she became a frequent exhibitor of flower paintings at London and provincial galleries. She continued exhibiting until 1898, by which time her work had been hung on at least 50 occasions in no fewer than 13 galleries. She exhibited only once at the Royal Academy, in 1889; her painting of primroses was selected for mention by the art critic of *The Queen* along with works by three other artists out of a large number of flower subjects "of quite average merit". In the following year she exhibited at the Grosvenor Gallery in Bond Street, and her work was again noticed by *The Queen* as "among the more strongly representative" contributions by women artists. This was the last year of the Grosvenor Gallery; opened in 1877 and a favourite of the Pre-Raphaelites during the 1880s, it closed in 1890 in the face of competition from the rival New Gallery. Among other prestigious London galleries at which Henrietta exhibited were the Royal Institute of Painters in Watercolours (founded in 1832 as the New Watercolour Society), and the Royal Society of British Artists. Her paintings were also shown at galleries in Birmingham, Manchester, Liverpool and Glasgow.[7]

During the late 1880s and early 1890s, some of Henrietta's flower paintings were reviewed by *The Queen* in a feature entitled *Select Works by Lady Artists*. The artists submitted sketches of their paintings to the newspaper, and these were reproduced together with a short commentary on the original. On 25th May 1889, for example, Henrietta's painting *Daffodils* was illustrated — "prettily arranged and extremely well painted". The artist was credited with taste in the selection of her subjects and with manipulative power. The issue of 7th September 1889 included *From the Shrubbery*, "inspired by the artist seeing a relative entering the room carrying a mass of wild daffodils and bay leaves". Henrietta painted the large blooms of *Narcissus horsfeldii* against a backdrop of dark foliage. Her study of *Apple Blossoms*, reproduced on 2nd November 1889, was highly praised: "one is always glad to see this lady's work, because she is one of the most thoroughly earnest and careful artists it is possible to meet with....she paints with all the care of a botanist as well as an artist".

The Queen continued to champion Henrietta's work. *Autumn Jewels*, published on 7th February 1891, was a composition of white autumn daisies, brightly coloured bramble leaves, a spray of pink blossom and some blackberries. The flowers were reflected in a bevelled glass mirror set in a *repoussé* brass frame of rich design — possibly a feature of the artist's home at Grove Lodge. *Christmastide*, reproduced, unseasonably, on 6th June 1891, depicted a bowl of Christmas roses with bay leaves and holly — "a really beautiful picture". Most of Henrietta's flower paintings were indoor studies, but *Primrose Day*, illustrated in *The Queen* on 23rd April 1892, shows a mass of primroses gathered in Winchmore Hill Wood by children who "have so loaded the hamper with both roots and bunches of the flowers that it has overturned by the stump of the tree where it was left". The wood, painted from nature, forms a background to the picture.

In time Henrietta's flower paintings became dispersed, and it is doubtful whether more than a few have survived. Just four examples have been traced —

A study of Christmas roses and violets painted in watercolour by Henrietta Cresswell in 1891. Signed and dated in the lower left-hand corner, it survives in private ownership.

all watercolours — in private ownership in the north of England. Two are unsigned, though they have been authenticated by the owner as Henrietta Cresswell's work. One of these is a study of marguerites and foliage in an earthenware vase, the other an apparently unfinished painting of large yellow daisies. The signed pictures, both dated 1891, show orange tea roses in a blue bowl, and Christmas roses and violets beside a dark green jug. Christmas roses and winter flowering violets were associated in *Alexis and his Flowers*, no doubt fresh in the artist's mind; her fondness for Christmas roses was expressed in a poem she wrote about the flower's Christian legend to which we shall return. Three of the paintings have the dark backgrounds which she favoured for her flower studies, and which are relatively unusual in watercolour. The signatures appear in the stylised form which she used frequently on her work — a large initial 'C' enclosing a smaller initial 'H', the rest of the name having the first 's' elongated in the antique manner.

These surviving examples of Henrietta's work confirm that she was indeed a talented flower painter. In a genre which was extremely popular in the late 19th century, especially among lady artists, it was a mark of achievement that her paintings attracted favourable criticism on a number of occasions, and that her name has been recorded as a frequent exhibitor at reputable public galleries around the country. Her love of flowers, which owed as much to their folklore and associations as to their botanical interest, was reflected in her charming and effective studies.

In tracing the art of the Cresswells, it remains to consider the very different work of Henrietta's second cousin Clarice Mercedes, daughter of Richard Henry Cresswell. She was still a child in the early 1890s, and her painting does not belong to the Victorian period, although it was heavily influenced by it. Her distinctive contribution to the family's artistic legacy will be explored in a later chapter.

CHAPTER 7

A Scattered Flock

The Lost Village

Henrietta Cresswell and her brother Francis did not remain long at Grove Lodge after the death of their father in November 1892. On 25th January 1893, Henrietta purchased from Arthur Goulding, a surveyor living in Holloway, the leasehold of two modern semi-detached houses on the north side of Middle Lane, about 70 yards from the junction with Green Lanes. The pair of houses had a 64-foot frontage onto Middle Lane, small front gardens, and rear gardens of about 100 feet. In 1893 they were the ninth and tenth houses from the Green Lanes corner; the seventh and eighth houses were an almost identical pair. They were built on land owned by the governors of Dr. Radcliffe's School, Steeple Aston, Oxford-shire.[1] The two-storey properties were of red brick with stone mouldings, sash

The last of Grove Lodge, Winchmore Hill. Photographed in 1961, whilst awaiting demolition, it had been a doctor's house for much of its life. A block of flats now stands on the site, on the corner of Station Road and Wilson Street.

windows and a slate roof. To one side of the porch, which was supported on slender stone columns, was a canted bay window at ground-floor level. A corbelled string course ran the entire width of the building at first-floor level, and a brick gable rose above the principal front rooms. The two ground-floor reception rooms and three first-floor bedrooms were spacious and well appointed. Only four houses of this design were built in the road; their external appearance compared favourably with the rather ponderous design of neighbouring detached and semi-detached properties which by the early 1890s were lining the north side of Middle Lane.

Henrietta moved into one of the two houses whose lease she had purchased — that nearer the Green Lanes — and let the other. In this way she was investing inherited wealth in property and deriving an income from it. The houses remained un-numbered throughout the 1890s, but all were given names; Henrietta called hers Cheslyn, the name of the Leicestershire family from whom she was descended through her great-grandfather Richard Cheslyn Cresswell (*c*.1754–1824). His mother Sarah Cheslyn (*c*.1720–1782) was Henrietta's great-great-grandmother. Through pride in her ancestry, she introduced the name of the 17th century owners of Langley Hall in Leicestershire to a suburban street in Winchmore Hill![2]

No.16 Station Road, Winchmore Hill, in 1992 — little changed externally since it became the home of Henrietta Cresswell in 1893. It was then known as Cheslyn, Middle Lane.

From the front of the house Henrietta had an uninterrupted view of open fields extending towards Compton Road, and of trees bordering Highfield Park beyond. It was from the bay window of Cheslyn that she painted one of her last watercolours of Winchmore Hill — the 1897 picture of Ford's Grove Farm mentioned in Chapter 6. Looking across Middle Lane to the eastern side of Green Lanes, it shows the dilapidated, open-pale wooden fence of the tree-lined stackyard, in which there are haystacks, barns and cowsheds.[3]

It seems likely that Francis Cresswell had planned to move out of Grove Lodge even before his father died, no doubt wishing to establish his own medical practice in separate premises and provide a good modern home for his young wife Emily. In the early part of 1893 he moved into a new house lower down

The house in Middle Lane, Winchmore Hill, into which Francis Cresswell moved in 1893. He named it Cotterstock after his wife's home village. It is now 42 Station Road. Photographed in 1992.

Middle Lane, still on the north side, and roughly midway between Grove Lodge and Cheslyn. Horace Regnart, who knew Francis Cresswell, implies that Francis had the house built himself; certainly he was the first owner, and it was a spacious and distinctive property, unlike any others in Middle Lane. It was built well back from the road, at an angle which would have permitted road widening at a later date — a scheme proposed but never implemented. The two-storey, detached, double-fronted house had a strikingly modern appearance for its date. The ground floor was in unfaced brick, the first floor in stucco. There were tall casement windows with leaded upper lights, a shallow roof behind a gable with vertical half-timbering, and deep eaves. The house owed more in its design to the arts and crafts movement than to late Victorian suburban architecture. It was an impressive residence for a young, newly married doctor anxious to develop a successful practice. Francis named the house Cotterstock, recalling Emily's former home and the place where they were married.[4] With them in the house were their maids Frances Emily Gamble, who had served the Buttanshaw family in Leicestershire and Northamptonshire, and her younger sister Matilda Letitia Gamble, also from Sileby near Leicester.

Although Francis had failed to secure a position as medical officer to the Edmonton Union, he acquired other professional interests outside his practice. By 1892 he had become medical officer to the Liverpool Victoria Legal Friendly Society and the National Medical Aid Society. Subsequently he joined the North London Medical and Chirurgical Society and was elected its vice-president.[5] Many years later a former patient recalled his poor eyesight, inherited from his father, which necessitated the use of a magnifying glass as well as spectacles; "we have vivid recollections of him striding along with a prancing gait and his hands behind his back, or making his rounds by bicycle, clad in a brown tweed cycling suit and peaked cap which matched the sandy colour of his beard".[6] Horace Regnart said he was a most interesting man to talk to with a wonderful accumulation of knowledge.

The first child of Francis and Emily Cresswell was born on Tuesday 9th May

1893. He was christened Dirk, the Dutch form of Diederich, the name of his great-uncle who had died four years earlier. Dirk was born immature, with a partially inflated lung, and was not expected to live. Consequently his baptism was performed at St. Paul's Church on 10th May by the vicar, Alfred Drought, and the infant died at his parents' new home, attended by his father, later the same day. Infant mortality remained high in late Victorian England, but even so the event must have been one of great sadness for the family. Just over two years later, on Sunday 5th May 1895, the couple had another baby boy. He too was given only one christian name — Frank, the form to which his father's first name had often been abbreviated. He was baptised at St. Paul's Church by the vicar on Trinity Sunday, 9th June, during an afternoon service which included the Litany and Catechism. Happily, he grew into a healthy young lad.[7]

Not long after moving into Cotterstock, Francis became involved in securing land at Winchmore Hill to be used as a playing field by St. Bartholomew's Hospital. The evidence for his involvement is a statement many years later by Henrietta that "my brother Frank [Francis] was mainly responsible for Bart's Recreation Ground being in Highfield".[8] In 1892, various athletic clubs at St. Bartholomew's had combined with the hospital's Abernethian Society (a medical reading and debating society) to form the Amalgamated Clubs. Faced with the increasing difficulty of finding suitable cricket and football grounds to rent, they decided to purchase land somewhere accessible from London. A committee was formed for the purpose, and in July 1893 William Bruce Clarke, an orthopaedic surgeon at the hospital, approached the Great Northern Railway on behalf of the committee to enquire about the cost of tickets for medical students travelling to and from a proposed new recreation ground near London. The general manager of the railway company replied: "I have been looking into the arrangements that can be made for the Hospital Students if they take a pleasure ground a few miles out of London, and I find that we can issue to Students, on production of a Card of Membership, tickets at a fare and a quarter for the return journey with a minimum of threepence". He went on to say that this would apply whether students travelled singly or together, but that the same fares would be offered to visitors and competing teams only if they travelled in parties of at least 10.[9] No doubt Winchmore Hill was already in mind by this date.

On 8th November 1893 approval was given by the medical officers and lecturers at Bart's to the purchase of 10 acres of land on the Highfield Park estate at Winchmore Hill for use as a recreation ground.[10] The plot lay between Highfield House and Green Lanes; the main road frontage, opposite Highfield Row and the New River, was 600 feet long. The site was rectangular, except for the irregular course of its southern boundary. The land was bordered by trees to the south and east, but to the north and west straight boundaries were formed across the open fields of the estate. The purchase was completed on 5th April 1894 by conveyance between trustees for the Bart's medical school and the executors of the late Alfred Walker of Stone Hall, Winchmore Hill, who had owned the land.

The medical school thereby became the landlords, and the Amalgamated Clubs were tenants.[11]

Purchase of the site was financed partly by mortgaging the ground to the trustees of the Brackenbury Scholarship at Bart's. This yielded over £2,200 towards a purchase price of nearly £7,700, the remainder being derived from investment income. Use of the Brackenbury Scholarship fund for this purpose provides a further link with Francis Cresswell's involvement in the project, as he himself had been the holder of a Brackenbury Scholarship whilst at the medical school in 1883. He was well placed to advise the school not only on the availability of suitable land in Winchmore Hill, but also on possible means of financing its purchase. It was no doubt a source of satisfaction to him that he had been instrumental in saving from building development a portion of land which he had enjoyed as a childhood playground, whilst at the same time providing a much needed recreational facility for the school at which he had received his medical education.

By early 1895, levelling, draining and fencing of the ground had been completed, and a pavilion had been built on the northern boundary with access from Green Lanes. The ground was formally opened on Saturday 8th June (the day before Frank Cresswell's baptism), when cricket and lawn tennis matches were played between past and present students. In the same year a sinking fund was established into which was paid the rent received from students for use of the ground, and from which were financed annual maintenance charges, repayment of the mortgage to the Brackenbury trustees, and enlargement of the medical school's scholarship endowment fund. In 1895 only a handful of houses could be seen from the ground; within 10 years it was surrounded on three sides by building development.[12]

Francis Cresswell and his wife took an active part in the life of the community. In October 1897 the first exhibition of the Winchmore Hill Arts and Crafts Society was held in the village hall in Wilson Street. Under the presidency of William Thomas Paulin, the society encouraged amateur art and handicrafts at a time of renewed interest in creative home activities. Francis and Emily were amongst those who gave demonstrations at the exhibition. The event was a great success, and was repeated on 31st May and 1st June 1899. By this time the Cresswells were members of the committee. The second exhibition attracted even more entries; Emily was thanked for assisting with craft demonstrations and a musical entertainment, her husband for taking part in the judging.[13]

In 1901 Emily became secretary and treasurer to the St. Paul's ladies' working party for home and foreign missions, which met at least monthly during the winter, and she continued in this capacity for three years. The members made useful articles for sale in aid of missionary work; they provided their own materials, and were required to contribute at least three large or six small articles in the session. During the winter of 1901–2 the meetings took place at Rose Cottage, Vicars Moor Lane, formerly the home of Francis Cresswell's grandmother, later occupied by the vicar Alfred Drought, and, after his sudden death in 1901, the residence of Miss Julia Mann, the blind sister of Edward Mann, the brewer, who lived at nearby Roseneath House. At that time about 20 ladies attended the working party, but by the following winter the membership had grown to 47. On 12th November 1902 a sale of work was opened by the Marchioness of Ely (of Eversley Park, Green Dragon Lane), Emily Cresswell running the "woollen and plain work" stall. Emily's musical ability was again evident at a People's Concert held by the St. Paul's Literary Society in the schoolroom on 11th December 1901, when she performed two songs to a large audience.[14]

Francis and Emily gave generously to parish causes, as John Cresswell had done. They both paid annual subscriptions to the St. Paul's day and Sunday schools. Emily supported the annual Sunday School treat, and Francis subscribed to the Church Lads' Brigade from its formation in 1897. Early in 1895 they both gave donations to the soup kitchen and coal funds, as did Henrietta: "by means of the liberal response....to the appeal, which was made by the Vicar, on behalf of the exceptional distress that prevailed during the recent severe frost, much timely and sorely needed relief was afforded, in food and fuel, to those who were in want of those necessaries". Among other causes supported by Francis were a fund for the provision of a new reredos at St. Paul's Church, dedicated in February 1899, an appeal held during 1901 in memory of the late vicar, Alfred Drought, to provide his daughters with an annuity and to pay for a memorial brass in the church, and a presentation to the new vicar, Arthur Dewdney, on the occasion of his marriage to Miss Ina Paulin of Broadfields in July 1902. Between 1894 and 1900, Emily's father Francis Buttanshaw, still Vicar of Cotterstock, preached at St. Paul's Church on seven occasions during visits to Winchmore Hill. In 1894 and 1895 he was there in July, in 1897 and 1898 in January. The last occasion was on 12th August 1900, when he was the preacher at both morning and evening services.[15]

Following her move from Grove Lodge, Henrietta Cresswell continued the good work which she had already undertaken for the parish. In 1893 she organised with Annie Villiers of Highfield House a jumble sale to pay off the balance of the debt on the new font erected in St. Paul's Church. The event was referred to as a "rummage or American sale", and was later claimed to have been the first jumble sale ever held in the parish. It took place in the village hall on Saturday 13th May, and raised more than enough to pay off the debt. The vicar expressed his thanks to Misses Cresswell and Villiers who had started the project to provide the font, "and who now have the gratification of bringing it to such a successful issue. A handsome Font now finds a place in our Church, and will probably be used and admired and valued by many future generations".[16]

Henrietta reached her 40th birthday on 15th February 1895. She had witnessed great changes in Winchmore Hill, and greater changes still were soon to occur. She was a countrywoman at heart, with no love for the "crowds and cities and struggling suburbs". She was hearing the call "to wild places, to country sights and sounds, to the unspoilt corners of the land", which she had heard in the depths of Winchmore Hill Wood in the far-off days of her childhood. During the closing years of the century, her thoughts turned to an escape from the encroaching tide of bricks and mortar — from the loss of cherished views,

Henrietta Cresswell, c.1895, aged about 40. The mannish hairstyle, adopted in her late thirties, attracted some mischievous comment, but caused her little embarrassment.

the felling of centuries-old trees, the widening of country lanes to become suburban streets, and the building of houses on fields where lately cattle had grazed and harvests had been gathered. She sought tranquillity in a distant part of the land, far from the spreading metropolis.

Just how her attention came to be drawn to it is not recorded, but on 25th February 1899 the columns of *The Dumfries and Galloway Standard* carried the following advertisement:

> NUNHOLM HOUSE TO LET. Entry at Whitsunday. NUNHOLM HOUSE contains Three Public Rooms, Four Bedrooms and Two Attic Rooms, good Kitchen and Scullery, Pantries, Wash-house and Lavatory (with hot and cold water); also, Coach-House and Stable. Excellent Spring Water. There is also a good Kitchen Garden well stocked with choice fruit-bearing Trees, &c. Neat Policy Grounds and Shrubberies. The House is delightfully situated on the banks of the Nith opposite to Lincluden Abbey, within a quarter of an hour's walk of Dumfries. Rent moderate. The House may be seen on Tuesdays and Fridays, between Two and Four Afternoon. For further particulars apply to JOHN HENDERSON, Solicitor, Dumfries.

The advertisement was repeated twice during March. Henrietta must then have entered negotiations with John Henderson and Sons, solicitors acting on behalf of the owners, to secure a tenancy of the property. Towards the end of that year she reached agreement to occupy Nunholm House at an annual rental of £45, and left Winchmore Hill to settle in her new home north of the border. Her cousin Anastasia, with whom she was already close, moved from Devonshire to join her there. The family had long expected that the two cousins would eventually share a home.[17] Though Henrietta was now separated from her childhood home by a distance of well over 300 miles, her connections with Winchmore Hill were by no means at an end — not least because she retained ownership of the two leasehold properties in Middle Lane, and derived an income from them, for the rest of her life.[18]

After the Cresswells had left Grove Lodge it was occupied for a few years by a Mr. William Law. Then in 1900 it became the home of John William Jackson, the doctor who had secured John Cresswell's position as medical officer for the Winchmore Hill District of the Edmonton Union. Dr. Jackson, who had previously lived at Oakbank on the Green, at Eskbank in Vicars Moor Lane, and at Rowan Tree House on the Green, remained at Grove Lodge until 1912. Thereafter it continued to be a doctor's home for many years.[19]

By the end of Queen Victoria's reign the population of Winchmore Hill had reached well over 4,000. In the opening years of the century, building development was concentrated on Highfield Park, Middle Lane, Compton Road and Green Lanes. Had she remained, Henrietta would indeed have been surrounded by houses within a few years. Francis and Emily lived in Winchmore Hill long enough to see this process underway. During 1903, on fields almost immediately opposite their home in what had now become Station Road, work was in progress on the erection of a large new parish hall and institute for St. Paul's Church. The site had been chosen after failure to secure one on the Green. The building comprised a basement for boys' clubs and a gymnasium, a parish hall accommodating about 400 people, rooms for a men's club and girls' club, a church meeting room, kitchen and caretaker's premises. The design provided separate access to the different parts, permitting simultaneous occupation and use. The main entrance was in a new road formed between Station Road and Compton Road, to be known as King's Avenue. The institute was intended for religious and secular parochial meetings, concerts, private dances, "and various other proper forms of entertainment". The full-time caretaker, who was offered room, coal, light, 21 shillings a week and special fees, was required to be a regular Communicant.

The red-brick building, illustrated by artist's impression in the June 1903 parish magazine, was a bold and imposing example of the emerging Edwardian institutional style, applied to numerous public buildings throughout the country in the years leading up to the Great War. It was the gift of William Thomas Paulin and his daughters Ina and Irene in memory of his wife Fanny. The opening ceremony was performed by the Bishop of London on Monday 7th December 1903.[20] Useful though it was, the new parish hall had a commanding bulk out of scale with its surroundings.

In the following year, the view from Francis Cresswell's home was further curtailed by the erection of a postal sorting office across Station Road and opposite the entrance to the new parish hall. Also in red brick with stone dressings, its pleasing architectural detailing included a royal coat of arms, and the legend "Postmen's Office" over the doorway, both carved in stone. To the Cresswells, it was no doubt just another sign of the process of urbanisation which was gaining momentum. Together with the parish hall, it must have generated unwelcome noise and activity.

Within the next few years, the remaining fields bordering Station Road and Compton Road succumbed to residential development. The houses, characterised by ornamental gables, corner towers, finials, wooden-railed balconies and stained glass, were architecturally distinctive compared with many other contemporary schemes.[21] The portion of Green Lanes between these two roads was furnished with a modern shopping parade known as the Broadway. To those who felt no pain at the retreat of the countryside, the emerging Edwardian suburb — varied, well designed and convenient — created a favourable impression. As the tide of building spread to the fringes of the neighbourhood, however, more voices of regret were heard. In 1906, the editor of *The Enfield Observer* was saddened by the destruction of orchards to the north of Green Dragon Lane: "in place of the extent of fruit trees that for so long have filled the spring air with scent and sweetness, have arisen a long line of garish brick villas. For those to whom this pretty old part of the district has become endeared, the mutation which modern life imposes is indeed hard to bear".[22]

The changing character of the district may have strengthened Francis Cresswell's desire to move with his family from Winchmore Hill, but the decision to do so was motivated chiefly by the advancement of his son's education. Frank had received a preparatory education at a school referred to as Somerville House, Winchmore Hill. No trace of its whereabouts has been found, and it may simply have been a private house in which informal tuition was given to a few pupils. No doubt Frank showed promise in these early years, because at some point his father decided that he should have a first-class secondary education, and that, more specifically, this should be at Loughborough Grammar School in Leicestershire. Emily had of course lived in Northamptonshire, a few miles from the Leicestershire border, and her father had been Rector of Smeeton Westerby, between Leicester and Market Harborough, from 1879 to 1887. The family servants, Frances and Matilda Gamble, had both come from Sileby, near Leicester, and their parents had continued to live there. The area would have been well known to the Cresswells, and it is most likely that Francis was persuaded of the merits of Loughborough Grammar School through his wife's family or a close friend. The school claimed to offer the educational and social advantages of public schools, and prepared many pupils for university or the Civil Service. The recommendation in its favour must have been strong, for a place was secured for Frank at the school, and in the late summer of 1904 the family moved from Winchmore Hill to the Leicestershire village of Barrow-upon-Soar. The Misses Gamble, who went with them, no doubt welcomed the opportunity to return to their childhood surroundings, for Sileby was adjacent to Barrow. Loughborough was just three miles away, and in September 1904 the nine-year-old Frank began his first term as a pupil at Loughborough Grammar School.[23] His father's medical practice in Winchmore Hill was taken over by Dr. Edwin Wallace Goble of Compton Road, who later moved to Grove Lodge, thereby restoring a link between that property and the Cresswells which continued until Dr. Goble's death in 1939.[24] With the departure of Francis, Emily and Frank Cresswell, Winchmore Hill ceased to be home to any members of the family after a period of 62 years.

Sisters Apart

It will be recalled that Christiana, cousin to Francis and Henrietta, was living with her three daughters in Barnes, South West London, following the death of her husband John Henry Jennings in 1890. Some time after this she moved to less agreeable surroundings in Webb's Road, South Battersea, a busy thoroughfare running south from Battersea Rise, between Wandsworth Common and Clapham Common. It had been built up around 1880 with shopping parades, and most of the residential accommodation consisted of rooms above the shops.[25] Close by, in Bolingbroke Grove, was the Bolingbroke Hospital, founded in 1880 by Canon John Erskine Clarke, Vicar of Battersea and related to Christiana on her mother's side of the family. It was here, on 7th February 1896, that Christiana died of intestinal cancer at the age of 47. She was attended in her illness by Cecil

Rupert Chaworth Lyster, resident medical officer at the hospital. Formerly assistant medical officer at the Charing Cross Hospital, he became well known in the scientific world for his pioneering work on the use of X-rays and radium in the treatment of cancer and other diseases.[26] Christiana's death left three orphaned children — Mary, aged 12, Frances, 10, and Margaret, 8. They had faced sadness and insecurity in their early lives, and more sorrow was yet to come.

The sad years of Christiana's widowhood were a time of hope for her sister Beatrix. In 1890, the year of her visit to Oberammergau, she became engaged. Her own, brief words will best describe the attachment:

> 1890 witnessed another episode of my life which I will sum up as "he came, I saw, and was conquered". Then ensued that trying ordeal for both parties — a long engagement. It lasted six years — neither of us had money on which to marry — he cut the knot abruptly, by suddenly marrying someone else. But I have never regretted the experience.

The identity of her fiancé is not revealed, and the matter is unrecorded elsewhere. It was not the first occasion on which an engagement failed to lead to marriage in the Cresswell family, and it would not be the last.[27]

Beatrix lived in patient expectation at Lugehay House throughout these years, but was finding home life "very uncongenial....I felt caught and caged". She had never been close to her sister Anastasia, and now their tastes and interests were drifting entirely apart. Beatrix had her own circle of academically inclined friends. One family with whom she stayed in London during the 1890s were the Gladstones of Pembridge Square, Bayswater. John Gladstone, a retired professor of chemistry, had had a distinguished career in science and education.[28] By 1891 he had become a widower and was living at 17 Pembridge Square with two unmarried daughters and six servants. It was also during the 1890s that Beatrix acquired a bicycle, and with it a new found freedom. A photograph of the period shows her with her cycle outside the front door of Lugehay House. "I rode all over Dartmoor, which in those first days of the drop-frame cycle was regarded as a remarkable feat." She contributed articles to *Cycling*, under her own name or her "Maid of the Moor" pseudonym. The tourist editor of this magazine gave her an introduction to the Homeland Association, founded for the encouragement of touring in Great Britain, and their editor, Prescott Row, invited her to write the text for a guide book to Dartmoor.[29] This was the first of a long line of illustrated "Homeland Handbooks" to places in the West Country written by Beatrix. Issued at "popular prices", they contained "everything likely to interest the intelligent visitor regarding the History, Traditions, Worthies, Antiquities and Literary Associations of the neighbourhoods with which they deal". Each book was written by a well qualified author with special local knowledge. As a native of the West Country, with a detailed understanding of its history, topography and botany and an accomplished literary style, Beatrix was an ideal person to undertake this task in her area.

Dartmoor and its Surroundings first appeared in 1899. In it Beatrix introduced

Beatrix Cresswell, with her bicycle, outside the front door of Lugehay House, Teignmouth, in the 1890s.

the traveller to the moor and described excursions and walks from its principal centres. Her affection for the area is clear from her introduction:

> The writer of this book can remember, when a little child, being taken by her father nearly every day to see [the moor] in the distance, and being told that when she was old enough she should go to the blue hills, a promise duly fulfilled, and begetting that love of the Moor which never perishes....I have had to learn the Moor by experience, hard walking, excursions often very fatiguing, and not seldom losing the way....the best part of Dartmoor must be seen on foot: indeed, it has truly been said that you cannot feel the spirit of the Moor until the turf is beneath your tread.

By 1905 the book had run to four editions. The fourth edition was edited by William Crossing, a Devonshire writer and antiquary. In his preface he says: "the authoress has stated that she hardly hopes to do more than instil her readers with a love for the district, and in this I think she will be successful". Elsewhere in the book he takes issue with the author's advice on approaching moorland mires: "except when the mists hide them", she had said, "the mires or bogs should be avoidable, though in some places a certain amount of 'bog-trotting' may be demanded of you". The editor considered this to be a dangerous practice in the more extensive mires.

Beatrix's second handbook — *Teignmouth, its Past History and Present Interests* — was published in 1901. Her home town for nearly 40 years, it was an obvious choice of subject. "Teignmouth", she wrote, "has been stigmatized as a place that has no interests, an assertion that I hope this little book will go far to disprove". However, she is regretful and indignant "that during past centuries more has been done to destroy past interests than to make present ones. Especially is it to be lamented that one charming site after another passes into the hands of those whose only idea of benefiting by the soil is to load it with as many small houses as possible".

Guides to Dawlish and Newton Abbot and their surroundings, and to Exeter and its cathedral, appeared in 1902. In the following year Beatrix extended her coverage to Somerset with a handbook to Taunton, and in 1904 this was followed by a guide to the Quantocks, with chapters on stag hunting by another author. Over the next five years, Barnstaple, Bideford, Bude and part of the North Cornwall coast were covered. Her contributions to the series continued into the 1930s.[30]

When Beatrix's sister Anastasia moved to Dumfries with her cousin Henrietta, she still owned the freehold of Lugehay House, Teignmouth. In 1901 the title was conveyed to Henrietta, who continued to receive rental income from the property until 1906, when it was sold to Mrs. Theodora Drew, an actress. In 1900 Beatrix and her mother had moved out of Lugehay House to somewhat smaller accommodation at 10 Barton Terrace, Dawlish. This tall, three-storey house, one of a similar pair in a short terrace, was built during the second half of the 19th century. Barton Terrace, begun in the 1820s and extended up to the late

Victorian period, was in a pleasant situation overlooking the valley of Dawlish Water some 600 yards back from the seafront.[31]

Beatrix's mother Frances was a severe invalid during her last years, and Beatrix looked after her, sacrificing her literary work in order to do so.[32] Frances died at Dawlish, of senile decay, on 31st January 1904, aged 83. Her will is of some interest because of the provisions made in it for other members of the family — notably the Jennings children — and for the disposal of family heirlooms. The terms of the will were subject to a settlement made in contemplation of her marriage to Richard Cresswell in 1843. Her son Richard Henry and her daughter Beatrix were appointed trustees with responsibility for the distribution of investment income from her estate. This included a legacy for her granddaughter Clarice Mercedes and an annuity for her daughter Anastasia. Her niece Henrietta was given a particular responsibility in relation to the orphaned Jennings children — to hold in trust pecuniary legacies to be given to them if and when they reached the age of 21 or were married, and to undertake their care. If she refused that responsibility she would forfeit a legacy bequeathed to her in the will. This provision created a further bond between the Winchmore Hill and Devonshire branches of the family. Among the chattels bequeathed by Frances were a sword once owned by her distinguished relative Sir Alured Clarke, a writing table which had belonged to Richard Cresswell's grandfather Mark Noble, and her own collection of coins, seaweeds and scientific instruments. All these went to her son Richard Henry. The will is a remarkable embodiment of family loyalty, responsibility, tradition and foresight which, in one way or another, involved all the surviving blood relations of the testator's late husband except his nephew Francis and great-nephew Frank.

Soon after her mother's death, Beatrix moved from Dawlish to Exeter. She had been fond of Exeter ever since she was taken there as a child in the early 1870s. At that time George Gilbert Scott's restoration of the cathedral was in progress; she remembered seeing the boarded partition which separated the nave and quire during the work, and recalled the thrill she experienced when the boarding was removed to reveal the view through the "golden gates" into the quire. Apart from this, Exeter meant shopping and restaurants, and staying at the home of a family friend in the cathedral close; it was then that she grew to love the city and its society. "It is not often that the wishes of our youth are fulfilled", she wrote later; "it is a great joy to me that one of mine has been granted, the wish I always had to live in Exeter".[33] She occupied a house in Wonford Road, in the St. Leonard's district, about half a mile south east of the city centre. This was a fashionable early Victorian suburb of spacious houses built on the Baring St. Leonard's estate. Beatrix's home, No.23, was on the north side of the road, a few yards west of the junction with St. Leonard's Road. It was a two-storey, end-of-terrace, stucco-fronted dwelling with a pillared porch and cast-iron verandah to the ground floor, similar in character to neighbouring properties. She was to remain here for the rest of her life, during which time she would study and report on the history and antiquities of Exeter and Devon to an extent that would perpetuate her name among future generations of local historians.[34]

Much of Beatrix's work survives in the form of unpublished manuscripts. A typical example is her *Arms of the Bishops of Exeter*, a 21-page volume containing hand-coloured representations of the coats of arms with their blazons and the names and dates of their holders. The volume finishes with the arms of Bishop Bickersteth, appointed in 1885, though his arms and those of his predecessor, Bishop Temple, have not been coloured. Beatrix has titled the volume in a crude Gothic script, under which she has written "an early effort, very bad".[35] Her lack of artistic skill is more clearly evident in a collection of drawings of Devon-shire church fonts, begun in about 1904 and later bound into one volume. The 150 pencil sketches display poor detailing and awkward perspective; unlike other members of her family she was not an accomplished artist.[36] In 1907, she be-came a member of the Devonshire Association, a learned society for the ad-vancement of science, literature and art. She also became a frequent contributor to *Devon and Cornwall Notes and Queries,* a quarterly journal devoted to the local history, biography and antiquities of these counties.[37] In 1908 her extensive notes on Exeter churches were published as an appendix to *Notes and Queries,* appear-ing later the same year as a separate illustrated volume of over 200 pages. In her introduction, she regrets the loss of city centre churches: "as each one vanishes we wonder which will be the next victim to the mania for what is called 'im-provement', in which name every succeeding generation sweeps away the work of those who imagined themselves to be making lasting improvements on the face of the earth in days gone by". This and other work of hers is prefaced with a Latin motto taken from the Exeter Cathedral clock — *"Pereunt et imputantur"*: "[The hours] pass away and are reckoned to our account".

Exeter Churches is a well balanced work, giving due weight to modern as well as ancient churches, though Beatrix is dismissive of early 19th century architec-ture: Holy Trinity (1820) "exhibits all the want of architectural features common to the churches of that time", while St. Edmund's "had the misfortune to be erected in 1833, therefore, as a building, there is nothing more to be said for it". Within St. Edmund's she observes an oak screen installed in 1895 by Henry Vivian Panton, rector of the parish. Beatrix could not have known that, in later years, in another parish many miles from Exeter, this same priest would com-mit for burial her own sister. Later 19th century architecture meets with more approval: St. Michael's, Mount Dinham, consecrated in 1868, "is undoubtedly the most beautiful modern church in Exeter"; in the new St. David's, then re-cently completed, "every feature....has been thoughtfully considered, not only what it was going to be, but what it was going to mean". The architect of St. David's was William Douglas Caröe (1857–1938), some of whose work else-where will be noted in due course for its personal associations with members of the Cresswell family. It is clear throughout her book that Beatrix shared her brother's enthusiasm for the pre-Reformation church: in welcoming the restora-tion for charitable purposes of the 15th century St. Katharine's Chapel, for ex-ample, she writes: "it is one of the most satisfactory parts of the church revival of the 19th century that these old religious foundations should be restored for such good works as their original founders would heartily have approved of". Elsewhere in her book she recounts the story of Catherine of Aragon's arrival in Exeter in 1501, her rest disturbed by the squeaking weather-cock on the steeple of St. Mary Major, hard by the cathedral:

> As she lay sleepless....above the gusts of wind came the creaking and moaning of the vane from the church of the Blessed Virgin close by; as if on her very arrival in England the fabric of the Church bemoaned the future havoc every parish church would endure on account of this Spanish girl coming into the land.[38]

Exeter Churches includes black and white drawings by the author's niece Clarice Mercedes Cresswell of armorial bearings on monuments in the churches. Beatrix's accompanying descriptions provoked a lively correspondence in *Notes and Queries*. Challenged on the accuracy of some of her notes, she replied:

> It always appears to me that monumental heraldry is very unreliable....arms are sculptured by those who know nothing of the subject, from information given by those who know little more; tinctures alter with time and dirt, and the worst occurs when a monument is repainted by church restorers.[39]

In 1910, Beatrix completed a "little pageant play" entitled *White Rose and Golden Broom*. The golden broom was the badge of the Plantagenets, to which she had alluded many years earlier in *Alexis and his Flowers*. The drama, set in the cloisters of Exeter Cathedral in about 1515, represents a fictitious episode in the life of Catherine Gordon, widow of Perkin Warbeck, executed in 1499 after his failed pretence to the English throne. The play, which included choruses sung to specially composed music, was performed on 15th June 1910 in the grounds of the Bishop's Palace, Exeter, by students of the University Extension Guild and their friends.[40] In 1911 Beatrix gave the first of a winter series of Saturday lectures organised by the University Extension College. Her subject was "Exeter Mayors", delivered in a "bright and crisp manner", with lantern slides, to a large and appreciative audience at the Royal Albert Memorial Museum.[41]

Around this time Beatrix was elected a member of the Council of the Devonshire Association. She made a study of the activities of the commissioners charged with preparing inventories of church valuables during the religious reforms of Edward VI's reign, and read her first paper to the Devonshire Association — "The Church Goods Commission in Devon, 1549–1552" — at their Dartmouth meeting in 1911.[42] In the following year her second volume of notes on Devon churches was published. This covered 26 parishes in the Deanery of Kenn, situated on the western side of the River Exe, along the Teign valley, and under the outlying commons of Dartmoor. She observed that the special characteristic of churches in this deanery was the rood screen. At the church of All Saints, Kenton, she noted the particular difficulty of deciphering Latin inscriptions painted on panels of the screen illustrating Old Testament prophets, and expressed her gratitude to her brother Richard Henry Cresswell "for the painstaking assistance he gave me in making out these inscriptions, and verifying them from the Latin Scriptures". She also has a special word of thanks for the late Vicar of Kenton, William Philip Strong Bingham:

> Personally, I cannot speak too gratefully of the kindness he shewed and the help he gave me. His were practical lessons on church architecture and archaeology, and the book from which he taught was Kenton Church. To his encouragement these Deanery notes owe what completeness they so far possess.[43]

As with her work on the Exeter churches, Beatrix's notes on the churches in the Deanery of Kenn attracted comment in *Notes and Queries*. A contribution by the Reverend Oswald J.Reichel (one-time president of the Devon and Exeter Institution) contained more than a hint of pompous academic rivalry:

> In these days of strict scholarship it is not sufficient for any one who undertakes to instruct others to be interesting in style and picturesque in description; but he may be expected to be fairly conversant with the new sources of information which are now rendered available by the printing of so many original documents.

Having criticised alleged inaccuracies and misinterpretations in Miss Cresswell's work, he concludes:

> One does not wish to seem captious. But is it quite fair to the reader, who may believe that he has before him the last word that can be said on the history of Devonshire Churches, to set down as facts what any attempt at verification would quickly have shewn to be unfounded legends of the past?[44]

Undaunted by this criticism, Beatrix went on to compile notes on churches in the remaining rural deaneries of Devon; this labour of love occupied another 10 years or so. Over the same period she produced other manuscripts and typescripts on a variety of ecclesiastical, archaeological and antiquarian topics relating to Devon, such as heraldry, stained glass, church bell inscriptions, fonts, and parochial and manorial chapels. Her published output included a number of short guidebooks to individual parish churches; these continued to appear until well into the 1930s.

The outbreak of war in 1914 caused little hindrance to Beatrix Cresswell's archaeological studies. On 21st July 1915 she read to the Devonshire Association, at their Exeter meeting, a paper on "Churchyard and Wayside Crosses in the Neighbourhood of Exeter". Acknowledging the work already undertaken on Dartmoor crosses by William Crossing (the not uncritical editor of the fourth edition of her Homeland guide to Dartmoor), Beatrix claims that ancient crosses in other parts of the county are more numerous than most people realise. She describes 16 crosses, with exact locations and measurements, indicating extensive fieldwork on her part. Commenting on the clumsy restoration of the cross at Poltimore, she asks "why those who undertake such repairs never go and look at some existing example of original work to see how they ought to be done". She argues that the crosses owe their preservation to the fact that they were boundary marks as well as Christian symbols, observing that a statute of 1541 forbade their destruction. Her paper ends with a suggestion appropriate to the time at which it was written: "that these broken crosses should be restored by the parishes in which they stand when Peace on Earth, which we so ardently hope for, is consummated; as a fitting commemoration of the Peace, and a memorial to those who have given their lives to secure the tranquillity and liberty of this country".[45] Soon enough, her closing words would reflect a bitter reality for the family of Cresswell.

In 1916 the Alcuin Club published Beatrix's *Edwardian Inventories for the City and County of Exeter*, transcribed from original documents forming part of a national survey of church treasures and ornaments ordered in 1547 in preparation for their disposal. This was later regarded by the Devonshire Association as "perhaps her most important work". In the following year she read to the association at their Barnstaple meeting on 25th July a paper on "Ancient Church Needlework in Devon", indicating the breadth of subject matter which she researched.[46] Her output continued during the postwar years, and we shall take note of some of her further work in due course.

The prewar years in Exeter had been a time of contentment for Beatrix. In 1918 she wrote of the kindness shown to her and the friendships made since her arrival in Exeter: "never, since the death of my father, have I been so happy, as in living my own life at 23 Wonford Road". Her friendships were of an academic nature, however, and in her social life she gained little pleasure from female company: "I have no love or admiration for my own sex, no sympathy for these present conditions of what, I feel sure, John Knox would have termed 'this monstrous regiment of women' ". Elsewhere she quotes with obvious approval some words of Mrs. Lynn Linton, written in 1868:

> The girl of all periods — she cannot be made to see that modesty of appearance, and virtue, ought to be inseparable. The girl of the period — a creature who dyes her hair and paints her face as the first article of her personal religion, whose sole idea of life is plenty of fuss and luxury, and whose dress is the object of such thought and intellect as she possesses....

"Will the Flapperlings of the 20th century", asked Beatrix, "be taught their behaviour in future years by the veterans of the Great War?".[47]

Faith of our Fathers

Beatrix's elder brother Richard Henry Cresswell, meanwhile, had begun the next stage of his clerical career. He had already forged a link with the parish of St. John the Baptist, North Kensington, early in 1880, when he began assisting there from time to time. His name first appears in the service book on the evening of Shrove Tuesday, 10th February 1880, when he preached from 1 Corinthians, Chapter 13, Verse 13: "now abideth faith, hope, charity, these three; but the greatest of these is charity". Referring back to this some time later, a writer in the Parish Notes said: "many of us, who have often listened with pleasure and profit to Mr. Cresswell's excellent short sermons, will quite believe that from such a text he preached so good a sermon that the congregation would wish to hear him often". On Good Friday 1880 he gave the addresses at the Three Hours' service for the first time. Then on Thursday 24th June, the Nativity of St. John the Baptist, he preached at the first Evensong of the Patronal Festival. The preacher at the second Evensong was Arthur Henry Stanton, the remarkable Tractarian curate of St. Alban's, Holborn, whose spiritual leadership and missionary zeal earned him a lasting reputation. Richard Cresswell was in good company. In the autumn of 1880 he became Sunday evening preacher at St. John's, an appointment which he held until 1887, when he changed places in the pulpit with Sidney Faithhorn Green, another assistant priest, who had hitherto preached on Sunday mornings.[48] Sidney Green, formerly Rector of St. John's, Miles Platting, Manchester, had been imprisoned for a year and seven months for contravention of the Public Worship Regulation Act, 1874, which forbade certain liturgical practices deemed to be excessively ritualistic.[49] Today they would be unremarkable in almost any Anglican church, but at the time were the cause of much controversy. On his release from prison, Sidney Green became a curate at St. John the Baptist, Holland Road. As at Christ Church, Clapham, Richard Henry Cresswell shared his ministry at St. John's with devout men who were leading a spiritual renewal within the Church of England.

George Booker, who was Vicar of St. John's from 1869 to 1889, had previously served as assistant priest at St. Barnabas, Addison Road, Kensington. It was to him that St. John's owed its origins, and we shall now look briefly at the early history of the church. In the late 1860s, the north end of Holland Road, adjoining Shepherds Bush, was only partly built up; fruit gardens and marshy open space extended beyond the West London Railway to Brook Green. The rapid development of the area after 1870 led to demands for a new church and parish. Under George Booker's leadership a site was purchased to the east of Holland Road. "Some day", he said, "though I may never see it, I know and am assured that a beautiful church will rise here to the Glory of God". A temporary church, seating up to 1,000, was opened on the site in February 1869. The worship was very simple, but even a modest ceremonial engendered considerable opposition in the neighbourhood. Matins and Evensong attracted the largest congregations, almost 600 attending these two services on Easter Day, 1869. A fund for the payment of assistant curates was established soon after the opening of the temporary church, though for some years the parish relied heavily on voluntary clerical assistance.

In due course, the architect James Brooks was commissioned to design a permanent church, and the foundation stone was laid at the Patronal Festival in 1872. Thereafter building proceeded very slowly, and by 1880, when Richard Cresswell first assisted at the church, only the apse had been completed. The new work, which was taking place around and alongside the temporary church, gained momentum from 1884, but it was not until 1889 that the chancel and side chapels were consecrated. In the same year George Booker resigned through ill health, William Martin Spencer was appointed vicar, and a district parish was established for the church. The parish was geographically confined, but growing in population. With the enthusiastic support of the new vicar, plans were brought forward to complete the church; the nave, aisles and transepts were ready for the Patronal Festival in June 1891. The preacher on this occasion was Henry Westall, vicar of the neighbouring parish of St. Cuthbert, Philbeach Gardens, who had officiated at the marriage of Richard Cresswell's sister Christiana in 1880.[50]

At Eastertide 1892, Richard Cresswell moved from Clapham with his wife Margaret Rosina and his daughter Clarice Mercedes to take up residence at 26 Melrose Gardens, West Kensington, a quiet street of three-storey, bay-windowed terraced houses off the Shepherds Bush Road, on the borders of Hammersmith. The house was in a terrace of four on the north side of Melrose Gardens. It was outside St. John's parish, but only just over half a mile from the church. At this time Richard was licensed as full-time assistant curate at St. John's.[51] He was by then deeply involved in the spiritual life of the parish, having witnessed its growth and development over a period of 12 years. He had experienced a change in emphasis to sacramental worship, to the point where the Sunday morning choral Eucharist had become the principal service, and he had seen the creation of a new church now almost complete except for the west front.

The building which had arisen around the temporary church, and which had eventually replaced it, was indeed a noble and dignified achievement. Constructed entirely of stone, its inspiration was early French Gothic, with steep-roofed apses and semi-circular flying buttresses. Inside, the soaring, clerestoried nave and chancel were stone-vaulted and of cathedral-like proportions. The cool, spacious interior created a distinctly medieval effect, whose mystery would soon be enhanced by an elaborate scheme of furnishing.[52] The setting was ideal for the solemn, high church ceremonial performed there.

On 13th June 1892, the annual festival of the English Church Union, which had been held at Christ Church, Clapham during Richard Cresswell's curacy there, took place at St. John's, Holland Road. Sidney Faithhorn Green, who had left the parish in 1888, returned to preach at Solemn Evensong. Then on 22nd June the first confirmation was held in the church, when the Bishop of Marlborough confirmed over 50 candidates. "It was a great happiness to all who were present, and we believe they were impressed with the reverence of the service, the earnest words of the Bishop, and the quiet devoutness of the young people." During the same year the ornaments of the church were increased with the provision of a festival chalice, a crucifix for the high altar, and a new font in Devonshire marble. The latter carried carvings by J.E. Taylerson, who had already executed other sculptures to adorn the church. A processional crucifix, inlaid with precious stones, was added in 1893: "many of the stones belonged to those who have passed within the veil". A well attended congregational meeting in December 1893 gave the vicar an opportunity to refer to progress made in the parish in recent years, to give details of proposals for the further adornment of the church, and to respond to questions and suggestions about the services. In speaking of the character of the worship he was evidently concerned to emphasise that this would continue to be distinctly Anglican: "we have taken our stand among the advanced guard of the Catholic Revival in the Church of England, and by God's help we shall keep to it, but without the least sympathy for anything that is merely Roman in doctrine and teaching or in our ritual and practice".[53]

Over the next few years, work continued on the beautification of the church, including the erection of a triple-arched stone chancel screen (later crowded with sculpture), the painting and gilding of the reredos, and installation of the first stained-glass windows. By the turn of the century, much of the interior arrangement and decoration of the church had been completed, though the west front facing Holland Road was still unfinished.[54]

In 1900, Richard Cresswell's last published work appeared. This was an English translation of the Liturgy of the Eighth Book of the *Apostolic Constitutions*, commonly called the Clementine Liturgy. It was published by the Society for Promoting Christian Knowledge in their Early Church Classics series. In his 30-page introduction, the author claims that this is the most ancient extant complete liturgy, probably written in Syria towards the end of the fourth century. He explains, however, that the document is apocryphal, refuting the idea that it was put forth by St. Clement of Rome and derived from the authority of the Apostles. The liturgy is in the form of a Mass to be celebrated by a newly consecrated bishop; as a deliberate falsification its historical value is limited, "but it has a distinct value on account of its being an entire liturgy, untouched by subsequent changes of custom, at least a century older than any other, and in its general form, in agreement with the unimpeachable evidence of writers anterior to 350".[55] The task of translation provided Richard Cresswell not only with a satisfying academic endeavour, but also with an insight into the liturgical traditions of the early church with whose unbroken continuity he and his late 19th century Anglo-Catholic brethren would have wished to identify.

Adjoining St. John's Church to the south was the vicarage, a lofty, brick, end-of-terrace house of three storeys, basement and attic, designed by George Edmund Street. Although built as a vicarage in 1872, it was not acquired for this purpose until 1900. Both sides of the north end of Holland Road were lined with terraces of equally tall Italianate houses, and it was to one of these, on the west side of the road, that Richard Cresswell and his wife and daughter moved in 1904–5. No.145 Holland Road was near the north end of a long terrace of houses

Interior of St. John the Baptist, Holland Road, Kensington, in 1920. Richard Henry Cresswell had been a curate here since 1892, witnessing the completion and beautification of the church as a centre for Anglo-Catholic worship.

between Addison Gardens and Hansard Mews, almost opposite the church. In common with its neighbours, the house had a pillared porch, bay windows and moulded cornices. At the rear, french doors gave access to a garden extending to the mews, beyond which the West London Railway ran in a cutting. This spacious property was to be Richard Henry Cresswell's last home.[56]

James Brooks, the architect of St. John's, had died in 1901, and it was left to J.S. Adkins, who had acquired Brooks's practice, to complete the west end of the church. He did so with a fussy and over-elaborate design of porches and turrets, quite different from Brooks's proposals. The work commenced in 1909, and Sunday 11th December 1910 was kept as "a day of High Thanksgiving for the completion of the Church".[57] Richard Cresswell had witnessed the physical and spiritual growth of the church over a period of 30 years, continuing to offer faithful and unobtrusive service throughout.

Saints and Heroes

By this time, Richard Cresswell's daughter Clarice Mercedes, still unmarried and living at home, had become an accomplished writer and illustrator. We have already noted the illustrations which she did for some of her aunt Beatrix's work. Clarice reached her 30th birthday on 10th February 1911, and her first book was published the following Christmas. Entitled *Roses of Martyrdom: Stories of the 'Noble Army of Martyrs' for Children*, it was illustrated by the author. The publishers were A.R. Mowbray and Company. The book tells the stories of eight Christian martyrs, several from the time of the last great Roman persecution in 303, some of them children. "We too, in these days, may not be called to die for Christ", writes Clarice, "but we must all try to live in His strength as perfectly as we can....that we may be, in these latter days, if not martyrs, in the noblest sense of the Greek word, nevertheless, witnesses to the divine truth of our blessed Faith".

The eight illustrations, one for each story, are charmingly done. Reproduced from delicate watercolours by Clarice, the figures are set against well composed landscapes or Classical interiors. The story of St. Devota, a child martyr of Corsica, is illustrated with a tender portrayal of her shrouded body being carried by boat over a moonlit ocean, led by a dove to her final resting place:

> They wrapped her in white, with sweet-smelling spices, set her lily and her palm in her hand, and carrying her out, put her in the little boat....the moon had risen, and poured her pale glory over the waves, the boat and its white-robed treasure....silvered in the white, quivering moonbeams, shone a little dove. It fluttered before the bows of the boat, as if inviting them to follow it.

The gentle, romantic imagery permeates this and other stories in the book. St.

Agnes, for example, was "slight and graceful as a white lily against the background of dark myrtles....so fair, that her high-born, delicate beauty, her white dress and her gold locks, coiled at her neck, presented an almost ethereal appearance". *The Church Times* described the book as "a most artistic and tasteful production". In it, Clarice demonstrates a feeling for the Classical world which suggests that she had already travelled in Italy: the orphaned St. Devota is brought up in a Roman household whose home is likened to that of the House of the Vettii at Pompeii; in retelling the story of St. Laurence the Deacon, Clarice describes the Roman Forum as "one of the most wonderful places in the world". Her Christian faith and upbringing, and her love of Classical antiquity — both evident in her first published work — were to have a profound influence on the course of her later life.

In the following year, Mowbrays published *Crown of the North and South, and other Stories*, in which Clarice recounts tales of some of the young heroes of history — ancient, medieval and modern:

> They smiled out of the past — boys and girls from East and West, from North and South...."though we were still so young", they whispered, "we did great deeds, and the promises of our childish years were fulfilled in our later days". And others answered: "though we did not stay to grow up *here*, we are not to be pitied. We have left you our stories and our names".

The author again provided eight illustrations, whose characters, with their slender, upright forms and angular features, owe something to the influence of Sir Edward Burne-Jones. The robed figures of Clytaemnestra and her daughter Iphigeneia stand in a Classical portico, smoke curls upwards from a brazier towards a crescent moon, and tall dark cypresses are silhouetted against a pale sky: "crossing the courtyard, where her trailing draperies disturbed a flock of doves feeding near the portico, she passed, amid a flutter of white wings, into the shadow of the outer colonnade". In another story, recalling the death of Dante at Ravenna, "the world was golden and purple with the pomp of Italian autumn, and beyond the city walls the pine forests sent up their incense of adoration to the September skies". These soft and serene visions are characteristic of the author, though she is equally at home in describing and illustrating tempestuous episodes. Her tale of Nero and Britannicus, rival claimants to the throne of Imperial Rome, is splendidly illustrated with a swirling, windswept scene under a dark, storm-laden sky, Britannicus crouching beneath the great statue of Caesar Augustus: "gusts of wind were plucking at the faded roses in his hair, whirling petal after petal to meet the last of the dead autumn foliage, driven thick from the Imperial Gardens by every blast of the storm".

Two more books for children, again illustrated by the author, appeared in 1913 and 1914 from the same publisher — *The Twelve Foundations* and *Saxon and Norman and Dane*. The latter, a collection of stories of medieval England, was dedicated to Clarice's aunt Beatrix, to whom she no doubt owed much of her

" The Lady held out her arms."

Illustration by Clarice Cresswell for her book Saxon and Norman and Dane, *published in 1914. The coloured plate, reproduced from an original watercolour, accompanies her story "The Princess of Peace". It is a vision of the Virgin Mary appearing to Princess Margaret of Norway, who was sheltering in the Orkneys in 1290 on her way to be married to the future King Edward II of England. The arranged marriage of the children never took place, as Margaret died where she was sheltering.*

love of history, mythology and religion. The tales are "all eloquently told and richly illustrated", said *The Times Literary Supplement*.[58] Then in 1915 there appeared her first novel — *The Making and Breaking of Almansur* — published by Chatto and Windus. Almansur was the eighth century Caliph of Islam, whose failure to oppress the Christians in Spain gives the novel its theme. Writing now for adults, Clarice employs a less direct style, but her descriptive power can still impress the reader:

> From Biscay and across Asturias the winds of October breasted the lower slopes of the Cantabrian mountains like the first waves of a hurricane. They tore through the ragged vines left from the vintage, and upwards, through walnut, chestnut, and pine, with ruin of branchage and leafage, to the long broken ridge of the summit.

This was not the last occasion on which Clarice would use the fury of the storm to create dramatic effect.

Clarice's last book for children, *The Ministry of Holda: Leaves from God's Story Book in Nature*, appeared from Mowbrays later in 1915. Holda was the benign and merciful goddess of spinning and agriculture in Teutonic mythology, identifying herself with Demeter, the Greek goddess of agriculture, in Clarice's text. She had already featured in aunt Beatrix's *Alexis and his Flowers*. Clarice uses her to introduce myths and legends from the "great Story Book of the Universe" — tales from France, Italy, Greece, Iceland, the Orient, and even London! The story from Sicily takes as its theme the fire of sacrifice:

> "Did not Elijah call down the flame from heaven, and by the might of the Holy Spirit, who came first upon His chosen in the likeness of tongues of fire, is not the miracle of the Holy Eucharist perfected daily upon our altars?".

The passage is a clear reflection of the sacramental worship offered by her father — a tradition in which she herself had been nurtured and through which her Christian faith found expression.

The Ministry of Holda is illustrated not by Clarice but by W.J. Taylor, whose home was in Holland Street, off Kensington Church Street. His eight watercolours, all of which are signed and two of which are dated 1914, are different in style from Clarice's — less precise in their representation of landscape and background, but good in their depiction of the human form. The year after Wilfrid John Taylor completed these pictures he answered the call to arms in the service of his country, enlisting with the Honourable Artillery Company on 23rd August 1915, and moving with their 1st Battalion to the western front on 23rd January 1916.[59] He was at the time engaged to be married to Clarice Mercedes Cresswell.

Wasted Genius?

Father Cresswell, as he was now generally known by his parishioners, had so far exercised his ministry under two vicars at St. John's, Holland Road. William Martin Spencer, who had replaced George Booker in 1889, completed 25 years in the parish in May 1914, and at a presentation made by the congregation "Father Cresswell spoke of his long and happy association with the Vicar".[60] Now just two years short of his 70th birthday, Richard Cresswell had served St. John's for 34 years. His ministry continued largely undisturbed during the Great War.

A little over a year after the outbreak of hostilities — during the first week of October 1915 — Richard Cresswell was called unexpectedly to Chelsea to give evidence to a coroner's inquest into the death of his niece Frances Jennings, second daughter of his late sister Christiana. Since the death of Christiana in 1890, Richard had had little contact with the Jennings children; Frances, now 30 years of age, had separated herself from the family, becoming an artist and occupying a top-floor studio flat at 125 Cheyne Walk, Chelsea. This was a four-storey building at the less fashionable end of the road, between Luna Street and Blantyre Street, overlooking the Thames upstream of Battersea Bridge. Frances was suffering from paralysis in one leg and had mental problems; her life had become lonely and unhappy. She had grown into a morbid and solitary woman who cared little for material comforts or human contact.

At about seven o'clock on the morning of Friday 1st October 1915, Charles Green, a labourer of 9 Luna Street, was working outside 125 Cheyne Walk. On looking towards the house he saw what appeared to be a bundle of clothes fall through the air and hit the front doorsteps. On going over to the house he discovered that it was a woman in her night attire. At five past seven a passing cyclist alerted Police Constable Littlewood to the incident. On reaching the house he found the woman greatly dazed and complaining of pain in her back. A doctor was called, and the patient was removed by police ambulance to Chelsea Infirmary, where she was detained with shock, a compound fracture of the thigh, and a spinal injury. She was identified as Frances Jennings. She had apparently fallen or flung herself out of one of the windows of her flat, 60 feet above the ground. Although regaining consciousness, she would not speak of the occurrence. Later the same day she died in hospital from her injuries.

The inquest was held on Tuesday 5th October. Isabel Derby, of King's Road, Chelsea, who had known Frances Jennings for about seven years, gave evidence of identification. Questioned about the state of mind of the deceased, the witness said that she was "a little unbalanced". In response to further questioning she added: "to a certain extent she was a genius". The coroner rubbed his hand over his chin as if perplexed, failing to observe where the evidence of genius lay. The witness went on to say that the deceased had often expressed a wish to die, remarking on one occasion: "Oh, I wish a Zeppelin would drop a bomb on me". Another witness, Violet Ormond, of Cheyne Walk, declared that the deceased was "altogether unusual". Asked what she meant by that, she replied "Oh, she was a genius"! The coroner's perplexity increased. A further witness, Emily

Sargent, also of Cheyne Walk, told the court that the deceased, whom she had known for about eight years, received an allowance of 31 shillings a week from a few friends. Violet Ormond and Emily Sargent were sisters of the painter John Singer Sargent.

Richard Cresswell's evidence was to the effect that he had last seen his niece alive in January 1901, and only once many years before that. He could not say what her state of her mind was, but she ought not to have been in want because she had been provided for in her grandmother's will. This referred, of course, to Richard Cresswell's mother Frances. Police Inspector David Ping stated that he had examined the deceased's rooms after the occurrence. The bedstead had been pushed towards the window; it appeared that the deceased had climbed onto the bed, pushed open the window and thrust herself out. In the room he discovered a piece of paper on which was written "I go to a happy death". The jury returned a verdict of "suicide whilst of unsound mind".

The affair was reported to have created "quite a sensation" in the neighbourhood. The singular evidence given by two of the witnesses as to the state of mind of the deceased prompted the editor of *The West London Press*, which had reported the inquest, to ponder the nature of genius. Quoting Goethe's dictum that "talent does what it can - genius what it must", he concluded that "genius contains something of the godlike and is therefore elusive....the real genius seldom commits suicide or does anything which bespeaks frailty....that miserably fraudulent old story that men and women of genius are almost necessarily frail or even immoral will not succeed. We hear of it in rather sombre art and literary circles, but it only means an excuse for aberration from the social or moral code".[61]

One can feel nothing but pity for poor Frances — detached from her family, friendless and depressed. Quite clearly she had had no contact with her surviving relatives for some time, although her uncle and cousin lived but a short distance away in Kensington. Close-knit though most of the Cresswells were, there is a strong inference that Frances's mother, in detaching herself from the family to join the studio life of the London art world, and then in marrying John Henry Jennings, had loosened the ties of kinship for herself and her children. It is perhaps significant that nowhere in surviving family papers is her marriage mentioned, although her sister Beatrix left recollections of her visit to Christiana only the year before the marriage took place. On the other hand, we shall discover that Frances Jennings's two sisters were to live to a good age, and that in due time one of them would offer support and companionship to the last of the Cresswells of Winchmore Hill.

Those who were acquainted with Frances Jennings during her final years knew little or nothing of her background or family. Least of all would they have been familiar with the story of her medieval ancestor the White Lady of Cresswell, who, in a fit of madness, took her own life by throwing herself from the roof of her home.

CHAPTER 8

Pastures New

The Place of the Nuns

During the opening years of Edward VII's reign, at a time when Beatrix Cresswell was pursuing her historical studies in Devonshire, and Richard Cresswell was keeping the faith in Kensington, their sister Anastasia was settling down to a new life with her cousin Henrietta in Dumfries.

When Henrietta moved to Dumfries late in 1899, she was no stranger to Scotland. She had travelled north of the border before, and had exhibited paintings at the Royal Scottish Academy and the Glasgow Institute of Fine Arts before 1898. Keen though she was to move away from the metropolis into an unspoilt corner of the land, the transition from a semi-detached villa in a growing suburb of London to a large, isolated residence on the outskirts of a county town in the Scottish borders was abrupt. However, she may have agreed with the English artist and critic who, around the time of her removal, wrote: "Dumfries has a distinct artistic character of its own, and you can but acknowledge that it is well worthy of its poetic name and a fitting place to contain the shrine of Scotland's greatest poet".

As well as being the burial place of Robert Burns, Dumfries was the judicial, educational and commercial centre for a wide area of South West Scotland. It had been a royal burgh and seat of the judicature since the 12th century; despite industrial and residential expansion during the second half of the 19th century, it retained several buildings of medieval origin. Public parks and footpaths extended some two miles along the winding east bank of the River Nith, on which the town was situated. On the west bank, united with Dumfries by bridges, was the separate municipality of Maxwelltown, sharing many administrative functions with its larger neighbour. The combined population of the two burghs was about 20,000.

The leading industries were tweed and hosiery manufacture; large mills were situated on both banks of the Nith. Other activities included leather tanning, the production of agricultural equipment, and dyeing. On the outskirts were extensive nursery gardens. The town was on the main line of the Glasgow and South Western Railway between Glasgow and Carlisle, with branch lines to Lockerbie, Kirkcudbright and Stranraer. Between the town centre and the railway station were streets of substantial mid-Victorian houses, whilst more recent terraced housing spread eastwards along the Annan and Lockerbie roads. A new building for Dumfries Academy, and new public baths and wash-houses, had been opened in 1897. Most buildings were of local red sandstone, giving the town a warm appearance.

Dumfries was surrounded by attractive countryside, popular for outdoor recreations and field sports. To the south west lay the peak of Criffel, the most easterly of the Galloway hills, overlooking the Solway Firth. Nearer the town were lower, rounded hills with more verdant slopes. To the east, Nithsdale and Annandale were separated by a line of undulating hills beyond Lochar Moss, partly reclaimed for farming. The town's sheltered position and mild climate had earned its inhabitants a reputation for longevity. It was perhaps no surprise that, in the words of a contemporary guide book, "many of the leisured classes find in it and the country houses round about a desirable place of residence".[1]

About a mile and a half north of the town centre, on the west bank of the Nith at its confluence with Cluden Water, were the ruins of Lincluden Abbey. Built by one of the Lords of Galloway in the middle of the 12th century for a community of Benedictine nuns, the abbey was converted by the Earl of Douglas into a college of canons in the late 14th century. Most of the surviving architectural features belonged to the latter period; the chancel walls of the 14th century church were remarkably complete. Facing the ruins on the opposite bank of the Nith, on land formerly owned by the convent, was the district of Nunholm. Here, some 150 yards from the river, and close to the main line of the Glasgow and South Western Railway, stood Nunholm House.

The chief features of the property were listed in the advertisement placed in *The Dumfries and Galloway Standard* in February 1899. The three principal rooms, four bedrooms, two attic rooms, kitchen and scullery constituted a spacious residence. The kitchen garden, grounds and shrubberies formed a sizeable small-holding which would support produce and livestock. The situation, little more than a mile from the centre of Dumfries, was secluded yet convenient. It was an ideal retreat for anyone seeking a quiet country existence within easy reach of life's daily necessities. When Henrietta and Anastasia moved in, they intended to make it their final home.

The two-storey house, built roughly in the shape of a T, was an enlargement of an 18th century dwelling of rectangular plan. It was constructed mostly of brick, with some rubble or ashlar dressings and additions. A substantial full-height two-bay wing was added in the 19th century. The front door was set into a curved porch formed in an angle between the original house and the later wing. The roofs were of slate with dormer windows to the attic storey and corniced chimney stacks. The uneven fenestration indicated different building periods. The rear of the house, facing towards the river, had a particularly piecemeal arrangement of windows, projections and roof lines. The walls were much overgrown with ivy and creepers. The interior had rooms of varying shapes, floor levels and ceiling heights, connected by narrow passages and two staircases.[2]

The house was reached from the Nunholm road along a tree-lined drive between fields, running straight for the first 180 yards then turning sharp left for the final approach. This rendered the house invisible from the road. However, the rear of the house was clearly visible, across pasture land and paddocks, from the adjacent railway line. From the garden, the railway was screened by a

Nunholm House, Dumfries, from the drive, in 1993 — the home of Henrietta and Anastasia Cresswell from 1900.

Rear of Nunholm House from the north west in 1993, looking across pasture land south of the River Nith. The house has retained the secluded aspect enjoyed by the Cresswells.

small copse. The drive formed the south eastern boundary of the property; beyond were tennis and cricket grounds and a bowling green. Apart from these, and a scattering of houses and cottages bordering the Nunholm road, the district was entirely rural. Its situation between the river and the diverging railway lines to Glasgow and Kirkcudbright had discouraged outward development from Dumfries. We shall return to a description of the garden of Nunholm House later in this chapter.

During the early 19th century the house had been owned by John Henderson, a Dumfries merchant. It remained in his family until 1891, when it passed to the trustees of the late George Henderson, one of whom was Thomas Hunter. Between 1843 and 1891 George Henderson of Nunholm was the owner of *The Dumfries and Galloway Standard*. After his death the newspaper passed to Thomas Hunter, later to become a partner in Thomas Hunter Watson and Company. Thomas Watson was the editor. At the time of the Cresswells' arrival at Nunholm the solicitors acting on behalf of the trustees were John Henderson and Sons. The names of Henderson and Hunter, and ownership of *The Dumfries and Galloway Standard*, had therefore been linked with Nunholm House for some time; these connections were not without significance for Henrietta's literary ambitions. The house had stood empty the year before the Cresswells arrived.[3]

For many years, Henrietta had exhibited pride in her ancestry and interest in her family history. Not long after her arrival at Dumfries she conceived the idea of writing down all that could be discovered about her family background. This took shape with the preparation of a manuscript volume of history, stories and pedigrees concerning the Cresswells and their related families. She called this the *Liber Cresswellii*. It is inscribed "*Franciscus Cresswell, Ex Dono Henrietta Cresswell*", indicating that it was intended for her brother Francis, or possibly his son Frank, to be handed down through the family. The volume, a transcript of which has been preserved, has been referred to extensively in this narrative.[4]

Henrietta began work on the project at Nunholm House in the autumn of 1905. In her foreword she says:

> Whereas I have found that as each generation dies out, much Family Knowledge is lost entirely, it has seemed to me that it will be a Good Deed if I should make a record, as far as I was able, of such History, Stories and Pedigrees as I could collect. The result is the collection of Fragments in this Book.

The work ranges widely over the Cresswells and allied families from the middle ages to the time of compilation. Only about a fifth of the text concerns the Cresswells themselves; the remainder is divided almost equally between the closely related families of Noble, Willink and Buttanshaw on the one hand, and more distant relationships on the other. Some emphasis is given to the nobility and landed gentry, and to famous (or notorious) deeds in which members of the families were believed to have been involved. At the other extreme, personal anecdote and recollection feature prominently in the more recent history. To an

extent the material is organised chronologically, although within that arrangement certain branches of the family are treated thematically, sometimes from
quite remote origins. The unbroken text, which describes genealogies in con-
tinuous prose, is at times difficult to interpret, despite the author's invocation
of the prophet Isaiah: "I have tried to arrange the way of the book so that way-
faring men, though fools, shall not err therein"! An index, included with the
original manuscript, has not survived. The history is, as its author admits, "a
collection of fragments". But it contains much information which, as Henrietta
rightly surmised, would otherwise have been lost. Anastasia contributed a section on the family of Clarke, who were ancestors on her mother's side.

Henrietta concluded her work on 4th April 1906 with an apology: "when I
began this manuscript I believed six weeks would suffice....but the work grew
under my hands and my book is the result of six months' steady work". In
compiling the history she corresponded with a number of more distant relatives, most of whom replied, and some of whom gave her much additional information. She acknowledges material collected by Anastasia "who has helped
me through all my work and saved me from many mistakes". She states that the
book is written for the whole family: "I hope no one who studies it will go quite
empty away. Old letters and stories give one glimpses of the life of long ago
when things were so different to this 20th century".[5]

Henrietta's writing illustrates from time to time the ease with which she
slipped into the language of the King James Bible — the result of an orthodox
Christian upbringing. Of the Cresswells' religious life whilst at Dumfries, however, there is slender evidence, though sufficient to indicate that they were involved with the Scottish Episcopal Church. For Anglican churchgoers this was
not surprising, but it placed them in a worshipping minority in a town which
had a long tradition of Scottish Presbyterianism. The first Episcopal chapel in
Dumfries, known as "the English Chapel", was built in the mid-18th century to
accommodate what was then the only Episcopal congregation in South West
Scotland. An early 19th century replacement had itself become inadequate by
the 1860s, and in 1868 a fine new church in Early English Gothic, with a 120-foot
tower and spire, was opened on a prominent site adjoining Lovers' Walk, in a
middle-class residential district close to the railway station. Dedicated to St.
John the Evangelist, the church was laid out in accordance with the recommen-
dations of the Ecclesiological Society. St. John's was the principal Episcopal church
in Dumfries, and it is almost certain that Henrietta and Anastasia were regular
worshippers there.

In 1883 John Richard Denham became Rector of St. John's. Unable to secure
agreement from his vestry that pew rents should be abolished, he resolved to
build a new mission church for Dumfries in which all seats would be free and
unappropriated. Built of local sandstone to John Denham's own design, the new
little church was erected on a corner site in Maxwelltown, on the west bank of
the river. The area was inhabited largely by mill hands and factory workers —
members of the working class on whose behalf the rector had fought for the
abolition of pew rents. The new church was a plain oblong building with a

rounded apse, low walls and a high-pitched roof. Dedicated to St. Ninian, it was opened on his feast day, 16th September 1891. Furnishings and embellishments were provided largely through the generosity of members of the congregation. The rector's continuing battle with his vestry resulted in the closure of St. Ninian's for over two years. In 1897 he resigned, and was replaced by Frederick Charles Moir, who served as Rector of St. John's until 1907. At this time, congregations at St. Ninian's usually numbered between 50 and 100, but at the Harvest Festival on 25th October 1908 the service register records "267 in Church. Many turned away". A photograph of the interior, taken at a Harvest Festival around this time, shows an open chancel screen decorated with flowers, fruit and foliage, and beyond it a flower-decked altar with an embroidered frontal. The names of Henrietta and Anastasia Cresswell appear in 1908 as donors of a set of altar linen for use at St. Ninian's.[6]

Patterns of Memory

During her years of residence at Dumfries, Henrietta's former home in Winchmore Hill was never far from her thoughts. On 31st December 1911, as the new year approached, she wrote a nostalgic reminiscence in verse of past new years celebrated with her family at Grove Lodge. Calling to mind loved ones who had passed on, she concluded:

> How often by my Mother's side I stood,
> On the old steps, to listen to the bells;
> When Southgate's chimes were heard across the wood,
> While from the north the Enfield chorus swells.
> Then all the happiest, holiest, New Year wishes
> Were ratified by sacramental kisses.[7]

Early in 1912, Henrietta's deep affection for the village of her childhood years found public expression in her major literary achievement and her only full-length published work — *Winchmore Hill: Memories of a Lost Village*. The book is central to the story of the Cresswells of Winchmore Hill — indeed its existence was largely responsible for this their story being written — and it has already been referred to extensively. Because it represented a significant part of her literary output whilst she was living at Dumfries, this is the appropriate place in the narrative to consider in some detail its origins, development, publication and impact.

The earliest clues to Henrietta's work on this book are two anonymous articles which appeared in the parish magazine of St. Paul's, Winchmore Hill, in October 1901 and January 1902. The first, entitled "Winchmore Hill in the Past", presented some of the history of the area and an indication of changes which had occurred over the previous 30–40 years. Apparently in response to an editor's footnote inviting the author to provide another contribution, the second article, entitled "Winchmore Hill and Neighbourhood", deplored the expected loss to building of much of the Grovelands estate, and dealt with neighbouring areas which had at one time been open space or woodland, such as Hornsey Wood, Tottenham Wood and Enfield Chase. Both articles appear to have been written by the same person. The material bears a striking resemblance to the chapter entitled "Chiefly Historical" in Henrietta's book — so much so that either one author drew on the work of another, or everything was the work of a single writer.

Henrietta's "Chiefly Historical" is an amalgam of both articles, reproducing the content but rearranging it in a generally more logical sequence. At the same time there is an almost obsessive insistence on word substitution and changes in grammar and syntax. Scarcely any passage escapes this treatment. Now and again Henrietta's chapter includes new material — usually of an anecdotal character such as a joke at the expense of Mr. Wade of Wades Hill, or a reference to the quaint figure of Scarborough the roadman (whom her father had painted). Occasionally she corrects inaccuracies or confirms uncertainties in the articles. Given her deep personal feeling for many aspects of the old village, expressed elsewhere, her references to them in this chapter are somewhat detached. Of her beloved Rose Cottage, for example, once her grandmother's home, she says little more than that "a part of the house is very old".

As Henrietta's chapter corrects errors in the articles, it is unlikely that it pre-dated them. The two possibilities, therefore, are that she wrote the articles first and then used the same material in her book, or that she based her chapter on someone else's work. We know that she was in touch with people in Winchmore Hill after she had moved to Dumfries, and quite probably received the parish magazine. Indeed, either she or Anastasia (or possibly both) appear to have been visiting Winchmore Hill in December 1901, as the January 1902 parish magazine reported that "Miss Cresswell" took part in the singing of a duet at a parish concert on 11th December. It would therefore be no surprise to find Henrietta writing for the parish magazine at this time. Similarly, material published in the magazine would have been available to her in Dumfries, and may well have been retained by her some years after publication.

The principal objections to the possibility that Henrietta wrote the magazine articles are based on content and style. Good though she was at writing vivid recollections of her own past, she was not a local historian, and is unlikely to have had the depth of knowledge revealed in the articles. Indeed, the few passages which appear in Henrietta's chapter but not in the articles are concerned with just the sort of humorous and incidental details found elsewhere in her work. More persuasive still is the argument that the stylistic changes in her book would have been quite unnecessary if she had been reusing her own text. The changes made appear to represent a deliberate attempt to avoid verbatim repetition. The style of "Chiefly Historical" differs from that of the rest of her book; despite the changes it does not read like the prose of Henrietta Cresswell.

The conclusion, therefore, is that Henrietta, feeling that a "historical" chapter was needed in her book, drew material from a readily available source which, by the time of publication, would have been forgotten, or never seen, by most of her readers. It is possible that she knew who the author of the magazine articles was and obtained their permission to reuse the material, though to do so without acknowledgment would represent a lack of courtesy were it to happen today. We shall probably never know who the author of the articles was, or whether the conclusion reached is wholly fair to Henrietta. What is certain, however, is that seeds for her book were sown as early as 1901–2; it is even possible that the appearance of the articles motivated her to write it. As the first article concluded, "it may make others think of the times gone by, for, notwithstanding 'improvements', the old times were good times".

Henrietta had completed the manuscript of her book by 1907, but another five years elapsed before publication. The first edition appeared early in 1912, to be followed by a second, enlarged, edition later the same year. It has often been asserted that the book was first published in 1907, on the basis that this date is printed beneath Henrietta's introduction. However, extensive enquiries have failed to produce any evidence of a 1907 edition. Unlike the two 1912 editions, it is not listed in the British Library catalogue of printed books, it has not been identified in the holdings of any other public library, it has not been located through the second-hand book trade, no long-standing resident of the Winchmore Hill area has ever claimed to have a copy, and it is not mentioned in any contemporary periodical circulating in the area. If it ever existed, it must have been a very ephemeral publication. Nonetheless, it is necessary to examine very carefully Henrietta's own introductory words before dismissing altogether the existence of a 1907 edition.

In the first 1912 edition, the 1907 introduction is preceded by a "Preface, 1912", written at Nunholm House, Dumfries in January 1912. This preface begins:

> I have been asked not to make any alterations to my original MS., but I think it best to call attention to the fact, that any discrepancies in dates are accounted for by some years having already passed since the book was written.

This statement has been adduced as evidence of an earlier edition, but careful reading of the preface leads more sensibly to the opposite conclusion. Why, for example, did Henrietta refer to "alterations in my original MS" if what she meant was alterations to the first edition of her book? And by saying that some years had passed "since the book was written" she does not imply that it had previously been published. She does go on to say that "in the present edition" it was possible to reproduce only a few of her father's pictures, but this reads more convincingly as an expression of hope that a future edition might have more pictures (which indeed it did) than as an expression of regret that the number of pictures in an earlier edition had had to be reduced. The preface closes with Henrietta thanking her friends "whose interest in my book has led to their undertaking its publication". This would be a strange acknowledgment to include for the first time in a new edition if one had already been published.

There is, however, a further argument for the existence of a 1907 edition, based on wording in a new preface for the second, enlarged edition of 1912:

> I must call attention to the fact that any discrepancies in dates are ac-
> counted for by my original MS. having been written several years ago.
> When it was first published I was begged to make no alterations in it.

This must mean, it is argued, that the original MS had been published "several years ago" — that is, well before 1912. But if that were true, would she not have said *"after* it was first published"? Surely she is saying that *at the time* of first publication (early in 1912) she was asked to make no alterations. Moreover, the new preface is entitled "Preface to the Second Edition", indicating that, if the January 1912 edition were not the first, it cannot have been anything other than a *reprint* of an earlier first edition. If that is all it was, why does the January 1912 preface not say so?

We have already encountered evidence that Henrietta may have started work on the book as early as 1901. The most likely course of events is that she was preparing the material for some time during her early years at Dumfries, that by 1907 she had completed the initial manuscript, and that for the next five years she was either seeking a publisher or looking for some means of financing publication, or both. No doubt she, or the publisher, also needed encouragement that there would be a market for the book. On the strength of all the evidence, the present writer has concluded that no 1907 edition ever existed!

The publisher's imprint on the first edition reads simply "Dumfries. Printed at the Standard Office. 1912". This refers to *The Dumfries and Galloway Standard*, the local newspaper whose owner, Thomas Hunter, was one of the trustees of the late George Henderson of Nunholm House. Thomas Hunter continued to enjoy a share in the ownership of Nunholm House during Henrietta's tenancy and occupation; he and others connected with the paper were no doubt the friends whose interest Henrietta acknowledges. It seems remarkable that journalists in Dumfries should have been interested in publishing a book about Winchmore Hill, but the author may well have borne the financial risk, and must have persuaded them that there would be a demand. Certainly she undertook to distribute the book herself from Nunholm House.

The stimulus for its publication, and one possible explanation of the delay in its appearance, came in the form of a sale of work arranged by St. Paul's, Winchmore Hill in the spring of 1912. This was in aid of a fund for the enlargement of St. Paul's and the completion of Holy Trinity, a daughter church in Green Lanes, Winchmore Hill, opened in 1908. In her January 1912 preface, Henrietta expresses her hope that the "Bazaar Book" will be a success. In a letter dated 6th March 1912 with which she sent a copy to the Guildhall Library, London, she says that the book "has been printed for a Bazaar" in Winchmore Hill. Preparations for the sale of work had been in hand since the summer of 1911; in

January 1912 it was agreed that the event should take place on Wednesday and Thursday 17th and 18th April, and that the stalls should represent "Japan". The opening ceremony was performed by the wife of John Pretyman Newman, who since 1910 had been the Conservative Member of Parliament for the Enfield Parliamentary Division (which included Winchmore Hill). The parish hall in Station Road had been transformed for the occasion: it was decorated with almond blossom and many of the stall holders wore Japanese costumes. The event was well attended, and receipts were £415.[8] There is no indication as to how much was raised by the sale of Henrietta's book, but presumably she gave a share of the proceeds to the church.

Two well known and widely quoted local authors have written about Henrietta's book in such a way as to add to the confusion over its origins. In *A Southgate Scrap-Book* (1948), Tom Mason says: "the first edition was published in 1907, and a later and cheaper edition was published in 1912 for sale at a bazaar held in St. Paul's Institute in aid of parish funds". This turns the story on its head, and does not mention the second (enlarged) edition of 1912 at all. In *Memories of Winchmore Hill* (1952), Horace Regnart recalls that he first knew Henrietta when she was in her twenties, and goes on to say:

> She wrote the book on Winchmore Hill to help a bazaar that was got up by Mr. Dewdney in 1903 or 1904 to raise some money to build Holy Trinity Church in the Broadway....she wrote a second edition of the book which, however, she did not publish as she thought she had given too many personal details about the inhabitants.

There is no other evidence that Henrietta had completed her book in time for the first bazaar in aid of Holy Trinity (actually held in June 1905). Presumably there is confusion here with the bazaar of 1912. In the second edition (November 1912) there are two additional chapters containing her recollections of some local inhabitants, but they are not of a kind likely to have caused embarrassment. It is possible that Henrietta had planned more extensive additions which she then curtailed, but it is more likely that Horace Regnart, who was an old man when he wrote his book, was suffering from failing memory. Certainly his recollections are unreliable in other respects. The story does however have a parallel in the work of Henrietta's great-grandfather, the Reverend Mark Noble, whose uncomplimentary remarks about many of the parishioners in his *History of Barming* remained unpublished.

The first edition of *Winchmore Hill: Memories of a Lost Village* (January 1912) had 112 pages and measured 5"x 7¼". It was bound in green, cloth-board covers, the front carrying a reproduction of one of John Cresswell's drawings showing cottages near the top of Church Hill. Although the author's name appears as *H. Cresswell* on the cover and in full after the introduction and preface, it appears simply as *H.C.* on the title page. There are 11 chapters, five plates reproduced from paintings and drawings by John Cresswell, and five of his line drawings in the text. No variations in binding or appearance have been found (except where libraries have subsequently rebound their copies). The book was reviewed in *The Dumfries and Galloway Standard* on 30th March 1912:

> Apart from its local interest to residents in Winchmore Hill, or those like
> the author having family associations with it, the book has a charm for
> the lover of country life in its closely observant description of the delights
> of bird nesting, of the hiving of the bees, and other episodes of the garden
> and the fields, and in its minute and sympathetic record of village life on
> the fringe of a great city.

No price and publisher were mentioned, but the author's address was shown at the head of the review. It would be interesting to know how many residents of Dumfries were persuaded to buy it!

The second edition (November 1912) was published in the larger format of 6¾"x 8½" and had 119 pages. The type was reset, and the publisher's imprint was changed from "Printed at the Standard Office" to "Thos. Hunter, Watson & Co., Ltd". The cloth-board cover carried the same picture. There were 13 chapters, 10 plates and five illustrations in the text. Several versions of this edition appeared, with variations in cover design, colour and other details. The basic version had a grey cover, its design identical to that of the first edition. A similar, red-covered version included a drawing of the pond on the Green on the front and back end-papers. Versions with the end-paper drawing also appeared in brown and blue covers; on these the cover design was enclosed within a double-line border, and the author's name was printed in full instead of as *H. Cresswell*. These versions also differed in having *Winchmore Hill* printed on the spine, and the plates within were re-ordered. The blue-covered version differed yet again in having gilt edging to the pages, gilt lettering on cover and spine, and a rearranged cover design which placed the illustration below all the lettering instead of in the middle. This version has been found with a light-coloured dust jacket bearing the same wording and illustration as the board cover, though differently arranged. Dust jackets may of course have been provided for other versions, but none has been traced. Yet another blue-covered version, with special binding, was offered for sale in a limited edition. A copy later presented by the author to the Southgate Local Museum is believed to be an example of this. It is remarkable that at least five distinct versions of the second edition of Henrietta's book were produced.

Announcing publication of the book, the November 1912 parish magazine of St. Paul's, Winchmore Hill, mentioned that the price would be three shillings, "with a limited number of copies in handsome binding, suitable for Christmas presents" at five shillings. There was a display advertisement in *The Recorder for Palmers Green, Winchmore Hill and Southgate* on six occasions between November 1912 and March 1913. It referred to the "second edition, much enlarged", and quoted prices of three shillings cloth, and three shillings and sixpence cloth gilt, gilt edges, post free from the authoress in Dumfries. The advertisement was changed during this period to indicate that copies were also available from Mrs.

Barnes at Sherborne House [Vicars Moor Lane], and from Mr. Walter Pole, the Broadway, Winchmore Hill. The five-shilling version was not mentioned in these advertisements. The book did not sell quickly: it was still on sale at Pole's in 1926, and a Palmers Green bookseller had difficulty in disposing of remaining copies, but it was out of print by 1931. Nowadays, copies of the second edition turn up occasionally in the second-hand book trade, but it is rare for the first edition to do so.[9]

The Recorder reviewed the book on 19th December 1912, devoting more than a whole page to it. The reviewer recalls from personal experience how Winchmore Hill looked in the early 1880s: "the scene....was one of beautiful rural simplicity....one could not have found a more perfectly rural spot a hundred miles from London. Yet it was never visited by the tripper class even then". The reviewer finds that Henrietta's descriptions confirm this impression, and, after referring to several episodes in her book, concludes:

> I shall have to read this very interesting book again, and probably again. I have books about other villages I know in various parts of England, but none can compare to this....it is the best of the kind I have ever read, and I commend it to all who love to read of the old days in the district they live in.

Lest it should be thought that a local reviewer might be biased in favour of a local author, it is worth noting the equally complimentary remarks of a writer in *The Times Literary Supplement* as late as 3rd July 1930. Within a review of a new prose and verse anthology of Middlesex, readers are reminded of "an exquisite piece of work by a writer very little known — 'Winchmore Hill: Memories of a Lost Village', by Miss Henrietta Cresswell. Nothing in the anthology before us, strong as its list of literary masters is, and skilfully as the selection has been made, offers quite the local passion and the minute and sweet painting of that book".

On 4th September 1931, *The Palmers Green and Southgate Gazette* published a letter received from Edmund Blunden (b.1896), the English pastoral poet then living at Yalding in Kent. In it he refers to Henrietta's book as "one of the most gracious, melodious prose-poems of the kind". Later writers have said of the book that it "can stand unabashed beside Mrs. Gaskell's *Cranford*", and that it "has much of the flavour of Flora Thompson's *Lark Rise to Candleford*".[10] Henrietta's account of the railway construction, in her last chapter, has been quoted by at least three authors for its gentle yet vivid effect.[11] Given the praise lavished on her book by writers over a long period, it is fair to conclude that Henrietta Cresswell has left us with an outstanding word-portrait of a Victorian village, and we are lucky indeed that that village happens to have been Winchmore Hill.

Writing for Pleasure

The Recorder, in which Henrietta's book was reviewed and advertised, was a lively and informative but short-lived local newspaper circulating in Winchmore Hill, Palmers Green and Southgate. It first appeared, as a monthly paper, in 1907, increasing to fortnightly in 1910. It reverted to monthly publication in 1915, and closed in the following year. Whilst living at Dumfries, Henrietta was both a reader and a contributor. In 1912, for example, she was quick to correct a report that the railway through Winchmore Hill "was opened somewhere about 1874 or 1875". Her letter, written from Nunholm House and published in the 20th June issue, gave the correct date of 1st April 1871, and went on to explain that the opening was delayed by a slipping embankment between Winchmore Hill and Enfield: "in fact, it was considered so unsafe for some time that I remember people who went often to London would on no account go by train to Enfield".

For *The Recorder* of 13th February 1913, Henrietta contributed a reminiscence of Udall and Childs, an old-established drapery business on Winchmore Hill Green which she had known in her childhood. Her article was prompted by recent demolition of the shop which the firm had occupied at Wood Corner

Udall and Childs, the drapery shop on Winchmore Hill Green, as Henrietta Cresswell knew it in her childhood. Founded as Udall's in 1799, it moved to the premises shown here in the 1840s. This engraving is reproduced from an account rendered by the firm for goods supplied to the National Schools, Winchmore Hill, in 1877. By this time the business was trading under the name of George Childs, the only son.

beside the path into Winchmore Hill Wood. She explained that Udall's first shop, which also sold groceries, existed when her father came to Winchmore Hill in 1842. This was the shop visited by Charles and Mary Lamb when they were living in Enfield. It was in a different position at Wood Corner from that occupied by the shop that Henrietta remembered; some years before she was born the firm gave up the grocery business and moved to the larger premises which she knew. The shop became Udall and Childs after a daughter of Mr. and Mrs. Udall married Mr. Childs and took it over. Their son George Childs came into the business after his father died, but later went into partnership elsewhere with a Mr. Child making dressmakers' dummies, and the firm of Child and Childs became known as the "Children's" business! Such are the byways of local history which, were it not for the retentive memory and fondness for recollection possessed by Henrietta Cresswell, would have been lost for ever.

In a letter to *The Recorder* of 31st July 1913, Henrietta turned her attention to a wholly different subject. In response to a correspondent's recollections of Teignmouth, formerly her uncle's home, she described the attractions of eating "cockles and cream" at an inn called Coombe Cellars, on the south shore of the Teign estuary near the village of Coombe-in-Teignhead: "I would recommend him next time to try them for himself. The rich Devonshire clotted cream takes the place of salad oil in the dressing, and is most delicious". She explains that the inn was frequented by the bargees bringing china clay down the River Teign. In recalling visits to the inn with her Devonshire relatives, she provides a rare autobiographical fragment of her younger days which does not relate to Winchmore Hill:

> The old inn was most picturesque, with its cob walls and thatched roofs. In the old days we beached the "Nancy Lee", and went up to the balcony facing west, with a magnificent view of the golden sunset behind the three tors — Hey-tor, Rippon-tor and Saddle-tor. Tea consisted of a soup tureen full of hot boiled cockles, a bowl of clotted cream, vinegar, pepper, bread and butter and a glass dish of jam, a large pot of tea, milk and sugar, at a charge of ninepence. After tea the correct thing was to play a game of skittles, for which no charge was made.

Henrietta's next contribution to *The Recorder*, on 11th September 1913, was about a holiday in her home district of Galloway. She described South Kirkcudbrightshire as "the South Devon of Scotland" for its beauty, mild climate, and profusion of wild flowers. Her account is of a cycle ride from Kirkcudbright to Dundrennan Abbey, on to the coast at Auchencairn, then through Palnackie to Dalbeattie. She writes in the first person plural, but does not say who accompanied her; however, we can imagine Henrietta and Anastasia cycling abreast through the quiet Galloway countryside, along wooded glens and over heather-clad moors, the distant hills of Bengairn and Screel seen "in an evening glow, partly shrouded in mist veils".

Henrietta wrote of her beloved Galloway with the intensity of feeling that had inspired her recollections of the lost village of Winchmore Hill. Her links with *The Dumfries and Galloway Standard* have already been noted, and it is no surprise that she should have contributed to that newspaper as well. In the issue of 20th July 1912 she wrote at length of the countryside immediately west of Dumfries, which she called "my wild garden in Galloway", and which she would visit from Nunholm. She refers to her enjoyment of "many a picnic-of-one in my lovely wild garden", and there is no mention of Anastasia accompanying her. The countryside she visited was one of low, tree-studded hills, scattered farms, and fields bordered by dry stone walls or hedgerows rich in wild flowers. Within five miles of Dumfries, and easily reached by bicycle, it lay between the Shawhead and Lochanhead roads, either side of the old military road to Lochfoot.

She finds the countryside deserted, and hardly anyone else picks the wild flowers. During the summer she brings back the showy blossoms to decorate her house. Her first visit to the "wild garden" in 1912 was on the Feast of St. Valentine, when she enjoyed evergreen ferns, hedges of copper beech, mosses and lichens, and the dark leaves of holly and ivy. In the spring her "garden" first appears in its full beauty, and she takes her reader through the seasons, and through the great variety of flora in the neighbourhood, describing its delights with the eye of a nature lover and the knowledge of a botanist. There is one favourite field which she calls her "botanical meadow", because of the great variety of flowers growing there. In a copse she finds "the earliest primroses and great beds of wood anemones that recall my old home in North Middlesex". She informs the reader that in Devonshire marsh marigolds are called "drunkards" because of their love of moisture. She also refers to countryside further from home which she can visit only occasionally: "in the wild rockery of Glenstocking is my special preserve of the grass of Parnassus, one of the most lovely of the rare wildflowers of the British Isles". A few years hence we shall find Henrietta again at Glenstocking, on the Solway Firth south of Dalbeattie, still gathering *Parnassia palustris*. Her article, a veritable litany of wild flowers, concludes with advice on how to pack them safely so that they do not fade on the homeward journey: "all that is needed is to pack them very tightly as soon as they are gathered in a tin box or American leather bag, which excludes air and retains moisture".

During the course of her article, Henrietta quotes one verse of a poem called *The Blessing of the Flowers: A Legend of Legends* — one of several she wrote on the subject of flowers and their associations. Her ability to capture images and events in mellifluous prose was rarely matched by a good poetic instinct; her poetry seldom rises above the mediocre and is sometimes banal. In no fewer than 23 four-line stanzas, *The Blessing of the Flowers* assigns to various trees and flowers a religious purpose, and concludes with the verse quoted in her article:

> And when I see a flowering gean,
> Under a bright blue sky,
> I think of Angels, dazzling white,
> Descending from on high!

The first two lines of the above were slightly reworded in the version printed in the newspaper.

This and several other flower poems by Henrietta are preserved in the album of flower lore started by her uncle Richard in Devon. Another long poem — *My Primrose Maid* — sings the praises of this "sweetheart among the flowers". There are allusions here to the primrose in a London setting — in a coster's barrow, on Hampstead Heath, on a theatre's steps, in hospital wards, and, in a particularly mawkish verse, on the death bed of an infant:

> I have seen her decking a baby's bed,
> With freshness and coolness, bringing relief;
> And when the innocent soul had fled,
> Soothing the stricken mother's grief.

Was her little nephew Dirk in mind here, perhaps?

The snowdrop is celebrated in two further poems, one recalling its traditional association with the Feast of Candlemas, the other welcoming its early appearance on St. Agnes' Day, 21st January. The latter, of three verses, is the most rhythmically interesting of this group of flower poems:

> Dear little snowdrop
> Clothed with humility,
> Yet you have golden gems
> Hidden in there;
> I know when the angels made
> Robes for St. Agnes,
> They saved up the fragments
> For snowdrops to wear!

It will be recalled that the story of St. Agnes had appeared in Clarice Cresswell's *Roses of Martyrdom*, published in 1911.

The final poem in this group, *The Legend of the Christmas Rose*, echoes a passage in Chapter 2 of Beatrix Cresswell's *Alexis and his Flowers* of 1891, in which the legendary blossoming of Christmas roses in Bethlehem at the first Epiphany is retold. Henrietta illustrated this chapter in her cousin's book with Christmas roses, and in the same year depicted these flowers in a watercolour.[12]

Whilst in Dumfries Henrietta and Anastasia produced a private literary magazine for circulation to friends with whom they corresponded regularly — an idea previously adopted by Anastasia when she lived at Teignmouth. In this way the cousins maintained what Henrietta sometimes called "pen and ink friendships". The magazine prepared at Nunholm House was typewritten, and consisted of prose and poetry, most of it by Henrietta. In 1912 it included her poem *The Old Danger Board*, in which a decaying cross-shaped sign warning of danger on a hilltop assumes the appearance, in her mind's eye, of the cross of Calvary, changing her mood from one of sadness to one of contentment and hope:

It stood in simple bareness
Against a brilliant sky.
Its presence blest the hilltop,
I felt that Christ was nigh.[13]

It came naturally to Henrietta, and to other members of her family brought up in a strong Christian tradition, to discern in everyday things a religious symbolism and significance.

In the following year, Henrietta wrote a poem which combined her love of flowers with nostalgia for her Winchmore Hill childhood. It recalled the garden of the Cottage, her paternal grandmother's house in Vicars Moor Lane, demolished in 1869 for the construction of the railway. Compared with much of her verse, *My Grandmother's Garden* is a well composed piece, skilfully accommodating the sweet old English flower names and leaving behind a lingering fragrance. It is quoted in full as an epitaph to pre-suburban Winchmore Hill:

Sweet lavender, how it recalls
A garden that I erstwhile knew,
A weeping ash, a holly hedge,
Some winding paths, a mighty yew.

The garden where we used to play,
Where flowers bloomed the whole year round,
A haven on a summer's day,
Where rest and peace were ever found.

Dear flowers, with old-fashioned names,
Love-in-a-mist and Indian cress;
Crown-daisies and forget-me-nots,
And beds of love-in-idleness.

Fair-maids-of-France and boy's-love grew,
With kiss-me-at-the-garden-gate,
While mourning-widows' sombre hue
Cried pity for their sad estate.

Sweet rosemary and lavender,
Carnations, pinks and picotees,
What luscious fragrance filled the air,
Beneath the laden apple trees.

The vision fades, for all are gone,
The little house, two centuries old!
The dear in-dwellers of the home,
For whom my love can ne'er wax cold.

But still above the iron road,
Where crowded trains go rushing through,
And close beside a busy street,
There stands erect the ancient yew.

The "ancient yew" was almost the only feature to survive when the garden was excavated to make the railway cutting.[14]

In April 1913 Henrietta explored another aspect of the natural world with a two-part article for *The Dumfries and Galloway Standard* on "The Birds of Nunholm". Published on 5th and 19th April, it gives a detailed account of the bird life seen close to her home. She begins by describing her garden. This was about an acre in extent, and consisted of rough grass and shrubbery, with a small wood of mature trees. It was bounded on the north by large quickset and privet hedges, and on the south by a low red sandstone dyke. The railway line to Glasgow cut off a corner of the vegetable garden. A long avenue of oaks led to a lane running down to a ford on the River Nith. Surrounding the garden was farmland, supporting rotation crops of oats, potatoes and turnips. During their fallow year, the fields were grazed with Ayrshire cattle which sometimes broke through the hedges and ate Henrietta's cabbages. Rabbits were a problem when the turnips were growing. The whole area made an ideal bird sanctuary, although Henrietta regretted that rooks would not nest there. They did however visit her garden to feed, coming in flocks of 20 or 30 at a time from the direction of Lincluden Abbey across the river. She explains that they can be encouraged to build by drawing large bundles of sticks up into high trees to represent nests, a method used to create a rookery in the grounds of Cotterstock Hall, Lord Melville's home in Northamptonshire. Readers of her article may have wondered how she came by this knowledge, as they were not informed that Cotterstock had been the home of her sister-in-law Emily Christiana.

The feeding and nesting habits of other birds are described at length, and are compared with the author's observations elsewhere in the country. There is a reference to a visit to Tintagel, Cornwall, 30 years earlier, where she had seen a large flock of goldfinches. (It will be recalled that seaweeds collected by Anastasia at Tintagel, possibly on the same occasion, had found their way into the Cresswell Collection at Exeter.) Henrietta had not seen goldfinches at Nunholm, and was told that they had become scarce through superior cultivation of the land and destruction of wild thistles. Her informant was Robert Service, a Dumfries nurseryman and seedsman and a leading ornithologist. Born in 1854, he had lived in the area most of his life, and became an expert on the natural history of the Solway. In 1876 he had been appointed secretary of the Dumfriesshire and Galloway Natural History and Antiquarian Society, and in 1903 accepted the position of honorary secretary and curator of the Dumfries and Maxwelltown Museum. He contributed over 200 papers on local flora and fauna to scientific magazines. Henrietta made his acquaintance and benefited from his expertise. He died in 1911, two years before her article was written.[15]

Henrietta refers in her article to the building of a sparrow's nest "in the corner of a cast-iron balcony of a house near London, quite 35 feet from the ground". This may well have been Grove Lodge, Winchmore Hill, as she goes on to say that while the nest was being built she supplied rags of coloured wool and cotton, old hair pins, gold paper etc., all of which were woven into the nest with great care. This conjures up a picture of Henrietta leaning from an upstairs window of Grove Lodge, emptying the unwanted contents of her needlework basket onto the balcony! Asides such as this offer glimpses of Henrietta's earlier life, but the articles are chiefly remarkable for the mass of ornithological detail, so carefully observed and recorded, which renders her closing words almost an understatement: "I think my readers will agree that we see a great variety of feathered folk at Nunholm".

The outbreak of war in 1914 caused little disturbance to the settled life of Nunholm House, in which Henrietta and Anastasia, supported by their "little maid", entertained guests and pursued their leisure interests — writing, botany, poultry-keeping, gardening, fruit and vegetable growing, horse riding, cycling, embroidery and needlework. Perusing *The Dumfries and Galloway Standard* in November of that year, Anastasia noticed that there were Belgian refugees in the area, some of whom might wish to follow their traditional craft of lace making. This prompted her to write to the paper on 18th November with an offer of help:

> If there are any lace-makers amongst those [refugees] near Dumfries I should be very glad to lend them three lace pillows and patterns, of which I have a number for both fine and coarse Torchon lace. I could lend them three or four dozen bobbins, which is, of course, rather a small number, but they can be purchased cheaply in England, and lace thread can be purchased in Dumfries.

She recommended lace making as a good recreation for the dark winter evenings. Whether her offer was taken up we shall never know.

Boyhood in Barrow

In her article "The Birds of Nunholm", Henrietta recalls a rare visit by a small green and grey cage bird which she caught after a chase, but which died the following day from exposure. She later identified it as a Madagascar parakeet, having seen a similar example in the bird market at Leicester. Her presence in that city no doubt arose from a visit to her brother Francis, resident in nearby Barrow-upon-Soar with his wife Emily and son Frank since 1904.

Barrow owed its early industrial prosperity to its position on the canal network. The navigable portion of the River Soar, otherwise known as the Leicester Navigation, provided the village with a waterway link to the rest of the canal system through Loughborough to the north and Leicester to the south. Its significance as a transport artery declined after the arrival of the Midland Counties Railway at Barrow in 1840, but in the early years of the 20th century the village still valued its "water communication with all parts of the kingdom".

In 1901 the population of Barrow was 2,400. Many of the inhabitants were employed in the hosiery manufactory of Messrs. Black and Driver Limited, and in the lime works of John Ellis Limited. Limestone extraction had taken place around the village for centuries. The lime kilns of Barrow had produced building material for the surrounding area since the middle ages. John Ellis, formerly chairman of the Midland Railway, became one of the main producers during the 19th century. The pungent aroma given off by the kilns was believed to be a cure for consumption, and around the turn of the century it was common for London doctors to send tuberculous patients to the village for the "Barrow Cure". It is not known whether Francis Cresswell ever did so!

When the Cresswells came to Barrow, however, it was not simply an industrial settlement. The village was surrounded by good agricultural country, whose clay soil supported wheat, barley and oats, and it was the home of the celebrated Quorn Hunt. Almshouses founded by Humphrey Babington in the 17th century still provided homes for 11 aged men and eight aged women. Two mixed elementary schools offered places for over 400 children, while the secondary school, endowed as a grammar school by Humphrey Perkins in 1717, had moved into new buildings in 1902.

Holy Trinity Church, at the centre of the village, was a sizeable 14th century building in pink granite, restored in 1870. Cruciform in plan with a western tower, it had a tall and spacious interior which contained some fine woodwork and carving designed in the late 19th century by William Douglas Caröe. In 1904 the Reverend Thomas Stone became vicar, and remained the Cresswells' parish priest for most of their period of residence in the village. Three of his 17th century predecessors, William, Anthony and John Beveridge, were related to the better known William Beveridge who was born in the village *c.*1636, became a prebendary of St. Paul's and Canterbury Cathedrals, and served as Bishop of St. Asaph from 1704 to 1708.[16]

Barrow-upon-Soar was one of 32 North Leicestershire parishes in the Barrow Poor Law Union, formed in 1837 to meet the requirements of the Poor Law Amendment Act, 1834. In 1901 the combined population of these parishes was 25,500. The workhouse at Mountsorrel, about two and a half miles south of Barrow, accommodated 300 paupers. It had been opened in 1840 to replace an old workhouse situated in Barrow at the corner of Church Street and Grove Lane. This earlier property, formerly known as the House of Industry, comprised the inmates' living quarters, a board room, frame-workers' cottages and the master's house. It was offered for public sale in four separate lots in 1842. Lot 1, consisting principally of the master's house, was sold to Thomas Fewkes, clerk to the Barrow Union. The house was almost opposite the birthplace of William Beveridge in Church Street — renamed Industry Street later in the 19th century. It was the master's house which in 1904 became the home of Francis Cresswell and his family.

Industry Square and Industry Street, Barrow-upon-Soar, 1921. The three-bay, white-fronted house with dormer windows was the Poplars, home of Francis Cresswell and family from 1904. On the extreme left is the birthplace of William Beveridge, the early 18th century Bishop of St. Asaph. The tower of Holy Trinity Church is just visible in the background. The war memorial was erected in 1921, and the names Industry Square and Industry Street were dropped in 1922. The Poplars survives as 49 and 49A Beveridge Street.

When the Cresswells moved in, and throughout their tenancy, the house continued to be owned by descendants of Thomas Fewkes. A small portion of the south end of the original house had been divided off as a cottage and was separately occupied; the remainder, tenanted by the Cresswells, was known as the Poplars. A little to the south, Industry Street opened out into a triangular space known as Industry Square, at the junction with Nook Lane (formerly Grove Lane). To the north, beyond Bishop Beveridge's house, Industry Street curved to the right to emerge into what was then called Church Street, immediately opposite Holy Trinity Church.

The Poplars was a house of some age and considerable interest. External features were Georgian in appearance, but some parts may have been much older. Floors were of stone at ground level, with a cellar beneath, and massive timber beams ran the length of the building. The street frontage was stuccoed, with sash windows at ground-floor and first-floor levels and gabled dormers in the roof. The ground-floor windows were externally shuttered. The main front door, set beneath a fanlight within a simple moulded doorcase, opened straight onto a narrow pavement. The irregularly shaped rear garden was bordered on one side by cottages which had previously formed part of the workhouse premises. The House of Industry had come into being in the early 1780s, and most of the buildings on the site, including the master's house, probably dated from that period. There is conclusive evidence that the master's house existed in 1816.[17]

In 1904 the Cresswell household consisted of Francis, aged 43, Emily Christiana, 41, Frank, 9, and their maids Frances and Matilda Gamble. Francis continued to appear as a physician and surgeon in *The Medical Directory*, but there is no evidence that he had a general practice in Barrow. Local directories of the period do not list him as a general practitioner; the only doctor included in 1908, for example, is a surgeon named Alexander Skipton. Although *The Medical Directory* does not show Francis Cresswell as retired until 1917, it is believed locally that if he practised at all whilst living at Barrow it was more likely to have been in a teaching or consultancy role at a neighbouring hospital. Certainly his failing eyesight would have been a great drawback, and there is some evidence that he retired from medical practice in 1907–8.[18]

Whilst living at Barrow the Cresswells earned a reputation as kind and benevolent people — much admired in the community, but socially a little apart from many of their neighbours and acquaintances. This observation, based on recollection by a very elderly resident who knew them, is entirely consistent with the mark of benign superiority borne by several generations of the family — a product of gentle ancestry, inherited wealth, creative talent and individualism of character. Emily Christiana Cresswell was remembered by another local resident as a dignified lady. She contributed greatly to the parish church of Holy Trinity through her generosity and good works; many beautiful items of embroidery — frontals, stoles, burses and banners — were her handiwork. Hers was a world of village fêtes, vicarage teas and sales of work — a world whose well-bred respectability is captured in photographs of ladies in long, flowing dresses and flower-decked hats attending a grand bazaar held in July 1906 in aid of the new organ fund.

Social and recreational activities in Edwardian Barrow were provided by many organisations, such as the Church Lads' Brigade, the Rising Star Football Club, the Prize Band and the Sunday Morning Adult School, but the Cresswells seem to have been touched by few of them. The untroubled life of the village was rarely disturbed by anything more alarming than the periodic flooding of the road to Quorn, although the floods of August 1912 were exceptional, a 15-hour downpour raising the river to its highest recorded level and submerging the surrounding countryside.[19]

Meanwhile, the young Frank Cresswell was receiving the grammar school education which his father had planned for him on moving from Winchmore Hill. Loughborough Boys' Grammar School owed its foundation in 1495 to Thomas Burton, a wealthy wool merchant whose bequest of lands provided income for the upkeep of the school. No doubt Francis took pride in the fact that his son had secured a place at such an ancient foundation, and he may have observed that Frank's year of birth coincided with the 400th anniversary of the school.

Since 1852 the boys had been taught in buildings on a 16-acre site at the edge of the town, the main block consisting of Big School, classrooms, library and gymnasium. A separate building contained science classrooms, laboratories and a lecture theatre. Modest tuition fees included the provision of books, stationery and games facilities. Boarding was possible at an inclusive fee, but this was unnecessary in Frank's case.

Boys were admitted into the preparatory class at the age of eight. Thereafter, education "of a broad modern type" was given through to the sixth form. Class sizes were generally small — as few as 8-12 pupils in the upper forms. From the fourth form onwards boys were entered annually for the Oxford Local Examinations, for which the school was a special centre. The examinations were taken only with the agreement of parents, but participation was certainly encouraged. Specialisation to prepare for university, Civil Service or other examinations was possible in the upper sixth, but few other departures from the standard curriculum were permitted. Various leaving exhibitions and prizes were offered, including two exhibitions to Jesus College, Cambridge.

Games were compulsory on half-holidays, and encouraged at other times — football in the winter, cricket and lawn tennis in the summer. In 1907 a rifle club was started for boys in the upper forms; drill and weekly firing under the direction of a competent instructor were obligatory unless parents indicated their objection in writing. In many respects the school was run on public school lines, and some of the school rules reflected this ethos: "try and let the School have, and deserve, a good name in the town and district"; "don't disgrace the School Cap which you are required to wear"; "keep body and *mind* clean"; "no work at all is better than dishonest work".[20]

Frank's academic progress seems to have been hindered by laziness. His pupil record survives from the third term 1907, when he entered the upper third at the age of 12. He was then "good in the subjects he fancies", and won a prize for science. By the following summer term he was making "little effort to improve in subjects which do not interest him", but he did pass the Preliminary of the Oxford Local Examination, for which boys from the upper third had been entered for the first time. During the next year his performance was variable, with English his weakest subject. By the summer of 1910, at the age of 15, it was clear where his strength lay; out of a fifth form of 13 pupils he took first place in science but was poorly placed in languages. In the following term, however, when he entered the lower sixth, he produced "bad work in every subject". Thereafter there was some improvement, but his reports reveal careless work, lack of effort, and very poor results in scripture.[21]

One of Frank's reports from the upper sixth says "very energetic out of school". As he had little interest in games, this must have referred to his performance in the rifle club, which marked his greatest achievement in the school. It will be recalled that his grandfather John Cresswell had been a "crack shot" in the rifle volunteers, and Frank evidently inherited this ability. His father clearly approved of the activity, for in 1909 he subscribed towards the cost of four new rifles for the club. By 1910 Frank was consistently scoring high points for the school in shooting matches. On 14th May, for example, he was top scorer for the school in a match against the Loughborough Miniature Rifle Club, and on 12th July, when the school met the Falcon Rifle Club, he received special mention as the first pupil to achieve the maximum possible score. The 1911 season was very successful for the rifle club, the school magazine recording that "the Donegal Bronze Medal for the best shot of the year fell to Cresswell, one of the keenest members of the Club". He qualified for the medal again in 1912 and 1913, but as he had held it previously he passed it on to the runner-up. On 21st June 1913 he represented the school in the Astor County Challenge Cup at Thurmaston, travelling by train from Loughborough: "after a quick lunch the members of the team walked, ran, crawled and cycled to the Midland Station. Arrived at the hamlet of Syston the team succeeded in pinching past the ticket collector, who did not dare to molest them as they carried rifles". By July 1914, when Frank left the school, he was captain of the rifle club. He was then 19 years of age, and had been in the sixth form for four years.

His practical abilities were used to good effect the previous December at the end of term concert, when thanks were offered to the participants "ably assisted in their task by Stage-Carpenter Cresswell and his assistants, with whose work no possible fault could be found". Despite his poor academic record, Frank had started to prepare for entry to Oxford whilst in the upper sixth; as with so many young men of his age, the onset of war removed any prospect of a university education.[22]

For King and Country

Frank Cresswell was one of the first wartime recruits from Loughborough Grammar School. He joined the 4th Battalion, Leicestershire Regiment on 10th August 1914, less than a week after Britain had declared war, and commenced training immediately. By the end of the year he was stationed at Luton, Bedfordshire, awaiting orders to go to the front. "His shooting makes him a very useful recruit", said an article in the school magazine in the winter of 1914; "since the end of last term our Nation and Empire have been involved in the most terrible war the world has ever known....the duty of self-sacrifice is one of the needed lessons which we believe this war is intended to teach a Nation only too inclined of late to be eager for ease and comfort". On 15th February 1915 Frank received a commission as Second Lieutenant in the 9th Battalion, Leicestershire Regiment, and soon afterwards went to the western front. Meanwhile, the daily round of village life continued at Barrow, Mrs. Cresswell raising money for a choir stall fund, her husband lending microscopes for a demonstration given by Dr. Alexander Skipton and a colleague to the Church of England Men's Society.[23]

The opening months of 1916 saw the beginning of the allied advance which would culminate in the first battle of the Somme. Early in the year news arrived that Frank had been wounded in action, but his injuries cannot have been grave because in mid-March he was able to send to Mr. A.J. Smith, his former science master at Loughborough, a sample of the latest German high explosive for analysis. It was "employed in the aerial torpedoes which had been very troublesome in the sector of trenches occupied by his battalion".[24] Early in May, Frank obtained six days' leave in order to return home for his 21st birthday celebration. He was back in France on 14th May. Four days later, whilst in charge of a machine-gun section in the front line trenches near Arras, he was struck by an enemy bullet in the femoral artery and died almost immediately from the wound. News of his death reached his parents by telegram a few days afterwards, and this was followed by a letter from the Colonel of his regiment:

> He was out with a wiring party in front of the trench when one of his men was hit by machine-gun fire. Your son and two men started to drag the man in, and whilst doing so, your son was hit, and died shortly afterwards.

"Is it possible to imagine a finer end to a life, or to a family of which he was the last of the line?" wrote his obituarist in the school magazine. The Colonel's letter described him as "such a clever, keen boy, and always ready to do any job, and....always without fear". A letter from his Captain spoke of his wonderful courage.

Frank's obituary appeared in the school magazine towards the end of 1916. He was described as a capable and daring officer of brilliant gifts and promise, whose sunny nature endeared him to many. His strong individuality as a pupil at the school was recalled, his interests being scientific rather than literary. For recreation he preferred cycling and shooting to games. "In his long country rides with map and camera, he made friends with many a country joiner and blacksmith, and learned something of their skill. At the age of 19 he was the best shot and scientist of the Loughborough Grammar School." He used his mechanical gifts, inventiveness and scientific knowledge to good purpose in the army, and was machine-gun officer for his division. The writer gives examples of technical improvisation with which he overcame problems, and refers to his discovery of new varieties of German shells. "Many a German fell to his unerring rifle. His physical endurance was remarkable, and his spirits never failed." The writer concludes:

> A perfect Christian gentleman, a loyal and loving friend, a good soldier, brave in peril, decisive in action, resourceful in difficulty, a true son of Empire, the memory of Frank Cresswell will live in the hearts of all who were privileged to know him as a bright example of devotion to duty, and the embodiment in an exceptional degree of those gifts of body, brain and spirit which have made our race great.

The same issue of the magazine acknowledged "the great kindness of Mr. and Mrs. Cresswell in presenting to the school some valuable scientific apparatus which belonged to their son".[25] Frank is buried in the New Military Cemetery at Hannescamps, south west of Arras. His headstone, bearing the badge of the Leicestershire Regiment, is inscribed "Christ's faithful soldier and servant".[26]

It would be small consolation to his parents that Frank was spared the worst horrors of the battle of the Somme, which commenced on 1st July 1916. Perhaps they read in *The Loughborough Echo* an eye-witness account of the first day of the offensive, written by another Old Loughburian. After describing a successful attack on German positions, he recalls the mixed feelings of pride, thankfulness and deep sorrow which followed: "those that are lost to us have given of their best. It is for us who remain to see that that best was not given in vain".[27]

The following weeks of fierce fighting against strongly defended German positions advanced the front line at the expense of enormous allied casualties. By the end of September, significant progress had been made north of the Somme, but enemy strongholds on the River Ancre, north of Albert, remained to be captured. An attack on these positions, which included the fortified villages of Beaumont-Hamel and Beaucourt, began on 11th November. Among those taking part in the attack on Beaucourt were members of the 1st Battalion, the Honourable Artillery Company. At 5.45 on the morning of Monday 13th November the battalion advanced into dense fog, their flank resting on the River Ancre to maintain direction. The heavy casualties sustained on that day included Lance-Corporal Wilfrid John Taylor, fiancé to Clarice Mercedes Cresswell. He did not live to see the capture of Beaucourt on 14th November.[28] For the second time, grief had been visited on the Cresswells from the craters of the Somme.

When the news reached Clarice Cresswell she suffered a nervous breakdown and temporary partial paralysis.[29] As she turned the pages of her most recent book, *The Ministry of Holda*, she would surely have found new and poignant meaning in a picture painted by Wilfrid to illustrate her description of young Prince Omar, the Caliph's son, waiting to cross Al-Sirât, the Bridge of the Day of Judgement:

> Omar stood on the brink of a tremendous gulf, black as night, in whose awesome depths red flames quivered. Mist-wreaths floated across it, wherein mist-faces gathered and waned, peeping at him with bright eyes. Across the darkness lay a thin line, like a spider's filament, clear as silver, nigh his feet, lost in the gloom beyond the gulf's centre; and on either side, two angel-shapes hovered, suspended upon their great wide-spread wings.

Supported by this unbroken thread, Prince Omar passes over into Paradise.

CHAPTER 9

Broken Threads

In Memoriam

Within a few months of Frank Cresswell's death on the Somme, a fund was established to provide new oak choir stalls in his memory at Holy Trinity Church, Barrow-upon-Soar. The greater part of this work was financed from Frank's own bank balance, which amounted to just over £200. The work was put in hand towards the end of 1916. The stalls, carved by Mr. J. Hind, a local man, were described as "an excellent example of modern craftsmanship". They carried a plaque bearing the words: "In proud memory of 2nd Lt. Frank Cresswell who was killed in action at Arras on May 18th 1916 these choir stalls the gift of his mother were provided by his patrimony".

In the following year, the vestry meeting accepted an offer by Dr. and Mrs. Cresswell to place a stained-glass window in the south transept of Holy Trinity Church as a memorial to their son, "whose bright and promising career was so suddenly cut short". The tall, three-light window was commissioned by William Douglas Caröe, architect to the church at the time, from the London firm of James Powell and Sons. Designs were prepared towards the end of 1917, the order was placed early in 1918, and a year later the window was fitted in the east wall of the transept. The main centre light contained a Crucifixion inscribed "Look unto me and be ye saved — God so loved the world". The left-hand light carried a figure of St. Bartholomew above the Cresswell family arms; the saint may have been chosen to match the dedication of the church at Cresswell, Northumberland. The right-hand light illustrated St. Andrew, to whom the church at Cotterstock was dedicated; when Frank died his grandfather was still vicar there. The three tracery-lights above were inscribed: "Thanks be to God for his unspeakable gift". A suitable inscription "in fond memory" of Frank was spread across the bottom of the main lights. Beneath the window, and extending the full width of the transept, a war memorial was later erected in the form of a panelled reredos on which were recorded the names and regiments of those who had given their lives in the Great War. Frank's was one of 14 names from the Leicestershire Regiment. To complete their gift to the church in memory of their son, Francis and Emily donated two priests' desks, the first of which was in position early in 1920. Holy Trinity Church, Barrow, thus became the focus of remembrance of the youngest of the Cresswells of Winchmore Hill.[1]

Before the memorials were completed, Frank's mother suffered a further bereavement with the death of her father, the Reverend Francis Buttanshaw, on 19th December 1917. He had been Vicar of Cotterstock for 30 years and had reached the age of 89. He was buried in the churchyard on Christmas Eve by the Vicar of Oundle, and a simple stone cross next to his son's memorial marks his final resting place.² A brass tablet to his memory was placed by his parishioners on the north wall of the nave of St. Andrew's Church; on it is inscribed "he was a good man and full of the Holy Ghost". His three surviving children, Mark Noble, Charles and Emily, benefited from the will. As well as a pecuniary legacy, Emily received a silver ink stand given to her father by friends at Chinnor, Oxfordshire, when he left that parish in 1872, a silver cream jug which had belonged to her great-grandfather the Reverend Mark Noble, and a miniature portrait of that gentleman set in a bracelet clasp. Francis Cresswell received an album of photographs of English cathedrals. The children were also invited to choose from their father's collection of books, especially those written by the Reverend Mark Noble and including "the History of the College of Arms bound in cream morocco ready for Presentation to his Majesty King George III". Such were the treasured heirlooms handed down to another generation of the family; sadly, the Cresswells now had no heir to whom to pass their share of the inheritance.

Back at Barrow-upon-Soar, the return of peace was marked by the embroidering of a beautiful and exquisitely worked peace banner for Holy Trinity Church — the gift of Emily Cresswell. At the centre of the banner she embroidered the *agnus dei*. It was first used on Sunday 6th July 1919, a day appointed for special services of thanksgiving for the blessings of peace. A procession formed of members of the parish council, local organisations and ex-service personnel wound its way through the village to the church, which was filled to capacity. Later the same day, another service, led by the vicar, was held in Industry Square, almost outside the Cresswells' front door. Nearly two weeks afterwards, on Saturday 19th July, a much greater peace procession took place in the village; it was "generally agreed that there never was a better parade in Barrow, and the remark was heard that it was the best 'show' in any village in Leicestershire".³

Francis Cresswell never fully recovered from the overwhelming grief caused by the death of his son, and his health deteriorated steadily thereafter. Following a prolonged illness, he died of sclerosis on Tuesday 19th October 1920, at the age of 59. The funeral took place at 3 pm on 22nd October at Barrow Cemetery, opened in 1895 half a mile north west of the village. The service was conducted by the vicar, Thomas Stone. Among the many beautiful wreaths were floral tributes from the vicar and Mrs. Stone, Dr. Alexander Skipton, and the two maids Frances and Matilda Gamble. An obituary in the parish magazine referred to his "long period of bodily affliction, borne with much patience and Christian resignation", and mentioned that his weak eyesight required the use of powerful magnifying glasses, enabling him to read only a few letters of each word at a time:

> Yet, in spite of this great drawback, the stores of information which he had acquired were nothing less than marvellous, the variety of subjects with which he was familiar being as extraordinary as the accuracy of the

knowledge he had gained, and his memory was such that he must have remembered all he read....he surmounted all obstacles in the pursuit of knowledge, and attained to great eminence and skill, both in his profession and in many other branches of art and science.

Within little over four years, Emily had lost a son, a father and a husband.[4]

Francis did not live to see the unveiling of the village war memorial on which his son's name was inscribed. Situated in Industry Square, close to the Cresswells' home, it replaced a temporary war shrine near the parish church. The new memorial was dedicated by the vicar on Trinity Sunday, 22nd May 1921. The stone plinth, supporting a cross mounted on a slender column, carried the names of over 70 Barrovians who had fallen in the Great War. In the following year, the names Industry Street and Industry Square were abandoned, and Mrs. Cresswell's address became 49 Beveridge Street.[5]

Six months before her husband's death, Emily Cresswell became a member of the newly formed Parochial Church Council at Holy Trinity, whose first meeting took place on 21st April 1920. Most of her recorded contributions to the meetings were concerned with the war memorial in the south transept of the parish church, beneath the Cresswell window. In May 1922, for example, the council discussed the provision of three sculptures for the memorial, at a cost of £37: "Mrs. Cresswell said she had seen the figures and that the work was good

Frank Cresswell's name is amongst those inscribed on the Barrow-upon-Soar war memorial, almost opposite the Cresswell family home. Photographed in 1994.

and that she considered it was a very reasonable amount for the work". The figures were carved by Nathaniel Hitch, chief sculptor to William Douglas Caröe. The memorial was completed in 1923, and dedicated by the Bishop of Peterborough on Sunday 1st July. A sale of work organised by Mrs. Cresswell and a colleague later the same month raised sufficient to pay off outstanding debts on the provision of the memorial.[6]

On 13th September 1923 the death occurred of Thomas Stone, Vicar of Holy Trinity, Barrow, since 1904. He was buried in the cemetery next to Francis Cresswell, and in the same grave-plot as his son Lieutenant Tom Pearse Griffith Stone, who had been killed in Mesopotamia in 1917 at the age of 24. A memorial window to Lieutenant Stone, the gift of the vicar and his wife and daughter, had been placed in the parish church next to the Cresswell window. The Reverend Thomas Stone began his ministry at Barrow in the year in which the Cresswells moved there; their names had been associated since then as parish priest and faithful parishioners, and latterly in shared grief for loved ones lost in battle. The proximity of their memorials symbolised their earthly friendship.

Emily Cresswell ceased to attend meetings of the Parochial Church Council after the vicar's death. Little over a week later, on 22nd September 1923, the council were discussing the appointment of a new vicar, agreeing to recommend to the patron "that he be a man of neither extremely High Church or Low Church tendencies but one who would be able to steer the middle course". Such a man was found in the person of John David Thomas, who was presented to the living in 1924. In the same year, the Parochial Church Council agreed to apply for a faculty for the erection of a new oak pulpit in Holy Trinity Church, to be given by Mrs. Cresswell in memory of her husband. The hexagonal pulpit, designed by Caröe, was placed in the church in 1925. Through their gifts of embroidery, stained glass and carved woodwork, the Cresswells had done much to enhance and beautify their parish church for future generations.[7]

Declining health was now restricting Emily Cresswell's contribution to parish and community life, though she remained a faithful worshipper, and a supporter of local causes. One such was the Barrow Prize Band, re-formed after the war to play at local events and entertain the residents. Samuel Darby, who had become bandmaster at the age of 17 in 1876, retired in 1926 after 50 years' service. Among the subscribers to his retirement presentation was Emily Cresswell.[8]

Three years later, on Sunday 8th December 1929, Emily passed away at the age of 67. She was buried in her late husband's grave-plot in Barrow Cemetery at 1 pm on 11th December. The vicar, John David Thomas, conducted the service. The plot was marked by a floriated stone cross bearing Francis Cresswell's age and date of death on the horizontal arm, his wife's on the plinth below. The shaft was inscribed *"mors janua vitae"* ("death the gateway to life"). The grave, near the middle of the cemetery, was shaded by yew trees. An obituary in the parish magazine described Emily as "an indefatigable worker for the church, which she loved so well":

> The way in which she endured suffering, mental and physical, with such
> fortitude was a sermon for us all. Her attendance at church, almost to the
> last, in spite of much weakness and acute discomfort, was also an exam-
> ple for many to imitate.

In her last illness, Emily was attended by Dr. Cecil Richardson of Loughborough, as her husband had been nine years earlier. In recognition of this, "for
which he would receive no payment", Emily left him £300 in her will. Other
beneficiaries included her second cousin Clarice Mercedes Cresswell, who received the Jacobite "rebel ring" referred to in Chapter 2, her sister-in-law
Henrietta Cresswell who received £1,000, and her maids Frances and Matilda
Gamble who received £500 between them "in gratitude for long and faithful
service and friendship". Frances had by then served the family for no fewer
than 46 years, her sister Matilda for 36. The maids retired to a cottage in Sileby
Road, on the south eastern edge of the village. It was known as Cresswell Cottage, and the sisters lived there into old age — a continuing link with the
Winchmore Hill family who had resided in Barrow for a quarter of a century.[9]

Beloved Priest

As Francis and Emily had mourned the loss of their son, so had Clarice Mercedes
endured the pain of her fiancé's death on the battlefield of the Somme. Before
Wilfrid John Taylor went to the war, he discussed with Clarice her ideas for a
new historical novel, based on the Passion and Resurrection of Jesus. This appeared from Methuen and Company early in 1920 with the title *Pilate Gave Sen-
tence*. It was to be her last published work. It received a mixed review in *The
Times Literary Supplement*: "as a reconstruction of Judaea in the days of Christ it
is not particularly successful....but it is a book with a strong idea; and through
many weaknesses and failures of expression the idea in the end asserts itself
victoriously".[10] A central figure in the drama is Pilate's wife Claudia, through
whom the reader learns of the trial and crucifixion of Jesus. Her experience of
the tempest arising at the time of Christ's death speaks of a momentous hap-
pening:

> The storm that raged upon the face of the earth swooped upwards. That
> which earlier had been a solid zenith became a chaos of frantic haste.
> Great brown clouds, hot and ragged and lashed by the shrieking blast,
> tore across the heavens. Strange lights came and went. The livid slopes of
> the Mount of Olives and the roofs of Jerusalem leapt to sight from a welter
> of darkness, yellow glare, and rufous fog-wreaths, as the concealing mist
> was torn to shreds.

In words strikingly reminiscent of her father's 1885 vision of the evening sky over South London, Clarice again achieves dramatic impact through her vivid descriptive imagery. But her reflection on Claudia's state of mind after the Crucifixion contains a passage which in this context must have seemed extraordinary to any reader unaware of the author's personal loss. In her thoughts, Claudia sees the crosses of Calvary endlessly multiplied:

> They marked the passing of eld, youth mown down untimely, the millions fallen in war; lines and lines and lines of wooden crosses, in cold and heat, by white light and by red; the stars turned above them and the autumn leaves drifted round them; and stars and leaves were less thick than they.

Perhaps the reader who had noticed that the book was dedicated "in proud and loving memory of L/Cpl. Wilfrid John Taylor, 1st HAC...." would understand, and would appreciate the lines from William Morris's poem *Sir Peter Harpdon's End* printed beneath the dedication:

> ....truly I never thought
> That I should make a story in this way,
> A story that his eyes can never see.

At this time, Clarice was still living with her parents at 145 Holland Road, Kensington. On 26th January 1923 her mother, Margaret Rosina, died at the age of 77. In her will she left all her property to Clarice, not to her husband Richard Henry, who by now was suffering from heart failure. He survived another two years, dying at home on 16th March 1925, aged 78. His funeral and requiem, at St. John's, Holland Road, was attended by many priests, including William Martin Spencer, who had ceased to be vicar in 1916. Father Cresswell's biretta and stole were placed upon his coffin, in blessed memory of "our beloved priest". "We shall all miss him very much for his short and very instructive sermons", wrote a parishioner afterwards; "no priest could have been more devoted and obedient".[11]

During the last few years of his life, it had been Father Cresswell's custom to say Mass daily in the chapel of St. Peter and St. Paul, on the north side of the choir. It was therefore decided that improvements should be made to this chapel as a memorial to the departed priest. Following an appeal to old friends and parishioners by the vicar, Lester Pinchard, a permanent stone pavement and predella (or step) for the altar, and carved oak communion rails, were put in place by 1926. The altar rails were very medieval in character, and incorporated curious carved figures whose significance was explained in a contemporary description:

> The little dog represents Faithfulness; the four figures with hands over their mouth, eyes, ears, representing the admonition, see no evil, speak no evil, hear no evil, then there is the figure representing Love of Music with

The Reverend Richard Henry Cresswell, curate of St. John the Baptist, Holland Road, Kensington, photographed outside the church towards the end of his life. When he died in 1925 he had served the parish as an assistant priest for 45 years.

a pipe in his mouth and one holding a flower representing Love of Beauty, and one a loaf being of Charity and the eighth one with a young animal in her arms being Love of Helplessness.

The rails were made from grained English oak felled in Thame Park, Oxford-shire.[12] On the front of the predella were inscribed the words:

IN PIAM MEMORIAM RICARDI HENRICI CRESSWELL SACERDOTIS
QUI OBIIT A.D. XVI KAL.AP. MCMXXV CUJUS ANIMAM PROPITIETUR DEUS

("In blessed memory of Richard Henry Cresswell, priest, who died 17th March [*sic*] 1925, on whose soul God have mercy.")[13]

Following her father's death, Clarice Mercedes remained at Holland Road. Of her father's generation of Cresswells, only Beatrix and Anastasia, and their cousin Henrietta, now survived.

Wide-Watered Shores

So much was changing for the Cresswells and their related families after the security of the prewar years — the tragedy of Frances Jennings, the sacrifices of the war, the onset of illness and the passing of an earlier generation. It was as if the tightly knit threads of the Victorian family were unravelling, to break one by one. For Henrietta and Anastasia, even the settled life of Dumfries, enjoyed for almost 20 years, and largely undisturbed by the Great War, would soon be threat-ened.

Their troubles began with a change in the ownership of Nunholm House. During the prewar years, and right through the war, the house had remained the property of the late George Henderson's trustees, whose interests continued to be managed by John Henderson and Sons, the Dumfries solicitors. In January 1919, Henrietta was informed that the house would be sold by auction, at a starting price of £550. As the sitting tenant, she tried to buy the house privately, but, having failed to do so, she attended the sale on 29th January, bidding up to £725 for it. A certain Mr. John Ramsay outbid her, offering £740. He was a re-tired farmer, living with his wife, son, daughter and niece in a house called Renwick Bank, situated about eight miles north west of Dumfries near the vil-lage of Dunscore, on the road to Moniaive. After the sale, Henrietta asked him to name a price at which he would sell, but he refused to do so, wishing to move into Nunholm House to enable his 12-year-old son and 16-year-old daughter to attend Dumfries Academy without having to travel. His daughter was already lodging in Dumfries for this purpose, and he did not wish his son to have to do so. The train service from Dunscore Station, on the Cairn Valley branch of the Glasgow and South Western, was unsuitable for a daily journey to Dumfries. The terms of the sale of Nunholm House were that John Ramsay could take possession from Whitsunday 1919. Henrietta was given notice that her tenancy would be terminated from that date.

At a stroke, Henrietta and Anastasia were faced with the loss of the home which they had grown to love, and which they regarded as theirs in all but name. As soon as the notice of removal had been sent, however, Henrietta began to look for a new home, corresponding with house agents in Carlisle, Whitby, Scarborough and elsewhere in England. On 11th March she found a suitable house on Ullswater, in the Lake District, and purchased it soon afterwards. It was at Watermillock, near the north end of the lake, and was known as Lambgill. Her initial understanding was that she could take possession at Midsummer 1919, but it transpired that the occupant, a gardener, held a yearly tenancy and could not be removed until Lady Day 1920. The tenant refused to quit sooner than that, leaving Henrietta and Anastasia with the prospect of having nowhere to live for nine months.

In an attempt to assist her over this difficulty, John Ramsay offered to arrange for her to take a short-term tenancy of Renwick Bank, Dunscore, the house which he was vacating, but Henrietta declined this on the grounds that she would be put to the expense of a double removal, that the house was too remote, and that it would not comfortably accommodate all her household and effects. Instead she refused to move from Nunholm House until she was able to take possession of Lambgill, causing John Ramsay to bring an action in the Dumfries Sheriff Court requesting a decree for her removal.

Henrietta and Anastasia remained at Nunholm House pending the court hearing, which took place on 16th August 1919. Henrietta was represented by Mr. W. Moodie, a Dumfries solicitor. She submitted that she and her cousin were both "advanced in years", and that she had never intended to leave Nunholm House as long as she lived. Her defence was based on recent legislation which provided that a court may grant a decree of removal only if, "after considering all the circumstances of the case, including especially the alternative accommodation available for the tenant, the court considers it reasonable to make such an order". Her argument was that there was no sufficient alternative accommodation available at the time at which she was required to leave Nunholm House. Having secured Lambgill in the expectation that she would be able to move there by Midsummer 1919, she had ceased looking for another home. It was the misunderstanding over the date of entry to Lambgill which had changed the situation, and she should not be obliged to seek temporary accommodation elsewhere because of this.

Sheriff Milne was unconvinced by this argument. The mistake about the date of entry to Lambgill was hers, and her inability to gain immediate possession did not relieve her of the responsibility of finding other accommodation, nor did it entitle her to stay on at Nunholm House. There was nothing to prevent her renting another property, but she had made no effort to do so. Her case was weakened further by the fact that, after she had negotiated the purchase of Lambgill, its owner approached her with a request that the tenant, who it now appeared would suffer greatly from eviction, should be given the opportunity to purchase the property from Henrietta at no financial loss to her. She refused to agree to this, considering Lambgill to be a bargain and an investment, but in doing so she could not argue that she was legally bound to the purchase of Lambgill, and could have given it up in favour of other permanent accommodation into which she could have moved immediately. It was demonstrated that suitable houses had been available in Dumfries at the time — particularly one called Beechgrove House — which Henrietta could have taken, but she had decided that, if ejected from Nunholm House, she did not wish to remain in Dumfries.

Beechgrove was described by a witness as a house in many respects of a similar kind to Nunholm. It was available for letting at a rent only slightly higher than at Nunholm, but it had more accommodation. It was situated on the south side of Annan Road, in the district of Noblehill, on the eastern outskirts of Dumfries. The two-storeyed, red sandstone house had an irregular ground plan. A rear garden extended some 100 feet towards the main line of the Glasgow and South Western Railway, which ran in a cutting to the east of Dumfries Station. The area had developed in the late 19th century with small and medium-size houses spread out along Annan Road. Although some open views remained, it was more urban and less secluded than Nunholm, and Beechgrove House had much less land. Henrietta had rejected this and other properties in Dumfries because they were not suitable for the keeping of poultry and dogs for which she required at least half an acre of ground — although she admitted she did this for pleasure and not for profit.

Referring to her refusal of the offer of a tenancy of Renwick Bank, Sheriff Milne considered that there was sufficient room to accommodate the Misses Cresswell and their maid comfortably in that house. Although a niece of Anastasia [possibly Margaret Jennings] stayed with them from time to time, she could not be regarded as a member of the household. The cost of storing furniture would be more than offset by the saving in rent, which would be only £12 per annum at Renwick Bank. The house was described by a witness as being "in very good order" and "very much above the average for a country residence of its size".

The sheriff concluded: "in these circumstances I do not think that it would entail real hardship on the defender to take up her quarters temporarily in Renwick Bank until she is able to get entry to Lambgill, which is to be her permanent home, and that seems to me to be sufficient for the disposal of the case". Whilst expressing sympathy with her in the disappointment which she would suffer in having to leave the house which had been her home for 20 years, he reminded her that eviction was always a risk inherent in the status of tenancy, and the protection afforded by recent legislation was designed only to prevent hardship arising from some particular difficulty in finding alternative accommodation, which did not apply in this case. Consequently, the pursuer (John Ramsay) was entitled to the decree of removal which he sought, requiring the defender (in Scottish legal terminology):

....to flit and remove herself, her family, subtenants and dependants, with
their goods and gear, furth and from the house known as Nunholm House,
Dumfries, and that on or before the 1st day of October 1919, and to leave
the same void and redd to the end that the Pursuer may enter thereto, and
peacefully possess and enjoy the same.

The judgment, issued on 18th August 1919, awarded costs to John Ramsay.[14]
The title to Nunholm House had been conveyed from the trustees of the late
George Henderson to John Ramsay on 16th May 1919.[15] Following the judg-
ment, the new owner was free to take possession in the autumn; the Valuation
Roll confirms that he had done so by the fourth quarter of 1919.[16] Henrietta and
Anastasia therefore had just over a month in which to arrange their move and
find temporary accommodation.

Although it had been indicated at the Sheriff Court hearing that Henrietta
would be able to take possession of Lambgill, Watermillock, on 25th March 1920,
she did not in fact do so on that date or for some time afterwards. The hardship
which the existing tenant of Lambgill would suffer on eviction, and which had
been alluded to at the hearing, may have had something to do with this. Whatever the reason, we do know that, during 1920, Henrietta was residing at a
farmhouse named Coatston, in the parish of Glencairn, about 10 miles north
west of Dumfries. This was some two miles beyond Dunscore, on the west bank
of the Cairn Water. The hamlet of Wallaceton, on the Moniaive road, was just
under half a mile away on the opposite bank of the river, which was forded at
this point. Between Coatston and the river ran the Cairn Valley Light Railway,
opened in 1905 by the Glasgow and South Western between Dumfries and
Moniaive. Crossford Station was about a mile to the north. The postal address
of Coatston was Auldgirth, a village about four and a half miles to the east in
Nithsdale.

This was a rich agricultural district of pasture and arable farm land, the light
sandy soil supporting chiefly oats, potatoes and turnips. Most of the scattered
population were employed as tenant farmers, farm workers, ploughmen, shepherds or dairymen. Coatston was one of the larger farms in the area. In 1920 it
was owned by the Highlands and Islands Educational Trust, and John Irving
was the tenant farmer.[17] The house may have been more spacious than Renwick
Bank, but it was certainly more remote, and it is not clear why Henrietta should
have chosen to live there. John Ramsay would however have been familiar with
accommodation in the Glencairn area, as his former home at Renwick Bank was
only a few miles to the south, and a farm would have provided space for
Henrietta's livestock and pets. There is no firm evidence that Anastasia lived
there also, but as she had previously shared a home with Henrietta and would
continue to do so in the future, it is reasonable to assume that she lived at
Coatston.

The next evidence of Henrietta's movements comes in a letter of 13th August
1920 which she sent to her cousin Beatrix in Exeter. It was written from the
Temperance Hotel, Dalbeattie, and begins as follows:

My Dear Bee,

> I have been down to Glenstocking on the Coast about 9 miles from
> here to get you the Grass of Parnassus. I hope they will arrive decent but
> my box is much too big. I have hardly been able to fill it enough to pre-
> vent rattling.

The letter was preserved in the album of wild flowers which Beatrix had been
given by her father, and with it the specimen of *Parnassia palustris* and the handwritten note: "Sent me by Etta from 'Glenstocking', on the coast of Solway Firth.
August 14th 1920".[18] The flower evidently made the journey from Dalbeattie to
Exeter safely and in one day. The Temperance Hotel was in Station Road,
Dalbeattie, and it can be assumed that Henrietta was staying there whilst on
holiday in Galloway, visiting the "special preserve of the grass of Parnassus" to
which she had referred in her newspaper article eight years earlier.

It is probable that Henrietta was living at Coatston when she inscribed in a
copy of the second edition of *Winchmore Hill: Memories of a Lost Village*:

> From the Author, Henrietta Cresswell
> "Memories are pleasant patterns woven from broken threads".

At New Year 1921, one of her neighbours gave this book to another, adding the
following inscription:

> With all my best wishes to you and I am sure our delightful neighbour's
> charming book will help us to find peaceful thoughts.

Later that year, Henrietta and Anastasia moved south across the Solway Firth
to another temporary home. This was at Skinburness, not far from the seaside
resort of Silloth, on the Cumberland coast. Their stay here was a short one, for
they appear just once on the Register of Electors for the parish of Holme Low
(Skinburness and Blitterlees Ward) — in autumn 1921. Their place of residence
is shown simply as "Skinburness", and they have left no trace of precisely where
they lived in this small community.

Skinburness would have satisfied Henrietta's liking for solitary places. It stood
alone on a flat, sandy peninsula, bordered on the south and east by creeks and
marshes, and on the north and west by the wide Solway estuary. There was a
large hotel, and a scattering of houses. The Long House, where Sir Walter Scott
stayed while he was writing *Redgauntlet*, overlooked a beach of pebble and sand
lapped by the waters of the estuary. The silence was broken only by the call of
birds from the sea and across the marshes. Distant views of the Galloway hills
and the coast of Dumfriesshire would have reminded the cousins of the home
they had reluctantly left behind.

Kelly's Directory of Cumberland for 1921 described Skinburness as "a pleasant village and sea-bathing place on the coast of the Solway Firth, near Grune

Point, 2½ miles north-by-east from the railway station at Silloth. It consists of several residences and lodging houses and two or three farms". It was the site of a once considerable town, which Edward I had used as a base for his operations against the Scots. In 1301 he made it a free borough and permitted the abbot of the nearby Cistercian monastery of Holme Cultram to hold a weekly market there. Soon after that the town was washed away by the sea, and only a small hamlet survived. The opening of the hotel as a health hydro in the late 19th century attracted some visitors, but even by 1920 the place was still quiet and unfrequented.

The area was a paradise for the bird lover and botanist. Curlews, oyster-catchers and lapwings inhabited the mudflats and saltmarshes, whilst herring-gulls and black-headed gulls swooped noisily across the waters of the estuary. The sand dunes, coastal grasslands and marshes supported a great variety of wild flowers: along the peninsula towards Grune Point were banks of golden gorse, sea pinks and wild roses; on the saltmarshes grew sea lavender, sea asters and thrift; on the inland peat mosses were found purple heather, bog plants and orchids.

Silloth, about two miles to the south, was a Victorian seaside resort of wide, cobbled streets, separated from the seafront by a broad greensward dotted with clusters of Scots pine. The grid pattern streets were lined with mid-Victorian terraces, the whole dominated by the granite spire of Christ Church, completed in 1870. Several hotels faced the seafront across the green. Adjoining the town was Silloth Dock, handling substantial trade with home and foreign ports, and nearby was the terminus of the North British branch line from Carlisle, 21 miles away. A wooden pier extended some 1,000 feet into the estuary, and a steamer sailed to and from Dublin twice weekly. The population of just over 2,000 was considerably expanded during the summer months with the arrival of holiday-makers. The mildly invigorating climate was "frequently recommended by the medical faculty as being specially beneficial to invalids and people of delicate health". As in Dumfries, longevity was claimed to be an outstanding feature of the locality.[19]

By the beginning of 1922 Henrietta and Anastasia had left Skinburness and arrived at Watermillock, on Ullswater. There they took up residence at Lambgill, their intended home on leaving Dumfries. The October 1920 Register of Electors shows the occupants of Lambgill as Atkinson and Eliza Anne Walker — Atkinson Walker was a local gardener. A year later the Walkers were living at Horrock Wood, a house closer to the lake shore, and Lambgill is not listed. In the April 1922 register Henrietta and Anastasia appear at Lambgill, but parish records, to which we shall return, confirm that they were living there in January 1922. The Walkers were no doubt the tenants whose difficulty in removing from Lambgill had caused the delay in Henrietta's possession of it.

Since Victorian times the scattered rural parish of Watermillock, on the north west shore of Ullswater about two miles from Pooley Bridge, had been dominated by several well established landowning families — the Marshalls of Hallsteads, the Bushes of Beauthorn, the Swinburns of Gowbarrow and the

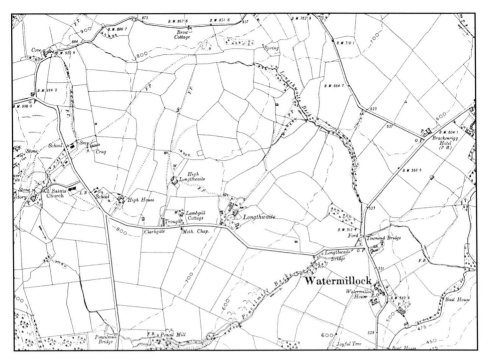

Watermillock, Ullswater. Lambgill (marked as Lambgill Cottage) lies to the east of All Saints Church, on the road to Longthwaite Bridge. Ullswater appears in the lower right-hand corner. The scattered nature of the parish, and the lack of an identifiable village centre, are evident from the map. The Watermillock mixed school referred to in the text is north of the church. From the 6 inch to the mile Ordnance Survey map, 1900.

Rumneys of Mellfell. Dr. Rumney, a 19th century owner of Mellfell, had three sisters who lived at Lambgill Cottage, as it was then called. The Marshalls and the Rumneys were heavily involved with educational provision in the parish throughout the 19th century: Thomas Rumney started a village school early in the century, and the Marshalls were benefactors of a new girls' school founded in 1832 and a boys' school in 1860. Miss Susan Rumney of Lambgill was schoolmistress of the girls' school from 1856 to 1892 — the last "well-to-do village lady" to run the school before the shift from middle-class philanthropy to a more professional system of education towards the end of the century. By the time Henrietta and Anastasia arrived, the boys' and girls' schools had merged to form the Watermillock Church of England Mixed and Infants Voluntary School, but some of the wealthy local landowners to whom the parish owed its well-being and prosperity were still in residence.[20]

In 1921, the population of the ecclesiastical parish of Watermillock was just 435. The Reverend Henry Paul Vivian Panton, whom we have met previously in Exeter, had been rector since 1919. In common with Chaucer's Parson, "wide was his parish, with houses far asunder". Watermillock had no recognisable village centre; isolated farmhouses and cottages were scattered amongst the lower fells, whilst the homes of landowning families were spread out along the lake shore. The landscape was one of farms, sheep pastures and wooded hillsides sloping down to the lake and backed by the steep contours of Little Mell Fell. The soil was clay and loam, and oats were the chief crop. The pastures were intersected by dry stone walls or, in places, by thick hedges, lines of trees and patches of deciduous woodland. From the rising ground there were wide views across Ullswater towards the fells on the south eastern shore. The parish was watered by several streams flowing into the lake — Pencilmill Beck, Longthwaite Beck and Ramps Beck. The well wooded lake shore was dotted with boat houses and jetties serving the larger properties standing near the water's edge.

The scenery was described as "delightfully picturesque and beautiful". Immediately to the west was Gowbarrow Park, an estate of 2,000 acres affording extensive views of the lake, and bordered by a deep ravine in which the stream cascaded over Aira Force, falling perpendicularly through a cleft in the rocks from a height of 70 feet. Nearby was Lyulph's Tower, an ivy-covered, castellated mansion, immortalised in Wordsworth's poem *The Somnambulist*. Ullswater, nine miles in length and a mile wide at its broadest part, owed its beauty to the configuration of the surrounding hills through which it followed a winding course in three distinct reaches. "In common with other lakes, situated amidst mountains, there is a replication of any loud sound that may be made. If a gun be discharged at Watermillock there is a loud reiterated noise like thunder, and two French horns produce the effect of a sweet concert."[21]

To naturalists the place had strong appeal. Red deer roamed over Gowbarrow, whilst foxes, otters, badgers and weasels made their homes in the surrounding countryside. Birds of the fells and mountains included buzzards, hawks and black grouse; curlews arrived early in March and stayed most of the year. On the lake there were many ducks, grebes, dab-chicks, sandpipers, herons and migrant geese. Wild flowers included mountain primrose, sundew, butterwort, saxifrage, bog asphodel, orchids and grass of Parnassus.[22] Winters could be severe and summers changeable; rain and low cloud sweeping across the fells could quickly give way to sparkling sunlight dancing on the lake and picking out the varying colours of the hillsides. In autumn the woodland became a profusion of gold and yellow, the bracken-covered fells a carpet of orange.

The church of All Saints, Watermillock, standing alone more than a mile from the lake shore and overlooked by Priest's Crag, had been completely rebuilt between 1881 and 1884. It consisted of chancel, nave, baptistery, north porch and a squat western tower surmounted by a diminutive spike. The walls were of red sandstone, the roof was of slate. Its oil-lit interior accommodated about 300 worshippers. At the time of the rebuilding, the ancient and overcrowded burial ground was doubled in size.[23] The rectory stood some 200 yards to the west, hidden among trees beneath the rocky slopes of Priest's Crag. Just south of the church the road forked; the right-hand turning descended across Pencilmill Beck to join the lakeside road above Hallsteads and the promontory of Skelly Neb; the left fork dropped more steeply towards the lake above Castlehows

All Saints Church, Watermillock, Ullswater, in 1992, surrounded by fields and fells. Henrietta and Anastasia Cresswell settled in this quiet Lake District parish in 1922.

Point. About a quarter of a mile from the road junction, near the point where the left-hand turning began its steep descent, stood the isolated dwelling known as Lambgill.

The house stood to the north of the road, at the end of a short, gated drive. On the opposite side of the road, in the corner of a field, was a tiny Wesleyan Methodist chapel built of wood with a slate roof. About 150 yards to the north of Lambgill stood the house and outbuildings of High Longthwaite Farm, accessed from the road at Clarkgate. To the west the ground rose steeply, but to the east there was an uninterrupted view across sloping fields to Ullswater and the fells beyond. The situation was altogether delightful; to Henrietta and Anastasia, now in their late sixties, it must have seemed an ideal retreat in which to spend their advancing years. It would surely have compensated amply for the loss of Nunholm House and the disturbances of the preceding two years.

The building date of Lambgill Cottage is uncertain. The plot which it occupied is shown on the Watermillock Inclosure Award of 1835. It is not listed in a local directory of 1847, but it does appear in 1858 as the home of a Mr. John Harrison. A construction date of *c.*1830 has been suggested; it shared with the nearby girls' school of 1832 a distinctive architectural feature in the form of a tall, round-headed window lighting the hall and staircase. By 1884 it had become the home of the Rumney sisters — Mary, Isabella and Susan, two of whom were still living there in 1901. Five years later it had been let as apartments, and

appears to have had a succession of tenants until the Cresswells took possession.[24]

Lambgill was never a farmhouse, nor was it large enough to have been the
home of a wealthy landowner. The white-fronted, two-storeyed, three-bay dwelling was set at an angle to the road, the drive approaching from the side and
giving access to a small yard at the rear containing a well. The front elevation
looked south east across a garden of lawns, trees and shrubs, at one corner of
which was a fountain. The ragstone walls of the house were unfaced at the rear.
The door and windows on the main frontage had chamfered stone surrounds
surmounted by angular drip moulds. The tall, round-headed window was at
the rear. The roof was of slate. The ground floor included an area of flag-stone
flooring, and the rooms were spacious enough to accommodate the furnishings
and household effects which the two cousins had accumulated. Among them
was a chair in turned woodwork made from a cherry tree which used to grow in
the garden of Barming Rectory, Kent, the home of Henrietta's great-grandfather
Mark Noble. The village carpenter there had fashioned it in the 1820s; it later
found its way to Winchmore Hill, where in 1890 John Cresswell was photographed seated in it; a century after it was made Henrietta was using it by her
bedroom fireside at Lambgill.[25]

*Front entrance to Lambgill, Watermillock, in 1992 — little changed since the Cresswells
lived there.*

The Hills Above

A life-long resident of Watermillock has offered a childhood recollection of the Misses Cresswell as "rather severe maiden ladies in long skirts". It is not hard to imagine the ageing spinsters enjoying the comfort of their home, tending their garden, walking the country lanes, and passing the time of day with other villagers. In a sense their life was sheltered, but the physical isolation, steep surroundings and harsh winter climate were challenging to the elderly.

Certainly the weather could be inhospitable. In January 1922 the log book of Watermillock Church of England School recorded heavy snowfalls, with deep drifts. On the 16th only eight children attended, and the assistant teacher, Miss Lancaster, was absent, "probably storm-bound". By the 18th conditions had worsened and the children were sent home at 12.30 pm "as some have so far to go". The inclement weather was accompanied by illness: between 6th and 20th February all schools in Cumberland were closed by an influenza epidemic. Notwithstanding these handicaps the children performed well; in May 1922 the diocesan inspector was able to report on "the happy demeanour and bright answering of the children in spite of very awkward teaching conditions, ill-health and consequent closures".

Each successive winter brought similar hardships. On a stormy day in February 1925 the children arrived at school very wet, "and are sitting round fire drying their clothes. Unable to follow timetable". In January 1926 the school was closed for a week by illness, and on 5th March the weather was "still very stormy....the drifts have been so deep and quite a blizzard blowing. After drying clothes and getting something warm to drink, the children went home". As early as 25th October that year there was again a "deep fall of snow....the chimney is smoking very badly today and there is no heat from the fires. Have had to allow the children to move about to get warm". During the winter that followed children were absent with colds, chickenpox, and ringworm on their necks and arms.[26]

When the weather was fine, however, the beautiful countryside and abundant plant and wild life afforded ample opportunity for the children to study the natural world. The school log book records excursions to nearby fields and fells to examine marsh plants, observe stream life, and identify wild flowers. Needless to say, such pleasures were enjoyed by Henrietta and Anastasia as well. In June 1922, for example, they were gathering wild flowers along the shores of Ullswater and beyond during a visit by Beatrix from Exeter; among the places noted are Watermillock, Gowbarrow, Matterdale, and "on the fell between Kirkstone and Ambleside". As to the whereabouts of one variety, *Geranium sylvaticum*, Beatrix has recorded "everywhere!".[27]

As at Dumfries, writing featured prominently among the cousins' indoor pursuits. During 1923 and 1924 Henrietta produced two contrasting essays which together demonstrate her affection for the past and her understanding of the present. The first is an account of what she calls her "great-grandmother's medley book". Although she does not say so, this almost certainly belonged to Sarah

Noble (née Pratchett), the wife of the Reverend Mark Noble, John Cresswell's maternal grandfather:

> Here it lies, on one of the shelves of the old Sheraton press; and its sides swell out with fatness; it is much too large for a bookcase, the back is of shiny red leather, and the covers grey boards, the pages coarse, drab-grained paper, but what wonders it contains! Prints and mezzotints, water-colour sketches, needlework pictures, illuminations on vellum, and fine etchings!

Among the book's contents was a sketch of the "old Parsonage" (presumably Barming) done by a relative, but few of the other items had family associations. There were early 19th century fashion plates, "coy maidens simpering and blushing, magnificent kilted Highlanders with mutton-chop whiskers....parsons cheek by jowl with Mendoza the prizefighter". Henrietta concludes that it would be a good idea "if the girl of today with time to spare were to start a medley book, on old-fashioned lines, for herself....half the charm lies in the infinite variety gathered together in love and friendship long, long ago".

The second essay, under the title "A Good Word for the Modern Girl", is altogether different. In contrast to her cousin Beatrix's disparaging remarks about contemporary females, Henrietta's piece is a broad-minded defence of the manners and behaviour of girls of the 1920s, which she contrasts with the stern superiority of some of their Victorian forebears. She castigates the "odious damsel" of Victorian fiction, standing upon her dignity and displaying nothing but arrogance to her inferiors. "Strange as it may seem these high and mighty young ladies really did exist, and were carefully trained to be stuck-up and overbearing." Henrietta challenges the belief that standards have fallen: "is not the pleasant spoken outdoor lass, who is hail-fellow well-met with all and sundry, in every way a greater ornament to her sex?". As the product of a strict, middle-class Victorian upbringing, Henrietta displays in her conclusion a refreshing independence of thought:

> If the girl of the present day does use over much slang, and is not so submissive to parental authority, she is at least natural and unaffected, strong in mind and in body, and infinitely more loving and self-sacrificing than the daughter who often could hardly "call her soul her own" under the stern system of hear and obey.[28]

Whilst living at Watermillock, both Henrietta and Anastasia wrote articles for *The Glasgow Herald*, a newspaper with which they no doubt had made contact when in Dumfries. As if to give further emphasis to her modern ideas, Henrietta contributed to the women's page of *The Glasgow Weekly Herald* of 4th April 1925 a piece about her short hair style, which we noted briefly in Chapter 5. Recalling the uncomfortable "knobby curl-papers" and tight plaits of her childhood, and the "granny-knot" of her twenties and thirties, she describes how, in middle age, she had her hair shingled: "a woman with short hair is better off than a man, as she does not need to shave. It is quick, clean, and to me more becoming than any other style, and made me look ten years younger". However, the fashion attracted mischievous remarks, such as "get yer 'air cut", and "when did you last come out of jail?", and once, whilst she was cycling in Annan, some children called out: "just look at that funny old man, riding in a woman's dress". Her most amusing experience was having to convince the guard of a train which she was boarding in Edinburgh that she was entitled to travel in a ladies-only compartment! That she felt pleasure rather than embarrassment in these situations was a mark of her independent spirit. Nonetheless, her contribution was anonymous, only a reference to "Auntie Winifred" (her paternal grandmother's pet name for her) providing a clue to the writer's identity.[29]

In their articles for "Women's Topics" in *The Glasgow Herald*, Henrietta and Anastasia often wrote over the pseudonyms Winifred Cheslyn and Charlotte Winchmore, the significance of which would of course have been completely lost on their Scottish readers. The subjects of their articles were mainly domestic or historical, reflecting their own knowledge and experience. During 1925, for example, Henrietta explained to her readers the finer points of chicken rearing, the advantages of breeding ducks, and the culinary uses of stinging nettles. In the same year Anastasia presented some aspects of the history of cradles, and dealt with irritating excesses in "domestic economy" — securing parcels with old pieces of tied-up string, writing letters on odd scraps of paper, and re-using candle-ends welded together. Her discussion of the latter topic, whilst giving the reader no indication of her place of residence, reveals to us that Lambgill was still at least partly dependent on candle light: "I often err in this way myself, but in a gasless country house it is very trying when the wick faints away and leaves one suddenly in the dark". This article begins with a reference to smooth, rounded stones picked up on the "wonderful pebble beach" below the Long House at Skinburness.[30]

With each move they made, the cousins kept alive memories of former homes through their writing and personal contacts — the Solway, Dumfries, and still, in the mid-1920s, Winchmore Hill. Henrietta's fondness for her childhood home found expression in later years through her friendship with Arthur Willis, a well known resident of Winchmore Hill. Three years younger than Henrietta, he came to live in the district in 1900 and took an active part in local affairs — as the founder of Winchmore Hill Ratepayers' Association, as a member and later chairman of the Southgate Urban District Council, and as a manager of St. Paul's School, Winchmore Hill. He was a Lieutenant-Colonel in the 1st Battalion Middlesex Volunteer Regiment, and became a Justice of the Peace for Middlesex. After he ceased serving on the urban district council he devoted much of his time to the study of local history; he valued highly the writing of Henrietta Cresswell, corresponded with her frequently, and met her from time to time during the 1920s when she revisited the district. He contributed many articles to *The Palmers Green and Southgate Gazette* under the pen names "Topical" and "Memorabilia", popularising Henrietta's work and her father's paintings and drawings. His bold and characteristic handwriting appeared in many documents of local interest, including the surviving transcript of the *Liber Cresswellii*. It is to Arthur Willis that we owe a good deal of our knowledge of the Cresswells and their work.[31]

Arthur Willis was proud of his friendship with Henrietta Cresswell, referring to "our happy chats about the district" and, with modesty, enlarging upon her recollections. In his late seventies he wrote:

> To add to, to amplify, and where necessary to clarify these records, is to me one of the delightful occupations of the advanced eventide of life. I cannot pretend to the pictorial skill of Dr. John Cresswell and his daughter, nor to the latter's much earlier personal knowledge of the district than mine, nor to her talented method of recording it.

His articles in *The Palmers Green and Southgate Gazette* sometimes quoted at length correspondence he had received from her. On 21st December 1927, for example, she wrote him a letter about the location of the Barrow Well at Winchmore Hill, in which she passed on information obtained from her father and demonstrated her own clear recollection of the features of the site. On other occasions Arthur Willis referred to memoranda he had made of conversations held with Henrietta about what he liked to call "local lore". These were still taking place as late as 1929, indicating that her occasional visits to Winchmore Hill continued throughout the 1920s.[32] It will be remembered, of course, that she still owned property in Station Road, Winchmore Hill.

Back in 1911, whilst at Nunholm House, Henrietta would no doubt have heard news of an interesting discovery made in Hedge Lane, Palmers Green. Workmen excavating a gravel pit unearthed some mammoth-bones, fossilised wood, and stones, believed to have been deposited there during the ice age. The objects were put on public display and aroused much curiosity, prompting a proposal that they should form the nucleus of a local museum. The cause was taken up by Arthur Willis, and other items were donated. Following an exhibition in 1923 the collection grew further, and two years later space was set aside at Broomfield House, Palmers Green, for a permanent display. This was formally opened as the Southgate Local Museum on 4th July 1925.[33] A week before the opening, Henrietta Cresswell donated to the museum a copy of the second edition of *Winchmore Hill: Memories of a Lost Village*, in a superior binding; inside was pasted a note in her own handwriting:

> Presented to the Southgate Local Museum by the Author, hoping that many interesting records may be preserved in it.

The note was written at Lambgill and dated 26th June 1925.

Among the "many interesting records" secured for the museum were over 200 drawings and watercolours, mostly of the Winchmore Hill area, executed by John Cresswell and described in Chapter 6. Acquisition of the collection began in 1924, when, at the suggestion of Arthur Willis, the Southgate Urban District Council asked Henrietta Cresswell "if she had amongst her father's papers any sketches which would be useful to the Museum". In response she donated 17 small drawings of Winchmore Hill. Further pictures were presented over the next five years, some by Arthur Willis, who had been given them by Henrietta. Among the latter were John Cresswell's earliest recorded watercolour, of Greenwich Park, and his painting of Trois Vase House, illustrated on page 60 and the front cover. By one means or another, the museum acquired most if not all of John Cresswell's drawings and paintings, thereby ensuring their preservation close to the district which they chiefly portrayed. Some of the pictures were framed and put on public display, but most were arranged in portfolios for inspection by visitors on request. In 1927, Mr. W.H. Pratt and Mr. E.J. Finch, two local residents who had taken a keen interest in the museum, were appointed honorary curators. Mr. Pratt described the Cresswell pictures as one of the finest collections of paintings and drawings of one small district anywhere in London: "I look upon the pictures as the chief things in our Museum". Mr. Owen Roberts, a local historian and former councillor, later said that "too much praise cannot be given to the two curators....and to Colonel Willis, JP, to whom the Borough is greatly indebted for securing the fine collection of....watercolours, pencil and crayon drawings made by the late Dr. John Cresswell". Arthur Willis also gave the museum some etchings made of pencil sketches by John Cresswell, the originals of which were too faded for permanent preservation. Amongst these were studies of riflemen at the Tottenham Butts, first drawn by John Cresswell in about 1861 during his service with the Middlesex Rifle Volunteers. In 1928 Henrietta made a gift of firearms to the museum, when she presented a pair of carriage pistols, once the property of her great-great-grandfather Henry Whitfield, Vicar of Bedfont, and then of her great-grandfather Richard Cheslyn Cresswell. Writing to her cousin Beatrix she said: "I have given....my Carriage Pistols to the museum. They were very perfect with powder flask, bullets, ram-rod etc. and were handsomely chased". Richard Cheslyn Cresswell always took the weapons in his carriage when he travelled across Hounslow Heath to visit his father-in-law at Bedfont.[34]

Back in Watermillock, Anastasia had been devoting some of her time to the running of the parish church. She was elected a member of the Parochial Church Council in January 1922, soon after her arrival in the village. Her first recorded contribution to its deliberations was in April 1923, when she proposed that a water supply should be laid from the main near the church gate to a stand pipe and tap at the church, "owing to the present great inconvenience of always having to carry water from the nearest house for every requirement". The proposal was adopted, but the work was not completed until October 1924. In January 1924 she and the rector's wife, Mrs. Panton, were given the job of getting the white altar frontal cleaned, and this was done by Easter. Her efficiency was rewarded with a further task — as a member of a committee deputed to acquire new curtains for the chancel, the existing ones being "very moth and mouse eaten". This matter took two years to bring to a conclusion; at Easter 1926 thanks were expressed for blue sanctuary curtains which had been presented to the church, the material having been made up by Mrs. Panton and Miss A. Cresswell. A year earlier, Anastasia "was accorded a most hearty vote of thanks for the beautiful piece of lace she had made and presented to the church for the super frontal". At the same meeting she was elected a parish representative to the Ruridecanal Conference, a responsibility which she took on again the following year.

Such was the routine of church affairs in which Anastasia involved herself — unremarkable maybe, but important to the smooth running of a rural parish. The brief minutes of the Parochial Church Council meeting held on 9th December 1925 hint at her loyalty in trying circumstances:

> A meeting was held in the School at 7.30 pm. It was a wet and stormy night and only the Rev. P.V. and Mrs. Panton, Miss Cresswell, [and] Mr. E.W. Mounsey attended. After the minutes of the previous meeting had been read and approved, there was no business on the agenda and not enough members present to make a quorum so the meeting broke up.

We can visualise the 70-year-old Anastasia battling her way through wind and rain along the half mile of exposed country road from Lambgill to the village school to fulfil her duty to the parish, only to re-emerge into the storm a few minutes later to face the journey home.

The last significant business in which Anastasia appears to have been involved as a member of the Parochial Church Council was a discussion of "the value of the envelope system for increasing the church collections by the contributions of those who cannot attend regularly". In April 1926 she recommended the system, telling the meeting "how well it worked in Toronto". This was presumably based on information from her Canadian relatives, if not on her own knowledge of the country. A year later, at the Easter vestry meeting on 18th April 1927, "much regret was expressed at Miss Cresswell's absence through illness, as her kindly aid had been much appreciated". Less than three months later, on Friday 8th July 1927, Anastasia died at Lambgill at the age of 72. She was buried two days afterwards in the peaceful, tree-shaded churchyard of All Saints, Watermillock, the burial service being conducted by the rector, Henry Panton. Her grave was marked by a granite cross on whose plinth a simple inscription recorded her full name, age and date of death. The news of her death was received with sorrow by members of the Parochial Church Council.[35] Charlotte Mary Anastasia Cresswell, born the daughter of a country clergyman in distant Devonshire, had been a loving friend and companion to her cousin Henrietta for most of her life — first during her frequent visits to Winchmore Hill, then in their shared homes at Dumfries, Skinburness and Watermillock. Her passing must have been a sad loss to her cousin. Unlike Henrietta, she was not a woman of wealth; when probate was granted in October 1927 her effects were valued at £24.

Although Henrietta attended Watermillock Church, she did not take the ac-

tive part in parish affairs that her cousin had done, and life without Anastasia
was lonely. Gardening, botany and writing were her chief pleasures. She continued to correspond with her cousin Beatrix in Exeter, signing herself "ever your
affectionate cousin". In a letter dated 3rd July 1928 she wrote: "My Dear Bee,
Your letter this morning was most interesting and as I am quiet and alone I will
answer some of it tonight....". She then deals with aspects of family history, and
folklore from Kent. There is also reference to a proposed long weekend in Dumfries, from 6th to 9th July:

> I am actually going to Dumfries from Friday to Monday to stay with Miss
> Maitland at 3 Albany, half way between Nunholm and the Town. I have
> not been there for seven years. I shall be at St. John's for Sunday. Albany is
> just above the Nith with a lovely view over the river to the Galloway
> hills....Miss Maitland is older than I am — she calls herself "nearly 80".
> She and Miss Copland built the Episcopal Church of St. Margaret's New
> Galloway between them. They were devoted first cousins. Miss Copland....
> owned nearly all Dalbeattie.

This provides evidence of Henrietta's continuing association with Dumfries and
with St. John's Episcopal Church there. On the day of her letter she had done
two hours' work in the kitchen garden at Lambgill and was tired: "it is nearly 11
and I must go to bed. I had to get a candle to finish writing this page but it was
not dark enough to be worth lighting the Aladdin lamp".[36]

For over a year Henrietta lived without a companion at Lambgill, but by the
spring of 1929 she had been joined there by her second cousin Margaret Jennings,
one of two surviving daughters of Anastasia's late sister Christiana. Margaret
was then 42 and unmarried; it will be recalled that Henrietta had been given a
special responsibility for her care, and we may assume that she had supported
her financially. Margaret was now able to reciprocate by offering Henrietta companionship in her old age.[37]

Two years later, on 13th March 1931, Henry Paul Vivian Panton, Rector of
Watermillock, died at the age of 68. The village school was closed for the after-
noon of his funeral on 17th March. He was buried in the churchyard close to
Anastasia Cresswell, and a simple stone cross was erected in his memory. As
Rector of St. Edmund's, Exeter, between 1891 and 1908, he had been known to
Anastasia's sister, Beatrix. He had then served as Vicar of Dunton Bassett, near
Rugby, moving to Watermillock in 1919.[38] This was the year in which Henrietta
originally purchased Lambgill, and it would be interesting to know whether her
choice of home was in any way influenced by the arrival of a priest who was
already known to the family.

Throughout the spring and summer of 1931 Henrietta continued to enjoy the
peace of her country home, supported by Margaret Jennings. The weeks were
marked out by Sunday churchgoing, and on fine days by walks round her lovely
garden. At the age of 76 she was unable to travel far, and her life was made up of
homely pleasures. She was sustained by her memories, formed into "pleasant

Watermillock churchyard, photographed in 1992. The Celtic cross on the left marks the grave of Charlotte Mary Anastasia Cresswell, who died in July 1927. The Latin cross on the right marks the grave of Henry Paul Vivian Panton, Rector of Watermillock, who died in March 1931. Between them lies Henrietta Cresswell, buried in October 1931. Her grave plot has remained unmarked.

patterns woven from broken threads". Autumn came, the bracken on Little Mell Fell turned to orange, the trees below Priest's Crag to yellow and gold. St. Luke's Day, 18th October, was a Sunday, and Henrietta attended Morning Prayer at 10.45. The sermon was preached on a text from St. Luke, Chapter 4, Verse 21 — "And he began to say unto them, This day is this scripture fulfilled in your ears". On returning to Lambgill Henrietta felt too tired for her customary walk in the garden, and after taking lunch retired to her bed. Over the next day or so her condition weakened, and at half past two in the afternoon on Tuesday 20th October, with Margaret Jennings at her bedside, she expired peacefully.[39]

Henrietta was buried on the following Friday, 23rd October, in Watermillock churchyard. The Reverend W.E. Hearn, Vicar of Matterdale, conducted the service. She was laid to rest between her cousin Anastasia and the Reverend Henry Panton, at the east end of the churchyard close to the boundary wall.[40] It would be difficult to imagine a more peaceful setting: on one side the ground rose steeply towards bracken-covered fells; on the other, wooded pastures sloped gently away towards distant hills. From the overhanging trees, withered autumn leaves fluttered to earth, and soon a brown mantle covered the last of the Cresswells of Winchmore Hill.

No headstone was erected over Henrietta's grave, and to this day the plot remains unmarked, its position identified only on the graveyard plan kept in the parish. Her will is silent on the matter, simply bequeathing all her property, including Lambgill, to Margaret Jennings. Her effects were valued at £2,300 for probate, so there was no financial reason for the absence of a memorial. It may have been her wish that she should not be commemorated in stone, preferring to be remembered by her writing and her art. A poem entitled *The Other Side*, which she wrote about five years before her death, expresses better than any epitaph the determination and faith which inspired her whole life:

> Effort is never lost, effort for right,
> The man who tries his best with all his might
> Gains in himself, yet more of strength and power,
> By overcoming self, from hour to hour.
> We must go up or down, we cannot rest,
> Sink to decay, or climb to reach the best;
> And though each summit shows us hills above,
> Our patience and our faithfulness to prove;
> We know full well, some hill will be the last,
> And rest must come when that is safely past.
> Some day we shall across the sombre tide
> With joy behold that glorious Other Side.
> God grant that, held aloft by faith and prayer,
> Our souls at last may land in safety there.[41]

During her last summer, *The Palmers Green and Southgate Gazette* published two stories by Henrietta about Winchmore Hill in the time of Charles Lamb. In them she combined her memories of the district with her knowledge of the essayist's life and her own fertile imagination. Given her earlier explanation of where the original Udall's shop had stood in Winchmore Hill (published in *The Recorder* on 13th February 1913 and noted in Chapter 8), she is cavalier with her local history in the first story, describing a visit by Charles and Mary Lamb in 1828 to the premises which the Udalls did not occupy until the 1840s. It is all the more surprising, therefore, that in a footnote to the story she claims that the description of Udall's shop is accurate. That apart, the story is yet another example of her elegant prose, guiding the reader effortlessly through the minutiae of a vanished world. It is also of interest in basing one of Mrs. Udall's daughters on Henrietta's aunt Sarah, who would have been 11 years of age in 1828 but who did not of course know Winchmore Hill at that time. She is identified as the child who before the age of eight "had made a whole set of shirts for her grandfather with hemstitched cambric frills!" — an achievement of Sarah Cresswell's to which Henrietta refers in the *Liber Cresswellii*.[42]

In her second story, Henrietta accompanies Charles and Mary Lamb in her imagination on a springtime walk from Enfield to Winchmore Hill, to visit their friend Tom Hood at Rose Cottage. Her description of the sights and sounds of the intervening countryside is delightful — standing comparison with anything in *Winchmore Hill: Memories of a Lost Village*.[43] Publication of this story and its predecessor brought forth from a Wood Green reader a highly appreciative letter which Henrietta treasured, and which was reproduced, in part, in *The Palmers Green and Southgate Gazette* some years later. The reader had previously lived in Winchmore Hill, and knew intimately the places featured in the stories. The letter to Henrietta concludes:

> Excuse my rambling letter please. I am writing chiefly to express my appreciation of your articles, and to show you how they have touched a sympathetic chord in my memory and to thank you for them. I am on the look out for more.[44]

Sadly, only one more contribution by Henrietta Cresswell was to appear in the columns of *The Gazette* — the posthumously published story of her childhood entitled "What Winifred Saw in the Twilight: A Winchmore Hill Phantasy of Seventy Years Ago". Referred to in Chapter 4 of this narrative, it appeared in the *The Gazette* on New Year's Day, 1932, with the editorial postscript:

> A melancholy interest attaches to the foregoing because it was the last story of Winchmore Hill which Miss Cresswell wrote, and since it was set up in type to await a favourable opportunity for publishing in our columns, Miss Cresswell....has passed away.

Its publication was a fitting tribute to an author whose affection for the Victorian village of Winchmore Hill remained undimmed throughout her life.

After Henrietta's death, Margaret Jennings continued to live at Lambgill. Among the property she inherited from her second cousin was the leasehold of the two semi-detached houses in Station Road, Winchmore Hill, which Henrietta had owned since 1893.[45] From these and other assets bequeathed to her she derived a sufficient income. In 1936, photographs were taken of all 114 families living in the parish of Watermillock at the time. They were placed in two albums and presented to Mr. E.O. Bolton in recognition of his 21 years' service as churchwarden. Among those photographed was Margaret Jennings, then aged 48, standing at the front door of Lambgill in a long, heavy overcoat, her straight hair parted to one side. In her arms she holds a white Persian cat, whilst a small dog stands at her feet. A rustic trellis frames the doorway, and the tall arched window lighting the hall and staircase is visible within. A half-gate of wood and chicken-wire is partly closed across the doorway, apparently serving as a barrier to animals.[46] As the years went by, Miss Jennings became increasingly reclusive, and by the outbreak of war in 1939 she was regarded in the village as a person of some eccentricity. During the war she is said to have offered shelter to a Belgian priest.[47]

Margaret Jennings, second cousin to Henrietta Cresswell, at the front door of Lambgill, Watermillock, in 1936. She continued to live alone in the house which she had shared with Henrietta, becoming increasingly reclusive as the years passed.

Assiduous Antiquary

With the death of Anastasia Cresswell in 1927, her sister Beatrix was now the sole survivor of the children of the late Reverend Richard Cresswell. Since the Great War she had continued her historical studies in Exeter, publishing further works from time to time. From 1918 she began to write occasional poems on historical themes, and these appeared in *The Devonian Year Book* over the next decade. First came *The Vision of Sir Walter Raleigh*, in 1919:

> The moonlight path across the tide
> To Ocean's furthest verge extends,
> A lad who wanders by its side
> Would fain discover where it ends:
> Surely upon some Golden Shore
> A daring mariner might know
> There lies the Realm of mystic lore,
> The Faerie Eldorado.

The idea is developed in four more stanzas. Two years later came *The Blind Earl's Vision*, in 10 stanzas. It tells the story of Edward Courtenay, third Earl of Devon, who became blind in old age. He lived at Tiverton Castle from 1345 until his death in 1419, and in his mind's eye sees the banner bearing the family arms flying proudly above the battlements:

> I hear the banner broad unrolled:
> It flutters overhead;
> My fancy paints the field of gold
> Streaming in sunshine, fold on fold,
> And the three torteaux red.

In a footnote, Beatrix interprets the heraldic devices for her readers. *A Legend of Lundy* was published in 1925. The theme of its nine verses is the granting of Lundy to the Knights Templar by King John on condition that they drive out the piratical Mariscoe family who were living on this inhospitable island: "Out of the strife of angry tides/It rose, grim rock and bare/With caverned depths and frowning sides/Defiant to the air". The last poem in this series appeared in *The Devonian Year Book* in 1927. In six verses it recounts the legend of "Old Squire Fry" of Yarty, in the East Devon parish of Membury. Robert Fry was born in 1666, became High Sheriff of Devon in 1724, and died in 1726. Tradition held that when the mourners returned from his funeral at Membury they found the squire sitting in his chair waiting for them:

> Gentle and simple from far and near
> Were asked to taste of the funeral cheer,
> And when they returned they found him there

> Beside the hearth in his leathern chair,
> With a glass of port and a wink in his eye,
> "You're late getting back," quoth old Squire Fry.

In the poem, Beatrix puts his age at "four-score and ten", but as a contributor to the transactions of the Devonshire Association later pointed out, this added some 30 years to his real age.[48]

For Beatrix, the poems formed a light-hearted diversion from what continued to be a serious literary output, not all of which was published. Between 1919 and 1925 she completed her notes on Devonshire churches, a massive project begun in 1902. In addition to the works already published — on churches in Exeter and the Deanery of Kenn — she produced no fewer than 24 typescript volumes, liberally illustrated with prints, photographs and drawings, some of the latter executed by her niece Clarice. In her general introduction she wrote:

> The history of England is written in her parish churches. For more than a thousand years they have garnered up the life of the past....it is in an endeavour to reconstruct their story [in Devon] that these notes have been written. They not only represent personal visits, often repeated, to every church, but also the collecting of information from every possible source....

The text, estimated to run to over a million words, was reproduced in a curious, rounded typescript on heavy paper — typically 300 sheets to each quarto volume. In 1926 Beatrix presented all the typed volumes to the Exeter City Library, where they were put into permanent binding to form part of the reference collection. The manuscript notes, even more extensive than the typescript, were retained by the author. The undertaking no doubt had a punishing effect on her typewriter, for in 1927 she recorded against some other typing in her collection: "done with the new 'Corona'".[49]

Completion of the "Church Notes" required a keenness of observation, clarity of thought, and purposefulness which were hallmarks of Beatrix's character. In 1927 these attributes, among others, were referred to in an analysis of her handwriting which she obtained from an Essex graphologist:

> Your writing denotes a rather phlegmatic temperament, though when you have a piece of work to do, or some duty, you do it with a dogged determination to finish it. You are unselfish and will often do a kind action for a friend or relation....you have much quickness of observation and a clear mind. In society you are at "home", though seldom demonstrative and in your circle you are all life and brightness. You are refined in your tastes and dislike anything low or vulgar.

To this Beatrix has added: "the character from handwriting is very good".[50]

Also in 1927 came Beatrix's next published work, a slender volume entitled *Rambles in Old Exeter*. She introduces it as neither a history nor a guide book, but as "the wanderings of one familiar with an old city, and loving it; who describes scenes, events, and localities in discursive fashion; now and then loitering to mention something irrelevant, suggested by the surroundings". The eight chapters concentrate on Exeter within the city walls, and are illustrated with drawings, engravings and photographs. The publishers were James G. Commin of High Street, Exeter. The same publishers were responsible for a 64-page volume by Beatrix which appeared in 1929 — *The Mavericks of Devonshire and Massachusetts*. Written at the request of Mr. Robert van W. Maverick, who paid for its publication, the book is a genealogical work tracing the history of his family, who were well established in Devon in the 16th century. The Reverend John Maverick left England in 1630 to become one of the founders of Massachusetts; his descendant Samuel Maverick, a 19th century cattle rancher in Texas, was notorious for not branding his livestock, thereby giving his surname to the English language. The book is based on original documents, wills and inventories.

The year 1930 saw publication of Beatrix's *Short History of the Worshipful Company of Weavers, Fullers and Shearmen of the City and County of Exeter*. This scholarly work was compiled chiefly from the company's minute books and documents. Most of the documents were in Latin, and Beatrix acknowledges the help of a kind, anonymous friend who transcribed and translated them for her — "a task beyond the writer's powers". The Weavers, Fullers and Shearmen were the only Exeter craft guild to have survived, and were probably always the largest and most important. The 134-page volume was published by William Pollard and Company of Exeter.

Beatrix's last substantial published work appeared in 1932 — *A Book of Devonshire Parsons*. In it she gathers together stories of the county's clergy from the middle ages to the 19th century. Her principal aim was to "rescue from oblivion" some of the lesser known Devonshire clerics, though a few well known names appear too. She confronts the bewilderment felt by priests and people during the upheavals of the Reformation, and there is a chapter on "The Sufferings of the Clergy", in which she describes hardships endured by many West Country clerics, some of whom were dispossessed of their livings. This chapter concludes with an account of William Yeo, of Wolborough, Newton Abbot, who was ejected from his curacy in 1662 for nonconformity. Thereafter he preached to his flock in the open air, often within the shelter of nearby Bradley Woods: "a deep hollow with slippery sides, attained by crossing the dancing stream....nature has spread mossy cushions on the stones, the trees roof it overhead; the amphitheatre seems specially formed for a place of worship, where the birds are choristers". Beatrix's description of the place carries strong echoes of the leafy goyle in which the little King Pepito had been found, all those years ago, in her very first book. *A Book of Devonshire Parsons*, published by Heath Cranton, was reviewed in *The Times Literary Supplement* on 5th May 1932. It was considered a "pleasant book....giving a fairly solid picture of parish life, difficulties and loyalties at various epochs, and the author is an interpreter of understanding". The only illustration in the book is a frontispiece drawing by the author's niece Clarice of the "Parson and Clerk" rocks at Teignmouth. It may well have been executed some years earlier, for by the time *A Book of Devonshire Parsons* was published Clarice was living far, far away.

Throughout this period, Beatrix remained active in the affairs of the Devonshire Association, continuing to serve as a member of its council for a few more years. The association's transactions contain numerous references to her work. In 1934 she was appointed to the Church Records Committee, but retired as a full member of the council in the following year. At the annual meeting held at Barnstaple in 1938 she was elected a vice-president, and played a prominent part in the proceedings on that occasion. After luncheon on 22nd June she accompanied members on a motor-coach excursion, first to Marwood, where she conducted them round the church, then to Braunton, where she recounted the legend of St. Brannock, the Celtic missionary to whom the church is dedicated, and drew attention to the font, bench-ends, a carved roof-boss and a palimpsest brass. The following morning she read a paper on Umberleigh Chapel, which used to stand some seven miles south of Barnstaple but had entirely disappeared. Once the property of the Abbess of the Holy Trinity, Caen, the chapel had a succession of female owners who came to be known as the "Ladies of Umberleigh". Its long and complex history was traced by Beatrix with close attention to detail, culminating in its suppression in the 16th century. During the afternoon of the 23rd, Beatrix showed members of the association round Tawstock Church, and then they visited Atherington Church to see ancient recumbent effigies removed from Umberleigh Chapel when it was dismantled. Tea was taken at the Rising Sun at Umberleigh.[51] Beatrix was now 76 years of age, but her energy and enthusiasm for historical research and archaeological investigation remained prodigious.

Hand in hand with her historical studies went her continued interest in botany. When her father died in 1882, his collection of algae, mosses and botanical drawings had passed to her brother Richard Henry, who in turn bequeathed it to his daughter Clarice. Following Richard Henry's death in 1925, Beatrix persuaded Clarice to donate the collection to the Royal Albert Memorial Museum, Exeter, where it has found a permanent home. The donation was made on 4th August 1925, after which all the specimens and drawings were remounted and classified by Miss Edith Aviolet, an assistant curator of the museum.[52] The Cresswell Collection of algae was listed in the 21st Botany Report of the Devonshire Association in 1929. Three years later, the association's 24th Botany Report included details submitted by Beatrix of various flora in the Torquay and Plymouth areas. She continued to observe and collect wild flowers throughout the 1930s. The last item to be entered in her father's 1881 album of wild flowers was placed there by Beatrix in 1939 — a dwarf mallow found at Hollacombe, North Devon, on 20th September. Against it she wrote: "I have never gathered it in Devon before".[53]

The preservation of that small flower marked the end of Beatrix's last summer. Following the outbreak of war she remained at 23 Wonford Road, Exeter, reaching her 78th birthday on 14th January 1940. Not long afterwards she was taken ill, and died peacefully at her home on Friday 16th February. The funeral took place in Exeter Cathedral at 1.45 pm the following Monday, the Bishop of Crediton officiating. Many friends from the city, including members of the Devonshire Association, were present. She was buried in the Higher Cemetery at Exeter. Reporting her death, *The Western Mail and News* described her as "one of the foremost antiquaries and church historians in the West of England". Her obituary in the transactions of the Devonshire Association referred to "her ability to present her matter for the consideration of the antiquarian without diminishing the interest of the less learned". She was an assiduous attender at the meetings of the association, "where her well known presence and apposite comments will be greatly missed". Her obituarist in *Devon and Cornwall Notes and Queries* remarked upon her "genial personality", and mentioned that shortly before her death she had submitted for publication a manuscript of *The Ladies of Umberleigh*; unfortunately there was little prospect of this appearing in print "in the near future" owing to lack of funds.[54]

In her will, made in 1918, she bequeathed her books, pictures, maps and manuscripts (including her handwritten "Church Notes") to Exeter City Library, which was also to benefit from a pecuniary legacy known as the Cresswell Bequest: "apart from the great love and interest I feel for the City and County of Exeter, I select the Committee of Management of the Exeter City Library in preference to any other Literary body, Institution, or Society in the County because being a body in charge of a public Institution I anticipate that it will continue for all time". The interest from the bequest was to be used to defray the cost of publishing her remaining "Notes on the Churches in the Rural Deaneries of Devon" in bound volumes similar to her *Exeter Churches*, and very precise instructions were given in the will as to the form of publication. Any surplus was to be used for printing documents, manuscripts or other works associated with the history of Devon, and for purchasing historical reference books. Her wishes were also expressed in a letter to the Library Committee: "it is my earnest hope that you should, Sirs, accept my bequest, and carry out the above mentioned conditions and suggestions....so that in a small measure I may know that where my heart is, there my treasure lies also".[55]

The bequest was accepted, but Beatrix's wishes were never carried out as intended. We will now move forward in time for a moment to discover why. When Beatrix's "Church Notes" came to be examined after the war, it was clear that extensive editorial work would be necessary to prepare them for publication. Alleging that her notes were marred by many inaccuracies, a member of the Library Committee considered the writing to be "of a pleasant and mildly interesting character", but to contain "antiquarian matter of no great moment". In a letter to Beatrix's niece Clarice in 1948, the Town Clerk tactfully explained that, for financial reasons, it would be impossible to carry out the terms of the bequest. Clarice's initial response was cool:

> I was always on very good terms with my Aunt, and her will was discussed by both of us in every detail in 1918. She asked me, as residuary

> legatee, to make the sacrifice of £1,000 *for the publication of her Deaneries*, and of course I at once assented willingly.

After further correspondence, however, Clarice agreed that income from the bequest could be devoted to the creation of a students' room at the library or to the purchase of rare books.

The matter was debated throughout 1949; in February 1950 Clarice wrote to the Town Clerk expressing impatience that, 10 years after her aunt's death, the legacy had not been used. Five years later she called at the library to see what had been done, and afterwards the Town Clerk wrote: "I confirm that it is intended in the restoration of the City Library to furnish and equip a Students' Room which will be called 'The Cresswell Room'". By this time the real value of the bequest had diminished to a point at which only limited furnishing and equipment could be afforded; the Cresswell Room did not materialise, and remaining funds were eventually absorbed into general library expenditure.[56] However, Beatrix Cresswell's lasting memorial is the large collection of books and manuscripts which she bequeathed to the library, and which are still in frequent use. Despite lingering doubts over the accuracy of some of her research, the collection represents a wide ranging and immensely detailed coverage of Devonshire's ecclesiastical, architectural and genealogical history, and a valuable resource for any student working in these areas.

In addition to the books and manuscripts, the Exeter City Library and the Royal Albert Memorial Museum received a collection of objects from Beatrix Cresswell's executors in 1940. Among them were several albums of botanical drawings mentioned in Chapters 4 and 5 of this narrative, and Henrietta Noble's album of paintings and sketches described in Chapter 6. The museum was given a substantial collection of costumes, toys and accessories, and bird and mammal specimens from North America. The latter were evidently obtained by Beatrix in Canada, and subsequently stuffed and mounted.[57] Two years after her death, her beloved city of Exeter was devastated in the blitz of May 1942; it is some consolation that she was spared this tragedy, and that, apart from a few items in the City Librarian's room, her donations to the library and museum escaped undamaged.[58]

Beatrix Feodore Clara Augusta Grace Cresswell was the last of her generation. There were now no surviving children of Richard Cresswell of Teignmouth, nor of his brother John Cresswell of Winchmore Hill. The next generation was represented only by Clarice Mercedes Cresswell and her cousins Mary and Margaret Jennings. So far as this branch of the ancient Northumberland family was concerned, Clarice was alone in carrying the name Cresswell into the post-war years.

The Passing of Eld

After her father's death in 1925, Clarice Cresswell continued to live at 145 Holland Road, Kensington. Her love of Classical antiquity, already evident in her writing, grew yet more intense. Her imagination was stirred by visions of Imperial Rome and its greatness. The social and economic recovery of modern Italy under the leadership of Benito Mussolini seemed to afford a parallel with the flourishing of ancient Rome under its strongest emperors. Clarice watched with growing admiration as *Il Duce* established firm political rule from the time of his appointment as Prime Minister in 1922 to the creation of a full Fascist government in 1928–9. As with others of her generation, Clarice's idealism closed her mind to the perils of dictatorship; years later she still spoke of Mussolini in hushed reverence as "the great man".[59]

Early in 1931 Clarice was staying in Rome. She wrote to her aunt Beatrix from the Albergo d'Lughetterra, referring to a gift which she had sent her aunt, but which had been damaged in the post: "tomorrow I will go round to the shop and pour the vials of my wrath on whoever addressed it....was the donkey much damaged, or could you bend his leg straight? Yes, of course it is absolutely the genuine Italian article — whatever may be its defects from the art point of view!". She goes on to describe the ceremony of the lambs, which took place at the church of Sant'Agnese fuori le Mura on the feast day of St. Agnes, 21st January. Wool from the lambs blessed on this occasion is used to make the Papal pallium. Enclosing a newspaper cutting about the event, she says to Beatrix "you would have loved the ceremony". She then refers to a flat in the Piazza di Spagna in which she is interested, but which is too expensive: "it is not certain yet when the other will be vacant. But I am not hurrying. It has to be as nice as possible to match Rome".[60] Her quest for accommodation was evidently successful, for later in 1931 she took up permanent residence in the city, a move consolidated by her reception into the Roman Catholic Church.

Little is known of Clarice's early years in Rome. In 1938 there is a record of her attending the ceremony of washing the high altar at St. Peter's on Maundy Thursday, 14th April. In a letter to her aunt Beatrix she describes the stripping of the ornaments and linen, the pouring of wine over the altar, and the scrubbing down with mops, all to the accompaniment of antiphons. She appeals to her aunt for information on the origin and meaning of the ceremony, which Beatrix seeks from a Roman Catholic friend in England.[61] Two years later, when Beatrix died, Clarice was unable to return to England for her funeral, and it is known that, as a British subject, she suffered hardship during the war. After the war she lived in the Via Clitunno, in the north east of the city, and by 1953 had moved about three quarters of a mile away to the Via di Santa Costanza.[62] From the Porta Pia, at the edge of the walled city, Santa Costanza was approached along the Via Nomentana, lined with palaces and villas standing in beautiful gardens. It was a residential area containing two historic churches. One of them, Sant'Agnese fuori le Mura, was where Clarice had attended the blessing of the lambs in 1931. On its high altar were preserved the relics of St. Agnes and her foster-sister St. Emerentiana. Both saints had appeared in Clarice's *Roses of Martyrdom*. Adjacent to the church were the well preserved catacombs of St. Agnes, where the martyr's body was buried *c*.300, and nearby was the fourth century church of Santa Costanza, built as a mausoleum for Constantia and Helena, daughters of the Emperor Constantine. This important Christian site was within a few steps of Clarice's flat. While she was living there, in 1954, the remains of a large Constantinian basilica were discovered on the same site.[63]

The five-storey apartment blocks in the Via di Santa Costanza were somewhat forbidding externally, but the accommodation within was cool, spacious and well appointed. Clarice's upstairs flat had marble floors, two bedrooms, a living room lined with books, and a small flower-decked balcony looking out across the street. Her devoted maid Tina took care of all her domestic needs, for "Clarice had a mind above anything practical like cooking or shopping". She was fluent in Italian, and taught English to Italian students at her home. She occasionally revisited England with one of her students. English friends stayed with her from time to time, and nothing pleased her more than to conduct them around ancient sites, explaining and interpreting their history with enthusiasm. As a white-haired lady in her late seventies she took some friends round the ruins of Pompeii in gruelling August heat for nearly seven hours, talking all the time. She had the gift of bringing the past to life in the hearer's imagination, recreating the buildings and repopulating the streets in the mind's eye.[64] Her ability to do so is well illustrated in *The Ministry of Holda*, where, some 40 years earlier, she had conjured a vision of the citizens of ancient Rome returning to the ruins of their fallen city:

> Senators, priests of Jupiter Capitolinus, Praetorians, soothsayers, poets, mimes — all were there. The moonlight pierced the open impluvium, and from its sheen the phantoms of those who once had trodden these splendid halls had taken to themselves a tenuous opalescence, wherein to deck their souls. They passed and repassed — all the pride and power and ambition and cruelty of Imperial Rome.

Clarice's only surviving relatives, her cousins Mary and Margaret Jennings, had both remained spinsters. Margaret lived at Lambgill throughout the war and for some years afterwards, becoming more of a recluse as each year passed. In 1957, at the age of 70, she relinquished her interest in the properties in Station Road, Winchmore Hill, bequeathed to her by Henrietta Cresswell.[65] In doing so she severed the last formal link between the Cresswells and Winchmore Hill. Two years later her elder sister Mary died at the age of 75, leaving Margaret as the sole survivor of the family resident in Britain.[66] Margaret, too, was a practising Roman Catholic, and in the late 1950s placed herself in the care of the Little Sisters of the Poor at their Botcherby Home on the eastern outskirts of Carlisle.

The Little Sisters had arrived in Carlisle in 1880 and established St. Joseph's Home for the Aged: "respectable old people, who are incapable of earning a livelihood, and have no means of support, are the deserving objects on whom

Clarice Cresswell, on the balcony of her flat in the Via di Santa Costanza, Rome, c.1957, when in her mid-seventies. She was the last survivor of that branch of the ancient Northumberland family whose story has been told in these pages.

the Sisters wish to bestow their care". The purpose-built home in which Margaret
Jennings lived was erected in 1892 — a tall, sombre, red-brick pile off Victoria
Road, Botcherby. Mass was celebrated regularly in the chapel by a Roman Catholic chaplain from the parish of Our Lady and St. Joseph, Warwick Road.[67]
Margaret Jennings was looked after in her declining years by the devoted sisters, and died in the home, aged 75, on 25th November 1962. She bequeathed
most of her estate to the Little Sisters "in gratitude for all they have done for
me". An old friend of Miss Jennings who attended her funeral wrote afterwards
to one of the executors, a Penrith solicitor, who had also been present: "I don't
think the Roman Catholic liturgy is nearly as moving as ours in the Book of
Common Prayer". With the same letter she enclosed a copy of *Winchmore Hill:
Memories of a Lost Village*, which Margaret Jennings had given her some years
earlier: "Henrietta's book", she wrote, "seems to me so interesting and so faith-
fully observed a record of one of London's villages I am sure some sociologist
would welcome it. Perhaps it could join the Cresswell Book? I hope both find an
appropriate home".[68] This is indeed a tantalising reference; the Cresswell Book,
whatever it may have been, has disappeared.

Clarice, now turned 80, had become not only the last Cresswell but also the
last of her family. Immersed in her historical and archaeological interests, and
surrounded by friends, she was doubtless undisturbed by the absence of relatives. She was still visiting friends in England from time to time, continuing to
enthuse over anything of antiquarian interest and entertaining her hosts with
lively, intelligent conversation. A return visit to Rome had been planned for the
grandson of an English friend in 1965, but it never took place. On 12th April that
year, the Monday of Holy Week, Clarice collapsed in her flat, and was discovered by her maid Tina; two months past her 84th birthday, she had suffered a
fatal stroke.[69]

Clarice left her flat and some other possessions to her friend and lawyer Dr.
Cino Bacchiani of Via Marcella, Aventino, Rome, "as a token of my appreciation
and as some small return for his unceasing and generous attention to my interests and affairs over many years". All her books and manuscripts she bequeathed
to the Biblioteca del Pontificio Istituto Orientale, in the Piazza Santa Maria
Maggiore. Her plate and silver she gave to Oriel College, Oxford, successor to
her father's college St. Mary Hall. After providing for the residue of her estate
to be handled by trustees, her will closes thus:

> I furthermore declare that I die in the Catholic Faith and I rest all my
> hopes of salvation on my Blessed and Beloved Saviour Jesus Christ our
> Lord.

The Cresswell flame was extinguished in a foreign land, far from the home
ground on which it had burned most brightly — the fruitful fields of Kent, the
bosky combes of Devonshire, the restless streets of London, the sylvan thoroughfares of Winchmore Hill. The folk whose joys and sorrows we have shared
have passed into history, but they have left for our enjoyment a legacy of words

and images by which they should long be remembered. More than that, they have reminded us, as their Victorian contemporary Jean Ingelow may have reminded *them*, that even in the midst of tears and sadness there can be precious memories to warm the heart:

> For life is one, and in its warp and woof
> There runs a thread of gold that glitters fair,
> And sometimes in the pattern shows most sweet
> Where there are sombre colours. It is true
> That we have wept. But oh! this thread of gold,
> We would not have it tarnish; let us turn
> Oft and look back upon the wondrous web,
> And when it shineth sometimes we shall know
> That memory is possession.[70]

Notes to the Chapters

Abbreviations

Barming MSS — *A History of Barming in the County of Kent: Collected from Authentic Material both Manuscript and Printed*, Revd. Mark Noble, 1802 (Centre for Kentish Studies, Maidstone, TR/1884/1). A genealogy associated with this document is identified separately in the notes.

CB Autobiog. — Cresswell Bequest: Beatrix Cresswell, MSS, autobiographical notes, various dates (Westcountry Studies Library, Exeter, msx920/CRE).

CB Flowers — Cresswell Bequest: Revd. Richard Cresswell, MS, *Wild Flowers, their Names and Associations*, Vol.2, 1881 [with later additions] (Westcountry Studies Library, Exeter, s582.13/DEV/CRE).

CB Noble — Cresswell Bequest: Album of watercolours and sketches, Henrietta Noble [and others], 1814 [with later additions] (Westcountry Studies Library, Exeter — deposited with Devon Record Office, Z19/2/11).

CB Notes — Cresswell Bequest: Beatrix Cresswell, MS, *Notes Concerning Many Things*, 1916 [with later additions] (Westcountry Studies Library, Exeter — deposited with Devon Record Office, Z19/15/7).

Crockford — *Crockford's Clerical Directory*.

DNB — *Dictionary of National Biography*.

HC — Henrietta Cresswell, *Winchmore Hill: Memories of a Lost Village*, 1912 (page references are to the second edition).

LMA — London Metropolitan Archives.

LPL — Lambeth Palace Library.

Lib.Cres. — Henrietta Cresswell, *Liber Cresswellii*, 1906 (MS transcript by Arthur Willis in Local History Unit, Enfield Libraries, 71 pp., D2353).

PGSG — *The Palmers Green and Southgate Gazette*.

PO Dir. — (Kelly's) Post Office Directory.

Recorder — The Recorder for Palmers Green, Winchmore Hill and Southgate.

St. Paul WH — St. Paul's Church, Winchmore Hill.

VCH — *Victoria County History*.

Most other repeated references are abbreviated after their first occurrence, thus: Tomlinson....pp.294–5.

Chapter 1 : Cresswell of Cresswell

1   W.W. Tomlinson, *Comprehensive Guide to Northumberland*, c.1910, p.294.
2   Hazel Reynolds (and others), *More Ghosts and Legends of Northumbria*, 1989, pp.33–4.
3   Barming MSS: *A Genealogy of the Family of Cresswell of Cresswell Court*, Revd. Mark Noble (Centre for Kentish Studies, Maidstone, P16/28/1).
4   Tomlinson....pp.294–5.
5   Barming MSS: *Genealogy*.... Presumably John (the younger) lived well beyond 1422, as his son George was active in 1509 — unless Mark Noble has missed a generation.
6   *Visitation of Yorkshire 1584–5*, Robert Glover, Somerset Herald, Deputy to William Flower, Norroy King of Arms (College of Arms, London, ²D.5, f.94). Although the Cresswell family seat was in Northumberland, the pedigree was recorded at Holderness, Yorkshire, where a member of the family was living at the time of the Visitation. A drawing of the Cresswell arms accompanying the Visitation report shows three squirrels, standing erect, in roundels, the blazon reading: "Gules, on three plates a squirrel sejant gules". Above the roundels is a crescent, denoting a second son.
7   *Burke's Landed Gentry*, Vol.1, 1965, p.174.
8   Barming MSS: *Genealogy*....
9   *Burke*....p.174. The Barming pedigree shows an additional generation — another John, living during the reign of Charles I (1625–49). There is also, at the College of Arms, a Cresswell pedigree collected by Sir Ralph Bigland (the younger) and extending to the year 1731 (Bigland Pedigrees, Vol.7, f.413). Unlike the Visitation reports, the Bigland Pedigrees do not form part of the official records of the College of Arms.
10   Lib.Cres., p.8.
11   Barming MSS: *Genealogy*....
12   Lib.Cres., p.5.
13   For the lineage, see *Burke*....pp.174–5. William's son, John (1748–81), had no male heir. His twin daughters Frances and Catherine were co-heirs. Frances married Francis Easterby, who purchased Catherine's moiety of the estate and assumed the name and arms of Cresswell in 1807. His first son, Addison John, who built the new Cresswell Hall 1821–5, married Elizabeth Reed. When she succeeded to the property of her cousin John Baker in 1818, Addison John Cresswell assumed the surname and arms of Baker also. The Northumberland family therefore became Baker-Cresswell, and so it has remained to the present.
14   Barming MSS: *Genealogy*....
15   Lib.Cres., p.1.

Chapter 2 : Town and Country

1   Heather E. Broughton, *Family and Estate Records in the Leicestershire Record Office*, 1991, p.8.
2   J. Nichols, *History and Antiquities of the County of Leicester*, 1815, pedigree of Cheslyn of Langley, Vol.3, Part 2.
3   *Index to the Act Books of the Archbishops of Canterbury 1663–1859*, British Record Society, 1929.
4   His last will, dated 31.7.1758, refers to a "dwelling-house" at Doctors' Commons and a house at Hackney. Henrietta Cresswell (Lib.Cres., p.10) says that he died at Tottenham, but there is no further evidence for this other than the fact that he is buried there.

5 F.T. Cansick, *The Monumental Inscriptions of Middlesex*, 1875, p.69. The inscription refers to "Mrs. Mary Cheslyn who died eleven days before him"; however, this is almost certainly Richard's daughter Mary, who was unmarried. A representation of the Cheslyn arms appeared above the inscription. A recent search of the graveyard failed to locate the tomb.

6 This was Clarice Mercedes Cresswell (1881–1965). Lib.Cres., pp.5–6.

7 Bigland Pedigrees, Vol.7, f.413 (College of Arms).

8 Lib.Cres., p.6.

9 *Law Cases* 1759–1763, Nos.65 and 66, 1763 (British Library, 516 m.19).

10 Barming MSS: *Genealogy....*

11 Faculty for creating Richard Cheslyn Cresswell a notary public, Faculty Office, 19.4.1775 (LPL, f.167). Petition and Fiat to admit Richard Cheslyn Cresswell a proctor, Court of Arches, 19.10.1775 (LPL, Kkk16/20).

12 Barming MSS. Lib.Cres., p.9. F. Clive-Ross, *The Church of St. Mary the Virgin*, East Bedfont, Middlesex, 1984, p.35. Henry Whitfield held the living of Bedfont for 42 years.

13 Lib.Cres., p.6.

14 G.D. Squibb, *Doctors' Commons: A History of the College of Advocates and Doctors of Law*, 1977, pp.v and 4.

15 Leonard W. Cowie, "Doctors' Commons", in *History Today*, June 1970, pp.419–21.

16 P.W. Chandler, "Doctors' Commons", in *London Topographical Record*, Vol.15, 1931. J.Elmes, *A Topographical Dictionary of London and its Environs*, 1831, p.166.

17 Squibb....p.53 ff.

18 Joseph Foster, *Alumni Oxonienses 1715-1886. The Records of the Honorable Society of Lincoln's Inn*, Vol.2, admissions 1800–93; Black Books, Vol.4, 1776–1845.

19 Petition and Fiat to admit Richard Henry Cresswell an advocate, Court of Arches, 7.7.1810 (LPL, Kkk17/34).

20 Squibb....p.199.

21 Squibb....pp.74n. and 199, quoting the account book of Thomas Sharp.

22 The engraving is included in Rudolph Ackermann, *The Microcosm of London or London in Miniature*, Vol.1, 1808 (reprinted 1904).

23 Squibb....pp.32-3.

24 Chandler....

25 Barming MSS: Letter from William Heatley Noble's daughter, Sarah Chattock, 12.6.1835.

26 The foregoing biographical information, taken from Lib.Cres., pp.16–19, is based on Mark Noble's autobiography. The latter appears to have been retained within the family.

27 Barming MSS.

28 Barming MSS.

29 St. Margaret, Barming, parish registers (Centre for Kentish Studies, Maidstone, P16/1/4). Barming MSS: Letter from Sarah Chattock.

30 Lib.Cres., p.29.

31 Barming MSS. In the extracts quoted, spelling errors have been corrected.

32 The Amhursts owned extensive estates in the area, including the whole of the parish of Barnjet, or West Barming, where the last members of the family resided. By 1840 all their property in the area had been sold.

33 The foregoing extracts are from the parish registers of St. Margaret, Barming (Centre for Kentish Studies, Maidstone).

34 Barming MSS. CB Autobiog.

35 Barming MSS.

36 CB Noble.

37 Lib.Cres., pp.29–30. St. Margaret, Barming, parish registers (Centre for Kentish Studies, Maidstone, P16/1/5).

Chapter 3 : A New Generation

1   Lib.Cres., p.30.
2   Cowie....pp.423–4.
3   *The Annual Register or a View of the History, Politics and Literature for the Year 1816*,
    pp.244–7.
4   Petition and Fiat to admit William Cresswell a proctor, Court of Arches, 4.5.1808
    (LPL, Kkk16/102).
5   Petition and Fiat to admit Henry Whitfield Cresswell a proctor, Court of Arches,
    29.1.1819 (LPL, Kkk18/38).
6   *Records of....Lincoln's Inn*, Vol.2, admissions 1800–93. For the career of Sir Cresswell
    Cresswell see DNB; his great-grandfather was William Cresswell, heir to the North-
    umberland estate, who died in 1772.
7   *Boyle's Court Guide*, 1817, shows Richard Cresswell's address as 39 Great Coram
    Street; however, this information may be a year or two out of date.
8   Baptisms and burials from the parish registers of St. Benet, Paul's Wharf (Guildhall
    Library, London, transcribed for the Harleian Society, 1909/1912).
9   Squibb....pp.98–101. Walter H. Godfrey, "Church of St. Benet, Paul's Wharf", in
    London Topographical Record, Vol.15, 1931; the church survives as the Metropolitan
    Welsh Church, Queen Victoria Street.
10 Lib.Cres., p.30.
11 Elmes....p.166.
12 Eliza Jeffries Davis, "Doctors' Commons, its Title and Topography", in *London Topo-
    graphical Record*, Vol.15, 1931.
13 Walter Dexter, "Roundabout Doctors' Commons", in *The Dickensian*, Vol.27, 1931.
14 Charles Dickens, *David Copperfield*, 1850, Chap.23.
15 Sir William Holdsworth, *A History of English Law*, Vol.13, 1952.
16 Henrietta Cresswell, in PGSG, 4.9.1931.
17 Quoted by Beatrix F. Cresswell in *A Book of Devonshire Parsons*, 1932, p.174. Sydney
    Smith also held the living of Halberton, Devon, but never resided there.
18 Biographical information on Sydney Smith from DNB, and Stuart J. Reid, *The Life
    and Times of Sydney Smith*, fourth edition, 1896.
19 DNB. "Memoir" prefacing *The Ingoldsby Legends*. Charles G. Harper, The Ingoldsby
    Country, 1906, Chap.2.
20 DNB.
21 The rhyming letter and epitaph are quoted by Henrietta Cresswell in PGSG, 4.9.1931.
22 DNB.
23 PGSG, 4.9.1931.
24 DNB. "Prefatory Memoir" to *The Poetical Works of Thomas Hood*. PGSG, 4.9.1931.
25 Kent's Directory, 1800, 1816. PO Dir., London, 1818–64 (various dates). CB Autobiog.
26 Cowie....p.426.
27 Lib.Cres., pp.37–8. CB Autobiog.
28 CB Autobiog. CB Noble.
29 Lib.Cres., pp.30,39–40.
30 Lib.Cres., pp.27–8.
31 In 1841 London Street was interrupted on its east side by an approach road to the
    newly opened terminus of the Blackwall Railway (now Fenchurch Street Station).
    The street survives, though wholly rebuilt.
32 The drawing, by G.M. Ellwood, is reproduced in E. Hermitage Day, *Some London
    Churches*, 1911, p.92, and shows St. Olave's, Hart Street, from New London Street.
33 Pigot's *London and Provincial Commercial Directory*, 1826–7, pp.202–210.
34 Lib.Cres., pp.28,39–40.
35 Lib.Cres., pp.40–1.

36   William John Charles Moens, *The Marriage, Baptismal, and Burial Registers, 1571-1874, and Monumental Inscriptions, of the Dutch Reformed Church, Austin Friars, London*, 1884. The church was destroyed by bombing in 1940. Lib.Cres., p.41, gives Diederich's date of death as December 1831, but his memorial in the Dutch Church recorded it as 30th December 1832. This also showed his age as 53, which does not accord precisely with the year of his birth quoted in Lib.Cres., p.28.

37   *Robson's London Commercial Directory*, 1835.

38   Thomas Cromwell, *History and Description of the Parish of Clerkenwell*, 1828. Cumming Street now runs only from Pentonville Road (New Road until the late 1850s) to Collier Street.

39   Lib.Cres., p.41. PO Dir., London, 1851–9.

40   Lib.Cres., pp.30–1,35.

41   Lib.Cres., p.31.

42   *The Gentleman's Magazine*, Sept.1827, p.278.

43   *Topography of Maidstone and its Environs*, pub. J. Smith, Maidstone, 1839.

44   Lib.Cres., p.32. CB Autobiog. Crockford, 1870, for career of Francis Buttanshaw.

45   St. Margaret, Barming, parish registers (Centre for Kentish Studies, Maidstone, P16/1/5).

46   Lib.Cres., pp.31–2.

47   *Topography of Maidstone....*

48   Lib.Cres., pp.29,32.

49   Lib.Cres., pp.32–4. Foster, *Alumni Oxoniensis....*

50   S.L. Ollard, *A Short History of the Oxford Movement*, second edition, 1932 (reprinted Faith Press, 1963), pp.38–40.

51   Ollard....pp.20,35,43–8. Geoffrey Faber, *Oxford Apostles: A Character Study of the Oxford Movement*, second edition, 1936 (reprinted 1974), pp.72–3.

52   Faber....pp.238,367–8,403–4. Ollard....pp.39,47–8. CB Autobiog.

53   *Index to Act Books.... Topography of Maidstone....*

54   Lib.Cres., p.34.

55   Album of plant drawings, Cresswell Collection, Royal Albert Memorial Museum, Exeter. The album is not attributed, and the drawings are not signed, but it is evident from comparison with his other work that they are by Richard Cresswell. The pages of the album are numbered 65–95, indicating earlier work which has not been traced.

56   *Index to Act Books....*

57   Lib.Cres., pp.34,56. CB Autobiog.

58   Lib.Cres., p.34.

59   *Topography of Maidstone....*

60   M.J. Peterson, *The Medical Profession in Mid-Victorian London*, 1978, Chap.5.

61   Peterson....Chaps.1–2.

62   Society of Apothecaries, Court of Examiners Entry Books of Qualifications of Candidates, 1840–1 (Guildhall Library, London, MS8241/12).

63   Pigot's *London and Provincial Commercial Directory*, 1826–7, pp.631–5.

64   *A Brief Historical and Descriptive Account of Maidstone and its Environs* by S.C.L., 1834.

65   *Memoirs and Letters of Sir James Paget*, edited by his son, Stephen Paget, 1901; the memoirs were written 1880–5.

66   Peterson....Chap.1.

67   V.C. Medvei and J.L. Thornton (ed.), *The Royal Hospital of St. Bartholomew 1123-1973*, 1974. Abernethy (1764–1831) bought a country house at Enfield in 1815, eventually retiring there. He is buried at St. Andrew's Church, Enfield.

68   Society of Apothecaries Entry Books....

69   Peterson....Chap.2. Medvei and Thornton....

70   Society of Apothecaries Entry Books....

71   Paget's *Memoirs*.... Additional information on lecturers from Medvei and Thornton. Lectures attended by John Cresswell from Society of Apothecaries Entry Books.
72   J.L. Thornton, "Sir James Paget's Notes on his Students", in *Annals of the Royal College of Surgeons of England*, Vol.21, July–Dec.1957. The original notebook of Sir James Paget is in the library of the Royal College of Surgeons of England.
73   Society of Apothecaries Entry Books....
74   *Topography of Maidstone*....
75   Lib.Cres., p.35.
76   Zachary Cope, *The Royal College of Surgeons of England: A History*, 1959, pp.135,139. Registration requirements from *The Lancet*, 1841. Additional information from the Worshipful Society of Apothecaries of London.
77   Society of Apothecaries List (pub.1853). C.R.B. Barrett, *The History of the Society of Apothecaries of London*, 1905, Chaps.23–4.
78   Royal College of Surgeons in London, Examinations Book, 1841, List of Members, 1841.
79   PO Dir., London, 1842.
80   Paget's Memoirs.... Cope....pp.137-40.
81   Lib.Cres., p.33.
82   Peterson....Chap.3.
83   Pigot's *Commercial Directory for Derbyshire*, 1842.
84   Society of Apothecaries Entry Books.... V.G. Plarr, *Lives of the Fellows of the Royal College of Surgeons of England*, 1930, p.181.
85   Minutes of the Board of Guardians of the Edmonton Poor Law Union, 1840–2 (LMA, BG/E/5). Lib.Cres., p.33.

Chapter 4 : Trois Vase House

1   William Robinson, *The History and Antiquities of the Parish of Edmonton*, 1819, pp.32–3.
2   HC, p.82.
3   Pigot's *London and Provincial Commercial Directory*, 1826–7, p.488.
4   VCH, Middlesex, Vol.5, 1976, p.191. Recorder, 24.11.1910.
5   Assignment of Lease, Parkinson to Radford, 31.7.1821 (LMA, Acc.588/14). PGSG, 22.7.1960.
6   *Draft Conveyance of a Piece of Land at Edmonton, Walker Gray Esq. to His Majesty's Commissioners for Building New Churches*, 30.8.1826 (copy in parish records of St. Paul WH).
7   Eric W. Spalding, *Looking Outward: The Story of St. Paul's, Winchmore Hill's Parish Church*, 1966, p.10.
8   Revd. George Hennessy, *Novum Repertorium Ecclesiasticum Parochiale Londinense*, 1898.
9   Revd. Sydney Smith, *A Letter to Archdeacon Singleton on the Ecclesiastical Commission*, second edition, 1837, pp.32–4.
10   Alfred Blomfield, *A Memoir of Charles James Blomfield, D.D., Bishop of London*, 1863, Vol.1, p.194.
11   Spalding....pp.10–11,16.
12   HC, p.80.
13   Correspondence concerning sale of Winchmore Hill Chapel, 1842–8 (LMA, Acc.1414/22).
14   St. Paul WH, register of baptisms. Pigot's *National and Commercial Directory of Middlesex*, 1839.
15   Information on Caleb Radford's family from Elizabeth Milewicz, University of Tasmania, a descendant by marriage.

16   Society of Apothecaries Entry Books....1832–5 (Guildhall Library, London, MS8241/ 6). Royal College of Surgeons in London, List of Members, 1835.

17   Winchmore Hill Independent Medical Club, Object and Rules, 1836 (Local History Unit, Enfield Libraries, 361.1 (18923)).

18   Stanley I. Richardson, *Edmonton Poor Law Union 1837 to 1854*, Edmonton Hundred Historical Society, 1968. Edmonton Board of Guardians, minutes....1839–40 (LMA, BG/E/4).

19   Information from Elizabeth Milewicz, St. Paul WH register of baptisms, and Census of Population 1841. Caleb Radford practised at Uckfield, Sussex, until 1854, when he and his family emigrated to Australia.

20   Peterson....Chap.1.

21   Peterson....Chap.3.

22   Lib.Cres., p.33.

23   Peterson....Chap.3.

24   Edmonton Board of Guardians, minutes....1838–44 (LMA, BG/E/3–7).

25   Peterson....Chap.3.

26   PGSG, 20.3.1936. Ordnance Survey plan, 25 inch to the mile, Middlesex Sheet VII 10, 1865.

27   The original, dated 1868, is held by the Forty Hall Museum, Enfield, together with other paintings by John Cresswell.

28   PGSG, 20.3.1936, 18.9.1936.

29   Rate Book, Parish of Edmonton, 1850, Bury Street Ward (Local History Unit, Enfield Libraries).

30   Henrietta Cresswell, quoted in PGSG, 15.1.1926.

31   Henry Cox, *A Short Autobiography*, 1929 (printed in Australia for private circulation). He emigrated to South Africa in 1860, later moving to Australia. His descriptions of church and chapel are in reverse order, but it is clear to which each refers.

32   Lib.Cres., pp.31–3.

33   Peterson....Chap.3.

34   HC, p.7.

35   Catalogue of Books belonging to Southgate Reading Society, 1844 and 1849 (Local History Unit, Enfield Libraries, EP027.2). PGSG, 15.12.1939.

36   Horace G. Regnart, *Memories of Winchmore Hill*, 1952, p.48. Henry Cox....PO Dir., Middlesex, 1847.

37   CB Autobiog. Foster, *Alumni Oxoniensis*....

38   Pusey's letter, in an envelope addressed simply to "Miss S. Cresswell, Winchmore Hill, Edmonton", is with CB Autobiog.

39   Ollard....pp.120–2.

40   Ollard....pp.75–6.

41   CB Autobiog.

42   Peterson....Chap.3.

43   Cromwell.... The chapel became a parish church in 1854. It was reduced in size in 1933, closed in 1972, and burnt out in 1983. The façade has been reproduced in facsimile on an office building which now occupies the site in Pentonville Road.

44   St. James, Pentonville, register of marriages (LMA, P76/J52/16).

45   HC, pp.21–2. Lib.Cres., p.35.

46   Lib.Cres., p.35.

47   St. Paul, WH, register of baptisms.

48   St. Paul, WH, register of baptisms.

49   Lib.Cres., p.36. St. Paul WH, register of baptisms. All Saints, Edmonton, burial register, 1855–66 (LMA, DRO40/A1/22). Mary's burial was the first in the Cresswell family grave at Edmonton, no trace of which remains.

50   HC, p.22.

51   Lib.Cres., pp.37–9,41.

52   *A Sale of Useful and Ornamental Articles in Aid of the Building Fund of the National Schools, Winchmore Hill*, 1859 (copy of handbill in the archives of Southgate District Civic Trust).
53   HC, pp.24–5,30,51.
54   HC, pp.25–6.
55   Winchmore Hill National Schools, log book, boys, 1862–1906 (St. Paul's School, Winchmore Hill).
56   HC, pp.31–2.
57   St. Paul WH, register of baptisms. HC, pp.40,57,73.
58   Henrietta Cresswell, in PGSG, 1.1.1932. Most of her descriptive recollections of childhood are written in the third person.
59   PGSG, 14.8.1936, 18.2.1938.
60   HC, pp.56,58,66,69–77.
61   HC, pp.33–5. E.J. King, *The History of the 7th Battalion Middlesex Regiment*, 1927, Chap.4.
62   All Saints, Edmonton, burial register....
63   The drawings, about 10 in number, are in the Cresswell Collection at the Royal Albert Memorial Museum, Exeter. One is dated 27.4.1849 (19/1927/18).
64   CB Autobiog.
65   HC, pp.68–9.
66   HC, pp.17,42–3,52.
67   HC, pp.51–3.
68   HC, pp.58,90–5. PGSG, 30.10.1936.
69   HC, pp.58,60.
70   HC, p.49. Nancy Hicks, "Highfield Park", in *Victoriana*, Edmonton and Enfield Workers' Educational Association, 1985. The Moderator lamp, in which the flow of oil to the burner was regulated, was patented in 1836.
71   HC, pp.62–7.
72   HC, pp.39–41. PGSG, 10.7.1936.
73   PGSG, 11.2.1938. HC, pp.26–30,91.
74   HC, pp.17–18,35,45,93.
75   CB Notes. The tale was copied into Henrietta Cresswell's manuscript book in 1912. An almost identical version of the story was told to Henrietta's cousin Beatrix by her father.
76   St. Paul WH, vestry minute book.
77   Edmonton Board of Guardians, minutes....1865–6 (LMA, BG/E/22).
78   CB Autobiog. CB Notes.
79   White's *History, Gazetteer, and Directory of Devonshire*, 1850, p.243. CB Autobiog. CB Noble.
80   CB Autobiog. The flower painting, preserved with these notes, was given by Edith Cardew to Beatrix Cresswell in 1908.
81   Album of plant drawings, Cresswell Collection, Royal Albert Memorial Museum, Exeter (19/1927/93). The album is signed "R. Cresswell".
82   George Fox Tregelles, "The Seaweeds of South Devon", in *Transactions of the Devonshire Association*, Vol.64, 1932, pp.289–91. Biographical note on the Revd. Richard Cresswell, filed with the Cresswell collection of marine and fresh water algae and botanical drawings at the Royal Albert Memorial Museum, Exeter. Other information from curator of natural history, Royal Albert Memorial Museum.
83   Information from curator of natural history, Royal Albert Memorial Museum, Exeter.
84   HC, p.65.
85   CB Autobiog.
86   Ollard....pp.25–6.
87   CB Autobiog. Guide to St. James the Less, Teignmouth, *c.*1980.

88   White's directory....pp.413–6.
89   CB Autobiog., plus information from John Grange, Lugehay House, 1994, and from title deeds in his possession.
90   Guide to St. James the Less.... The dedication was adopted by a late 19th century vicar, and has no historical foundation. The church survives, but the galleries and overhead pulpit have been removed.
91   St. Paul WH, preachers' book, 1844–71.
92   CB Autobiog. The names inscribed are J.C. Barber and H. Walrond, with the date 1856. H. Walrond occurs again on another pane. The inscriptions were seen by the author on a visit to Lugehay House in 1994.
93   Lib.Cres., pp.63–4.
94   Information from John Reed, Teignmouth.
95   Beatrix F. Cresswell, *Notes on the Churches of the Deanery of Kenn, Devon*, 1912, p.39, quoting from the diary of the Revd. Richard Cresswell. Unfortunately the diary has not been traced.
96   Ollard....p.88.
97   CB Autobiog.
98   Richard Cresswell (trans.), *Aristotle's History of Animals: In Ten Books*, Bohn's Classical Library, 1862 (reprinted 1897, 1907).
99   CB Autobiog.
100   CB Notes. This reminiscence was broadcast on BBC radio on 6.9.1938. The words of six verses of *Maryland*, written out by Christiana, are preserved with the papers.
101   CB Autobiog. Ollard....p.154.
102   CB Autobiog. In Memoriam, Miss B.F.C.A.G. Cresswell, in *Devon and Cornwall Notes and Queries*, Vol.21, April 1940, p.49.
103   CB Autobiog.
104   CB Autobiog.
105   CB Notes.
106   PGSG, 15.1.1926.
107   HC, pp.18,57.
108   Regnart....p.82.
109   HC, pp.110–1.
110   HC, p.111.
111   Lib.Cres., p.36. PGSG, 28.8.1936.
112   HC, p.112. Lib.Cres., pp.41–2.

Chapter 5 : Grove Lodge

1   PGSG, 6.1.1939. Grove Lodge is shown on the 1865 Ordnance Survey plan. Middle Lane was renamed Station Road in the early 1900s.
2   A watercolour painted by the younger Henrietta Cresswell in 1873 shows a single-storey building between Grove Lodge and the railway station. This also appears in a photograph taken from one of the station platforms in the mid-1880s. It does not appear on the 1865 OS plan. It may have been a stable or coach house. Grove Lodge was demolished in the mid-1960s.
3   HC, p.112.
4   HC, p.114.
5   Edmonton Board of Guardians, minutes....2.2.1870 and 9.2.1870 (LMA, BG/E/26).
6   Lib.Cres., p.42; this gives Frances Mary Willink's date of death as 19th March; the death certificate shows 20th March. All Saints, Edmonton, burial register, 1866–75 (LMA, DRO40/A1/23).
7   The inaugural train service is shown in an advertisement in *Meyer's Enfield Observer and Local Advertiser*, 1.4.1871.

8   Henrietta Cresswell, in PGSG, 4.9.1931. Rose Cottage was altered in the 1880s, and demolished after bomb damage inflicted during the Second World War. A blue plaque records the site of Thomas Hood's home.

9   CB Autobiog.

10   Lib.Cres.,p.36.

11   HC, pp.103–8. VCH, Middlesex, Vol.5, 1976, p.143.

12   Winchmore Hill National Schools, log books, 1862–1906 (St. Paul's School, Winchmore Hill).

13   *The Enfield Gazette*, 1.1.1926.

14   *The Enfield Gazette*, 1.1.1926. Regnart....p.26. Tom Mason, *A Southgate Scrap-Book*, 1948, p.101.

15   CB Autobiog.

16   Lib.Cres., pp.35–6. All Saints, Edmonton, burial register, 1875–82 (LMA, DRO40/A1/24).

17   St. Bartholomew's Medical School, student register, 1879–80 (St. Bartholomew's Hospital archives, MS1/2).

18   Peterson....Chaps.1–2.

19   Medvei and Thornton....

20   St. Bartholomew's Hospital School Calendar, 1880–90 (St. Bartholomew's Hospital archives, MS20). *The Medical Directory*, 1884.

21   *The Medical Directory*, 1884. *The Medical Register*, 1885. Information on house-physicians from the archivist, St. Bartholomew's Hospital.

22   *The British Medical Journal*, 27.3.1886.

23   PO Dir., London, 1874. The numbering of premises in this part of London Street had not changed since the early years of the century. The numbers ran consecutively on each side of the street.

24   PO Dir., London, 1876–90. Louis Zettersten, *City Street Names*, 1926, p.113. Charles Goad's Insurance Plan of the City of London, 1887. The court was demolished to make way for the headquarters of the Port of London Authority, completed in 1922.

25   Regnart....pp.27,54. Valuation List for the Parish of Edmonton, 1884 (Local History Unit, Enfield Libraries). PGSG, 28.2.1964. PO Dir., London Suburban, 1899–1900.

26   All Saints, Edmonton, burial register, 1883–present.

27   St. Paul WH, parish magazine, July 1890. Edward Kelly, *St. Paul's Church, Winchmore Hill*, 1987. The two memorial windows and brass tablets are still in place in St. Paul's Church, in what is now the Lady Chapel, but the brass tablets have been transposed.

28   St. Paul WH, parish magazine, 1887–92.

29   St. Paul WH, parish magazine, 1887–92.

30   Lib.Cres., p.36.

31   Regnart....p.27. PGSG, 11.2.1938.

32   Letter from Henrietta Cresswell, quoted in PGSG, 7.8.1931. HC, pp.36–7.

33   PGSG, 20.8.1926. *The Enfield Gazette*, 19.11.1926, 9.9.1927.

34   "A Lay of the Suburbs", in HC, pp.116–9.

35   PGSG, 11.5.1973.

36   Foster, *Alumni Oxoniensis*.... CB Autobiog.

37   CB Autobiog.

38   St. Paul WH, preachers' books.

39   Cresswell Collection, Royal Albert Memorial Museum, Exeter.

40   Cresswell Collection, Royal Albert Memorial Museum, Exeter (31/1925).

41   Cresswell Collection, Royal Albert Memorial Museum, Exeter.

42   PGSG, 23.9.1932. The article quotes a letter from "an authoress" whose name is not given, but who can be none other than Beatrix Cresswell.

43   CB Autobiog.

44   The diary entries are with CB Autobiog. Archibald Grosvenor is the Idyllic Poet in

Patience. Beatrix's expression "utterly utter" echoes the fashionable vocabulary of the Aesthetic Movement.

45 Beatrix is likening Winchmore Hill to a landscape in Canada. CB Autobiog.
46 CB Autobiog.
47 CB Flowers.
48 CB Autobiog. Information on ownership of Lugehay House from title deeds in possession of John Grange, 1994.
49 *Lloyd's Register of British and Foreign Shipping*, 1882–3.
50 CB Autobiog. The Canadian journal is with these papers.
51 CB Autobiog.
52 Richard Dalby, *The Golden Age of Children's Book Illustration*, 1991, pp.28–9.
53 CB Autobiog., and information from John Reed, Teignmouth.
54 D.J. Farley, *The Building of Christ Church Union Grove and its Vicarage* (undated typescript); the church survives. Crockford, 1872.
55 Lida E. Ellsworth, *Charles Lowder and the Ritualist Movement*, 1982, pp.40,60.
56 Christ Church, Clapham, vestry minutes, 1862–1959 (LMA, P95/CTC2/44/1).
57 Christ Church, Clapham, Parochial Magazine, Nov.1865 (LMA, P95/CTC2/59).
58 Crockford, 1880.
59 Christ Church, Clapham, register of baptisms, 1868–77, register of marriages, 1862–94 (LMA, P95/CTC2/2/1, P95/CTC2/12/1).
60 PO Dir., Home Counties, 1874.
61 Christ Church, Clapham, register of services and preachers, 1873–4, register of marriages, 1862-94 (LMA, P95/CTC2/20, P95/CTC2/12/1).
62 Christ Church, Clapham, register of services and preachers, 1873–80 (LMA, P95/CTC2/20-3).
63 Service announcements with Christ Church Clapham register of services and preachers, 1879–80 (LMA, P95/CTC2/23).
64 Christ Church, Clapham, register of services and preachers, 1881–2, register of baptisms, 1877–86 (LMA, P95/CTC2/24, P95/CTC2/3).
65 Charles Mackeson, *A Guide to the Churches of London and its Suburbs for 1889*, p.75.
66 The diary entries are with CB Autobiog.
67 Christ Church, Clapham, vestry minutes, 1862–1959 (LMA, P95/CTC2/44/1).
68 PO Dir., London Suburban, 1888. Of the 19th century houses in Union Grove, only the vicarage survives.
69 The set of 17 novels was presented to Exeter City Library as part of the Cresswell Bequest. Titles not mentioned in the text are: *The Survivors*, 1886; *A Wily Widow*, 1888; *My Lord Othello*, 1889; *A Woman's Ambition*, 1892; *Disinherited*, 1893; *A Precious Scamp*, 1894; *Cancelled Bonds*, 1895; *Without Issue*, 1897. Richard Henry Cresswell was also the author of a drama entitled *The Conversion of England*, and co-author of another entitled *In Danger*; these two works are not in the Cresswell Bequest.
70 CB Autobiog.
71 CB Autobiog.
72 CB Autobiog. PO Dir., London, 1879. Richmond Road has become a part of Old Brompton Road.
73 CB Autobiog.
74 St. Matthias, Warwick Road, register of marriages, 1871–97 (LMA, P84/MTS/5). St. Matthias's Church, which has been demolished, stood at the corner of Warwick Road and Earl's Court Square.
75 Andrew Saint, Victorian Society notes on Kensington churches, 1983.
76 The house survives, and is now numbered 36 Halford Road.
77 St. Mary, Richmond, burial register, 1879–85 (Surrey Record Office, Kingston, P7/1/23).
78 Lib.Cres., p.42.

79   Foster, *Alumni Oxoniensis*....
80   St. Margaret, Barming, register of baptisms, 1813–46 (Centre for Kentish Studies, Maidstone, P16/1/6).
81   Crockford, 1889.
82   Lib.Cres., p.44.
83   VCH, Northampton, Vol.2, 1906, pp.555–9. The appearance of the village has changed little in over 100 years.
84   St. Paul WH, banns book, 1852–96.
85   *The Northampton Herald*, 20.5.1892. St. Andrew, Cotterstock, marriage register (Northamptonshire Record Office, Northampton).
86   Edmonton Board of Guardians, minutes....1891–3 (LMA, BG/E/54).
87   *Meyer's Enfield Observer*, 18.11.1892.
88   Edmonton Board of Guardians, minutes....1891–3.
89   Winchmore Hill National Schools, minute book, 1892–1903 (St. Paul's School, Winchmore Hill).

Chapter 6 : A Family of Artists

1   CB Noble.
2   HC, p.7. The title page carries the words: "Illustrated with leaves from the Doctor's sketch book". The surviving paintings and drawings by John Cresswell (and just two by his daughter Henrietta) are in the care of the London Borough of Enfield, and are kept at the Forty Hall Museum. There is an analysis of the collection in Appendix B.
3   Only one picture in the collection is unidentified.
4   Algernon Graves, *The Royal Academy of Arts: A Complete Dictionary of Contributors and their Work from its Foundation in 1769 to 1904*, Vol.2, 1905, p.198.
5   PGSG, 28.8.1936. The illustrations accompanying this article are reproduced from copies made by Miss H.E. Ewing of the watercolours by Richard Cresswell.
6   Two of the watercolours — the waterfall in Green Dragon Lane and the Compton Road bridge — are reproduced in *Dr. Cresswell's Winchmore Hill* (London Borough of Enfield Libraries, 1980), though not attributed there to Henrietta. A copy made by Miss H.E. Ewing of the watercolour of Ford's Grove Farm is reproduced in PGSG, 20.8.1926.
7   Algernon Graves, *A Dictionary of Artists who have Exhibited Works in the Principal London Exhibitions from 1760 to 1893*, 1901, p.67. J. Johnson and A. Grentzner, *The Dictionary of British Artists 1880-1940*, 1976, p.128. Christopher Wood, *The Dictionary of Victorian Painters*, second edition, 1978, p.111. *The Queen, the Lady's Newspaper*, 25.5.1889, 6.12.1890.

Chapter 7 : A Scattered Flock

1   Middlesex Deeds Registers, 1892–3 (LMA, MDR1892/32/228-31, MDR1893/4/866). The properties later became Nos.12,14,16 and 18 Station Road, and are so numbered today. The one occupied by Henrietta became No.16.
2   PO Dir., London Suburban, 1899–1900.
3   PGSG, 20.8.1926, 11.2.1938.
4   Regnart....p.27; he gives the house the incorrect name Cottesmore. *The Medical Directory*, 1893. Curiously, the house does not appear on the 1896 25-inch Ordnance Survey plan (Middlesex Sheet VII 10), which incorporates revisions up to 1895, but

Francis Cresswell was certainly living there during the first half of 1893; the house later became 42 Station Road, and carried the name Cotterstock until comparatively recent times.

5   *The Medical Directory*, 1892–1902.
6   Miss E. McDonald, in PGSG, 24.11.1961. As a child Miss McDonald was a near neighbour of Henrietta Cresswell in Middle Lane from 1896.
7   St. Paul WH, register of baptisms, register of services.
8   Henrietta Cresswell, quoted in PGSG, 15.1.1926.
9   Narrative account of purchase of ground at Winchmore Hill in 1894 and its conversion to sports ground for Amalgamated Clubs (MS compiled by Mr. W. Bruce Clarke, St. Bartholomew's Hospital, 1907) and letter from Sir Henry Oakley, general manager, Great Northern Railway, King's Cross, to William Bruce Clarke, Harley Street, 26.7.1893 (St. Bartholomew's Hospital archives, SU7).
10   Land at Winchmore Hill [purchased by medical officers and lecturers of St. Bartholomew's Hospital, 1894] (St. Bartholomew's Hospital archives, MS73/4).
11   Extract from Deed of Conveyance between executors of the late Alfred Walker of Stone Hall, Winchmore Hill, and Samuel West, Alfred Bowlby and Thomas William Shore, 5.4.1894 (St. Bartholomew's Hospital archives, SU7).
12   Narrative account.... St. Bartholomew's continued to use the Winchmore Hill sports ground until 1937. It remained in use as a playing field until recent years, when the site was built on. A wall along the southern boundary still bears a stone tablet inscribed: "This wall is the property of St. Bartholomews Recreation Ground".
13   St. Paul WH, parish magazine, Dec.1897, Oct.1899.
14   St. Paul WH, parish magazine, 1901–2. Regnart....p.72.
15   St. Paul WH, parish magazine, 1894–1904, register of services.
16   St. Paul WH, parish magazine, March, May, June 1893.
17   CB Autobiog.
18   Abstract of title to leasehold dwellinghouses, Station Road, Winchmore Hill, 1957 (Reed, Graham and Little, Solicitors, Penrith).
19   PO Dir., London Suburban, 1892–1900. Recorder, 15.2.1912.
20   St. Paul WH, parish magazine, June 1903. Spalding....p.33. The building has been demolished, but the foundation stone, recording the benefaction of William Paulin, has been preserved in the churchyard of St. Paul's, Winchmore Hill.
21   VCH, Middlesex, Vol.5, 1976, p.145.
22   *Meyer's Enfield Observer*, 21.9.1906.
23   Loughborough Grammar School, pupil's record, Cresswell F., 1907. *The Loughburian* (Loughborough Grammar School magazine), various dates. A report of Francis Cresswell's funeral in *The Loughborough Echo*, 5.11.1920, states that he chose to live at Barrow in order to send Frank to Loughborough Grammar School.
24   PGSG, 11.8.1939, 24.11.1961.
25   Roger Logan, *South Battersea: The Formative Years 1851–1900*, Wandsworth Historical Society, 1977.
26   Ethel A. Woolmer, *The Story of Battersea*, 1924.
27   CB Autobiog.
28   CB Autobiog. *Who was Who 1897–1915*, 1920.
29   CB Autobiog.
30   The British Library Catalogue lists 12 guides in this series written by Beatrix Cresswell. Some ran into several editions, occasionally with slight changes of title in later editions. A few other titles not included in the BL catalogue have been identified. She was also the author of at least two volumes in the companion series of Homeland Handy Guides: these are included in a list of printed books by Miss B.F. Cresswell appended to her obituary in *Devon and Cornwall Notes and Queries*, Vol.21, April 1940, though this list is not complete.
31   Title deeds in possession of John Grange, Lugehay House, 1994. PO Dir., Devon,

1897, 1902. CB Autobiog. Information on Barton Terrace from Tricia Whiteaway of Dawlish; No.10 survives.

32   CB Autobiog.

33   CB Autobiog.

34   PO Dir., Devon, 1906. Ordnance Survey plan, 25 inch to the mile, Exeter, 1905. *Discovering Exeter No.2: St. Leonard's*, Exeter Civic Society, 1982. The house still stands, though renumbered, in a suburb which has retained much of its early 19th century character.

35   Beatrix F. Cresswell, MS, *Arms of the Bishops of Exeter*, *c*.1905 (Westcountry Studies Library, Exeter, s13/EXE/929.8/CRE).

36   Beatrix F. Cresswell, *Devon Fonts*, *c*.1904–12 (Westcountry Studies Library, Exeter, msx729.91/DEV/CRE).

37   Obituary Notice, Miss B.F.C.A.G. Cresswell, in *Transactions of the Devonshire Association*, Vol.72, 1940, p.15. In Memoriam, Miss B.F.C.A.G. Cresswell, in *Devon and Cornwall Notes and Queries*, Vol.21, April 1940, p.49.

38   Beatrix F. Cresswell, *Exeter Churches: Notes on the History, Fabrics and Features of Interest in the Churches of the Deanery of Christianity, Devon*, 1908.

39   Beatrix F. Cresswell, "Armorial Bearings in Exeter Churches", in *Devon Notes and Queries*, Vol.5, 1908–9.

40   Beatrix F. Cresswell, *White Rose and Golden Broom: A Drama of Old Exeter*, 1910.

41   *The Exeter Express and Echo*, 6.11.1911.

42   Obituary and In Memoriam, Miss B.F.C.A.G. Cresswell.... Beatrix F. Cresswell, "The Church Goods Commission in Devon, 1549–1552", in *Transactions of the Devonshire Association*, Vol.43, 1911.

43   Beatrix F. Cresswell, *Notes on the Churches of the Deanery of Kenn, Devon*, 1912.

44   Oswald J. Reichel, in *Devon and Cornwall Notes and Queries*, Vol.7, 1912–13.

45   Beatrix F. Cresswell, "Churchyard and Wayside Crosses in the Neighbourhood of Exeter", in *Transactions of the Devonshire Association*, Vol.47, 1915.

46   Beatrix F. Cresswell, "Ancient Church Needlework in Devon", in *Transactions of the Devonshire Association*, Vol.49, 1917.

47   CB Autobiog. CB Notes.

48   *A Short History of the Church* [of St. John the Baptist, Holland Road, Kensington], 1868–97 (printed as a series of articles in the Parish Notes, commencing in 1889). There are two undated MS volumes in the parish archives which contain material similar to, and in places the same as, the printed *Short History*. One of these, attributed to William Richard Halsey, who became verger of St. John's in 1889, also contains more recent material than the *Short History*. Some of the references to *A Short History of the Church* which follow include material drawn from these volumes.

49   *The Kensington Post*, 6.3.1981. Ollard....pp.139–40.

50   *A Short History of the Church*....

51   PO Dir., London, 1892–4. Crockford, 1900. Melrose Gardens survives relatively unchanged.

52   Bridget Cherry and Nikolaus Pevsner, *The Buildings of England: London, North West*, 1991, p.458. A planned west tower, and a flèche and lantern at the crossing, were not executed. The building survives, and surely has one of the finest church interiors in London.

53   *A Short History of the Church*....

54   *A Short History of the Church*....

55   For a note on the *Apostolic Constitutions* and its place in apocryphal literature see Montague Rhodes James, *The Apocryphal New Testament*, 1924, pp.xxiii–xxiv.

56   Survey of London, Vol.37, Northern Kensington, Royal Commission on the Historical Monuments of England, 1973. PO Dir., London, 1904–5. The vicarage and the terrace survive.

57   Cherry and Pevsner....p.458. *A Short History of the Church*....

58 *The Times Literary Supplement*, 10.12.1914, p.557.
59 G. Goold Walker (ed.), *The Honourable Artillery Company in the Great War 1914–1919*, 1930, p.515. Correspondence from the Honourable Artillery Company, 1998.
60 *A Short History of the Church*....
61 *The West London Press* (*Chelsea News*), 1.10.1915, 8.10.1915.

Chapter 8 : Pastures New

1   W. Dickie, *Dumfries and Round About: The Land of Bruce and Burns, of Scott and Carlyle*, fourth edition, 1910, pp.1–7.
2   Statutory List of Buildings of Architectural or Historic Interest, District of Nithsdale, Parish of Dumfries: Nunholm House, 1986, supplemented by personal observation and Henrietta Cresswell's recollections. She stated in 1913 that parts of the house were at least 350 years old, but there is no visible evidence of this.
3   Title deeds in the possession of Gordon Little, Nunholm House, 1993. Valuation Rolls, Parish of Dumfries, Northern Division, Nunholm House, 1898–1901 (Ewart Library, Dumfries).
4   Henrietta Cresswell, *Liber Cresswellii*, 1906 (MS transcript by Arthur Willis in Local History Unit, Enfield Libraries, 71pp., D2353).
5   Lib.Cres., pp.69–71.
6   Jean S. Maxwell, *The Centenary Book of St. John's, Dumfries*, 1968. St. Ninian, Maxwelltown, Dumfries, register of services, 1891–1957 (Ewart Library, Dumfries); the church on this site closed in 1963, but the building survives. *The Dumfries and Galloway Standard*, 6.5.1908.
7   Quoted in PGSG, 18.2.1938.
8   St. Paul WH, parish magazine, 1911–12.
9   PGSG, 1.1.1926, 21.8.1931. Mason....p.103. The grey-covered version of the second edition of *Winchmore Hill: Memories of a Lost Village* was reprinted in facsimile by Southgate Civic Trust in 1982, but with soft covers and a page size slightly reduced by trimming margins.
10 Edmonton Hundred Historical Society, newsletter, April 1975. VCH, Middlesex, Vol.5, 1976, p.143n.
11 Michael Robbins, *The Railway Age*, 1962. Terry Coleman, *The Railway Navvies*, 1965. Dick Sullivan, *Navvyman*, 1983.
12 The five flower poems by Henrietta Cresswell mentioned here are pasted into CB Flowers. They are undated, but were probably put there by Beatrix Cresswell, to whom the volume was given.
13 Quoted in PGSG, 28.1.1938.
14 Quoted in PGSG, 2.9.1932.
15 Hugh S. Gladstone, *Addenda and Corrigenda* to *The Birds of Dumfriesshire*, Dumfriesshire and Galloway Natural History and Antiquarian Society, 1911, pp.4–5.
16 PO Dir., Leicestershire, 1908, pp.33–4. Heywood Chilton, *Eighth Centenary of Holy Trinity Church, Barrow-upon-Soar*, 1938. Barry and John Wilford, *Bygone Barrow-upon-Soar*, Vol.1, 1981, Vol.2, 1995.
17 Roger Chappell, *Barrow-upon-Soar's House of Industry*, 1994. Industry Street was renamed Beveridge Street in the early 1920s. The Poplars is now 49 and 49A Beveridge Street.
18 Frank Cresswell's surviving pupil record from Loughborough Grammar School, starting in December 1907, shows his father as "retired". The report of Francis Cresswell's funeral in *The Loughborough Echo* states, somewhat confusingly, that "he joined his father in a practice he had had for 50 years, retiring from it in 1908".
19 Wilford....Vol.1, pp.18–19; Vol.2, pp.6–7.

20   Loughborough Endowed Schools, The Boys' Grammar School, School List, 1910. *Conduct*, Loughborough Grammar School, 1912.
21   Loughborough Grammar School, pupil's record, Cresswell F., 1907.
22   *The Loughburian*....1908–14.
23   *The Loughburian*....1914–15. Holy Trinity, Barrow-upon-Soar, parish magazine, 1914–16.
24   *The Loughburian*....second term 1916, p.3.
25   *The Loughborough Echo*, 26.5.1916. Holy Trinity, Barrow-upon-Soar, parish magazine, June 1916. *The Loughburian*....third term 1916, pp.4–5.
26   Information from Vivienne Everett, Barrow-upon-Soar.
27   Quoted in *The Loughburian*....third term 1916, pp.15–19.
28   G. Goold Walker (ed.), *The Honourable Artillery Company in the Great War 1914–1919*, 1930, pp.65–77,515. G. Goold Walker, *The Honourable Artillery Company 1537–1947*, 1954, pp.246,314.
29   Information on this, and on Clarice's engagement, from Jennifer Leatham, granddaughter of a friend of Clarice Cresswell.

Chapter 9 : Broken Threads

1   Holy Trinity, Barrow-upon-Soar, parish magazine, 1916–20. Chilton....p.18. James Powell and Sons, window-glass order book, 1917–20, f.128 (Victoria and Albert Museum, Department of Art and Design, Whitefriars archive AAD1/22-1977). The window and other memorials are still in place.
2   St. Andrew, Cotterstock, burial register.
3   Holy Trinity, Barrow-upon-Soar, parish magazine, Aug.1919.
4   *The Loughborough Echo*, 5.11.1920. Barrow-upon-Soar Cemetery, burial book, 1915–30 (Leicestershire Record Office, Leicester, DE502/15). Holy Trinity, Barrow-upon-Soar, parish magazine, Nov.1920.
5   R.H. Bennett, *A Short History of Barrow-upon-Soar*, 1938. Wilford....Vol.1, p.29; Vol.2, p.2.
6   Holy Trinity, Barrow-upon-Soar, vestry and Parochial Church Council minutes, 1920–34 (Leicestershire Record Office, Leicester, DE2933/147).
7   Holy Trinity, Barrow....Parochial Church Council minutes. Bennett.... Holy Trinity, Barrow-upon-Soar, Faculty for erecting a new oak pulpit, 1924 (Leicestershire Record Office, Leicester, DE2933/47).
8   Wilford....Vol.1, p.24; Vol.2, p.23.
9   Barrow Cemetery, burial book.... Holy Trinity, Barrow-upon-Soar, parish magazine, Jan.1930. Chappell.... A letter preserved in the Leicestershire Record Office (DE2933/127) confirms that the Misses Gamble were still living in Sileby Road in 1948; their cottage survives.
10   *The Times Literary Supplement*, 8.4.1920, p.224.
11   *A Short History of the Church* [of St. John the Baptist, Holland Road, Kensington]....
12   *A Short History of the Church*.... St. John Baptist Church, Kensington, Parochial Church Council report, 1926–7.
13   According to the Roman calendar, "Ante Diem XVI Kalendas Aprilis" signifies 17th March, ie. 16 days before the Kalends (or 1st) of April, the named day and the Kalends both being counted. The correct date of death, 16th March, should have been rendered "A.D. XVII KAL.AP.". The inscription is therefore one day out. The altar rails and inscription are still in place.
14   *The Dumfries and Galloway Standard*, 12.7.1919, 23.7.1919, 20.8.1919. Dumfries Sheriff Court, John Ramsay v. Miss Henrietta Cresswell, decree issued 18.8.1919 (Scottish Record Office, Edinburgh, SC15/7/37).

15   Disposition by William Andson in favour of John Ramsay, General Register of Sasines, County of Dumfries, Book 383, f.95–8, 16.5.1919 (included in title deeds in the possession of Gordon Little, Nunholm House, 1993).

16   Valuation Rolls, Parish of Dumfries, Nunholm House, 1919–20 (Ewart Library, Dumfries).

17   Valuation Rolls, Parish of Glencairn, Dumfriesshire, 1919–23 (Ewart Library, Dumfries). PO Dir., Dumfries and District, 1920–1. PO Dir., Scotland, 1928.

18   CB Flowers.

19   PO Dir., Cumberland, 1921, pp.256–7. Official guide to Silloth on Solway, *c*.1934. Skinburness is little changed today, apart from some inter-war building along the road to Silloth. The hotel is functioning, after a period of closure in the 1980s.

20   *Watermillock Parish History*, unpublished and unattributed script, *c*.1960, in possession of Thomas Coulthard of Watermillock. Jeremy Godwin, *Watermillock School: A Brief History*, 1979, unpublished script written for successive owners of the school building of 1860 which became a private house after closure of the school in 1954. M. Coulthard, *Watermillock Girls' School*, Cumberland, unpublished script, 1984.

21   T.F. Bulmer, *History, Topography and Directory of East Cumberland*, 1884, pp.557–61. PO Dir., Cumberland and Westmorland, 1929, p.258.

22   *Watermillock Parish History*....

23   Bulmer....p.558. PO Dir., Cumberland and Westmorland, 1929, p.258. Guide to parish church of All Saints, Watermillock, *c*.1990.

24   Watermillock Inclosure Award, 1835 (Cumbria Record Office, Carlisle, QRE/1/17). Directories for Cumberland etc., 1847–1929 (various dates).

25   PGSG, 3.4.1931. Lambgill and its surroundings have changed little since the Cresswells lived there.

26   Watermillock Mixed Voluntary School, log book, 1913–40 (Cumbria Record Office, Carlisle, SSR/41/1).

27   CB Flowers.

28   Henrietta Cresswell, in PGSG, 11.1.1935.

29   The identity of the author was revealed in PGSG, 11.2.1938.

30   *The Glasgow Herald*, March–April 1925.

31   Biographical note on Arthur Willis (1858–1942) (Local History Unit, Enfield Libraries, 92:352). Tom Mason, in PGSG, 14.11.1947.

32   PGSG, 22.2.1935, 28.2.1936, 10.4.1936, 6.8.1937, 5.8.1938.

33   Borough of Southgate Museum, Broomfield House, short guide, 1955.

34   Southgate Urban District Council, reports of Parks Committee, 1924–30. PGSG, 15.6.1934, 13.5.1938. Letter from Henrietta Cresswell to Beatrix Cresswell, 29.6.1928, with CB Autobiog. The present whereabouts of the carriage pistols are not known.

35   All Saints, Watermillock, Parochial Church Council minutes, 1922–8 (Cumbria Record Office, Carlisle, PR/132/19). All Saints, Watermillock, vestry meeting minutes, 1922–7 (Cumbria Record Office, Carlisle, PR/132/18). All Saints, Watermillock, burial register.

36   Letter from Henrietta Cresswell to Beatrix Cresswell, 3.7.1928, with CB Autobiog. The Aladdin lamp was a paraffin lamp whose light output was obtained from an incandescent mantle.

37   Margaret Jennings first appears at Lambgill in the Register of Electors for the Parish of Watermillock on 1.5.1929.

38   Watermillock School, log book.... Crockford, 1930.

39   All Saints, Watermillock, register of services, 1925–39 (Cumbria Record Office, Carlisle, PR/132/21). PGSG, 1.1.1932.

40   All Saints, Watermillock, burial register, graveyard plan with list of burial plots.

41   Quoted in PGSG, 11.2.1938.

42   Henrietta Cresswell, in PGSG, 21.8.1931. Lib.Cres., p.32.

43   Henrietta Cresswell, in PGSG, 11.9.1931.

44   Quoted in PGSG, 14.1.1938.
45   Abstract of title....
46   Guide to parish church.... The albums are preserved in the church.
47   Information from Mrs. H.A. Eccles, Lambgill, 1992.
48   *The Devonian Year Book*, London Devonian Association, 1919, 1921, 1925, 1927. W.H.
     Wilkin, "Notes on Membury — Part IV", in *Report and Transactions of the Devonshire
     Association*, Vol.61, 1929, p.359.
49   Correspondence concerning Cresswell Bequest, 1948–55 (Westcountry Studies Li-
     brary, Exeter). CB Notes.
50   Letter from Miss Falconer, Colchester, to Miss Cresswell, Exeter, postmarked
     31.10.1927, with CB Autobiog.
51   *Report and Transactions of the Devonshire Association*, 1931–8.
52   Information from Royal Albert Memorial Museum, Exeter. The museum's acquisi-
     tions register lists "pressed algae, mosses, drawings of fungi etc., microslides, manu-
     scripts and notes, pamphlets etc." (Ac.No.31–32/1925).
53   *Report and Transactions*....1929, 1932. CB Flowers.
54   *The Western Mail and News*, 17.2.1940, 20.2.1940. *The Times*, 19.2.1940. *Transactions
     of the Devonshire Association*, Vol.72, 1940. *Devon and Cornwall Notes and Queries*,
     Vol.21, April 1940.
55   Copy of letter from Beatrix Cresswell to Exeter Library Committee, 20.11.1918, with
     correspondence concerning Cresswell Bequest, 1948–55 (Westcountry Studies Li-
     brary, Exeter).
56   Correspondence concerning Cresswell Bequest, 1948–55 (Westcountry Studies Li-
     brary, Exeter). Correspondence between the author and the Local Studies Librar-
     ian, Westcountry Studies Library, 1997.
57   Royal Albert Memorial Museum, Exeter, acquisitions register (Ac.No.28/1940) from
     the executors of the late Beatrix F. Cresswell. The acquisition comprises 95 items, of
     which 62 are costumes, accessories and shoes, 12 are dolls and toys, 12 are bird and
     mammal specimens, 4 are items of embroidery, 3 are weapons, and 2 are miscella-
     neous. None of the objects was on public display or available for inspection at the
     time of writing.
58   Note by Mr. H. Tapley-Soper, City Librarian, 25.11.1942, with correspondence con-
     cerning Cresswell Bequest, 1948–55 (Westcountry Studies Library, Exeter).
59   Correspondence from Jennifer Leatham and John Schmolle, whose grandmother,
     Jeanne Marie Louise Freeth, was a friend of Clarice Cresswell.
60   Letter from Clarice Cresswell to Beatrix Cresswell, Feb.1931, with CB Notes.
61   CB Notes.
62   Correspondence concerning Cresswell Bequest, 1948–55 (Westcountry Studies Li-
     brary, Exeter) includes letters written by Clarice Cresswell from Via Clitunno 38 in
     1948–50. Jennifer Leatham visited her at Via di Santa Costanza 38 in 1953.
63   Alta Macadam, *Blue Guide: Rome and Environs*, 1994, pp.260–2.
64   Information from Jennifer Leatham.
65   Abstract of title....
66   Correspondence between Mr. Quintin Little, Solicitor, Penrith, and Miss Ruth
     Mothersill, Penrith, 1962.
67   Kevin A. Rafferty, *Portrait of a Parish (1798-1993) to mark the Centenary of Our Lady
     and St. Joseph's, Carlisle*, 1993, pp.42-3 (also quoting Bulmer....).
68   Correspondence between Mr. Little and Miss Mothersill....
69   Information from Jennifer Leatham.
70   From "Songs with Preludes: Regret" in *The Poetical Works of Jean Ingelow*, 1899. The
     poem includes the lines printed on the title page of this book.

Appendix A

The Barming Manuscripts of the Reverend Mark Noble: Later History

The *Barming Manuscripts* consist of Mark Noble's *History of Barming* dated 1802, together with drawings, pedigrees, letters and papers made or collected by the author.

After Mark Noble's death in 1827 the MSS were retained by his family, later becoming the property of Mark Noble Buttanshaw (1834–1904), a grandson. In 1895 he was asked by the Reverend Thomas William Carr, Rector of Barming since 1865, whether he would lend the MSS to assist with a history of the parish which the rector was writing. Buttanshaw, then living at Blackheath, replied that he was given the MSS on the understanding that he would not let them go out of his possession, on account of the remarks his grandfather had made in them concerning some of the parishioners, but he added: "I think now that they are dead long ago and you are writing a history of the Parish I am justified in letting you have the Book to refer to".

In subsequent correspondence, Buttanshaw assured the rector that he had no objection to his making use of the MSS for publication, although they were "never written for publication but only for Noble's own amusement", and he gave permission for copies to be made of sketches and pedigrees, subject to the latter being verified.

The correspondence between Buttanshaw and Carr continued for several years. In 1898 Buttanshaw gave permission for two memorial tablets to the Nobles in the chancel of Barming Church to be moved "provided they are re-erected in a suitable position". In 1903 Buttanshaw agreed that Carr should send the MSS to Miss Violet Thorold of Croydon for typing, provided that certain passages were omitted.

The typing was completed in 1903 at a cost of seven guineas. Obvious errors, principally in spelling, were corrected. The omissions included Mark Noble's preface, and the more vituperative references to parishioners. In a letter to Carr, the typist expressed her interest in the book:

> I....was more and more struck as I went on with the extraordinary amount of knowledge Mr. Noble had gathered. His work is a most interesting study of his own character....the parts you directed me to omit I did not read, so I did not come across anything unpleasant except in one or two isolated passages all of which I have forgotten.

The final letter, dated 8th June 1904, is from Buttanshaw to Carr, confirming that the book had arrived back safely, and expressing pleasure that he had had a copy made for the parish of all that was interesting.

When the typing was done, extracts and pedigrees relating to the Amhurst family were sent by request to Lord Amherst (formerly Amhurst) of Hackney, who contributed to the cost of the work.

The typed MSS, running to 370 pages, were bound into one volume, the copies of pedigrees into another. On the flyleaf of the main volume the rector inscribed:

> I desire that this Book with the accompanying Vol. of Pedigrees and the sketches, should be in the keeping of the successive Rectors of Barming, for the Church and Parish.
>
> November 16, 1905
> T.W. Carr.

The two volumes were placed in the church chest, made by a former churchwarden out of the oak pulpit from which Mark Noble had preached.

Mark Noble Buttanshaw died on 1st August 1904. He had been a solicitor and well known resident of Blackheath. The original MSS passed to his brother, the Reverend George Buttanshaw (1839–1907), Vicar of Allerton, Bradford. After his death they became the property of his nephew Charles Buttanshaw, who presented them to the Maidstone Museum in February 1924. They are now held by the Centre for Kentish Studies, Maidstone.

The typescript has remained in the possession of successive rectors of Barming, and is now kept in the rectory. At some time the accompanying volume of pedigrees, and the sketches, were given to the Maidstone Museum or its successors, and are now held with the original MSS by the Centre for Kentish Studies.

The foregoing information is based on correspondence, papers and inscriptions in the *Barming Manuscripts*.

Appendix B

The Cresswell Collection of Paintings and Drawings in the Care of the London Borough of Enfield

The collection, comprising almost 200 works by John Cresswell (1818–92), and just two by his daughter Henrietta (1855–1931), is kept at the Forty Hall Museum, Forty Hill, Enfield. The pictures are not on open display, though a few are framed and have been hung previously at Broomfield House, Palmers Green, formerly the Southgate Local Museum.

John Cresswell did not sign his pictures, but they have been authenticated by Henrietta as her father's work. The collection is discussed in Chapter 6, and its presentation to the Southgate Local Museum is referred to in Chapter 9. The subjects and dates of the pictures are analysed in this appendix. Generally the items are well preserved, few having been exposed to extensive daylight. About 30 per cent are in excellent or good condition, about 40 per cent fair, and the remainder suffer from varying degrees of staining, fading or tearing. The pencil drawings are the most vulnerable to these conditions.

A small number of paintings and drawings by John Cresswell and his daughter, known to have been amongst those given to the Southgate Local Museum, are not now in the collection at Forty Hall.

Pictures from the collection have been reproduced in various places from time to time, principally in:

> Henrietta Cresswell, *Winchmore Hill: Memories of a Lost Village*, 1912 (as half-tones only).
> *Dr. Cresswell's Winchmore Hill*, London Borough of Enfield, 1980 (watercolours reproduced in colour).
> Various issues of *The Palmers Green and Southgate Gazette* and *The Enfield Gazette and Observer*, especially 1924–37.

1. Pictures by John Cresswell, by Subject

(Modern place names are used first)

Winchmore Hill:

	Watercolours	Washes	Drawings
Barrowell Green	2	4	5
Broad Walk (Winchmore Hill Wood)		5	3
Bush Hill			1
Church Hill	2	1	4
Compton Road		1	2
Eversley Park Road (Cock Hill)	1		5
Firs Lane	1	3	5
Ford's Grove/Farm Road		7	11
Grange Park (Pike's Fields)			2
Green Dragon Lane	6	2	9
Green Lanes			3
Highfield Road	2	4	8
Hoppers Road (incl. Highfield Park)	4	7	14
Station Road (Middle Lane)	5	2	4
Vicars Moor Lane			1
Wades Hill	3	1	2
Winchmore Hill Road			1

	Watercolours	Washes	Drawings
Winchmore Hill (continued):			
World's End Lane	1	1	2
People			1
Edmonton:			
Angel Road			3
Bury Street	3		3
Church Street	2		
Silver Street	2	2	1
Palmers Green:			
Bourne Hill	1	2	2
Broomfield Lane			1
Fox Lane	3	3	2
Green Lanes		1	
Hazelwood Lane			2
Oakthorpe Road		1	1
Powys Lane	1	1	1
Tottenhall Road			1
Southgate:			
Waterfall Lane		1	
Elsewhere:			
Epping Forest		1	1
Goff's Oak			1
Greenwich Park	1		
Waltham Abbey			2
Wood Green	1		
Unidentified			1
Total	**41**	**50**	**105**

2. Pictures by John Cresswell, by Date

(Dating is approximate in many cases)	Watercolours	Washes	Drawings
1840–1849	4	3	5
1850–1859	4	5	9
1860–1869	15	24	46
1870–1879	11	10	8
1880–1889	4		4
Undated	3	8	33
Total	**41**	**50**	**105**

3. Pictures by Henrietta Cresswell

Only two examples survive in the Forty Hall collection, both of Winchmore Hill:

Watercolour (signed *HC* and dated):
        Roseville, the Green, 26th November 1870

Engraving:
        Gable of Winchmore Hill Station, from Grove Lodge, *c*.1875

Index

A GENEALOGY OF THE CRESSWELLS OF WINCHMORE HILL
AND RELATED FAMILIES, 1666-1965

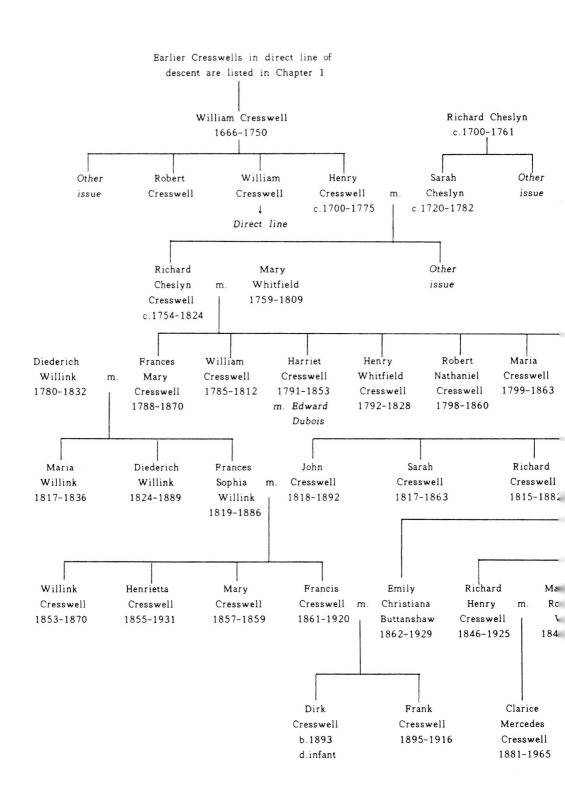

Earlier Cresswells in direct line of
descent are listed in Chapter 1

William Cresswell
1666-1750

Richard Cheslyn
c.1700-1761

Other
issue

Robert
Cresswell

William
Cresswell
↓
Direct line

Henry
Cresswell
c.1700-1775

m.

Sarah
Cheslyn
c.1720-1782

Other
issue

Richard
Cheslyn
Cresswell
c.1754-1824

m.

Mary
Whitfield
1759-1809

Other
issue

Diederich
Willink
1780-1832

m.

Frances
Mary
Cresswell
1788-1870

William
Cresswell
1785-1812

Harriet
Cresswell
1791-1853
*m. Edward
Dubois*

Henry
Whitfield
Cresswell
1792-1828

Robert
Nathaniel
Cresswell
1798-1860

Maria
Cresswell
1799-1863

Maria
Willink
1817-1836

Diederich
Willink
1824-1889

Frances
Sophia
Willink
1819-1886

m.

John
Cresswell
1818-1892

Sarah
Cresswell
1817-1863

Richard
Cresswell
1815-188.

Willink
Cresswell
1853-1870

Henrietta
Cresswell
1855-1931

Mary
Cresswell
1857-1859

Francis
Cresswell
1861-1920

m.

Emily
Christiana
Buttanshaw
1862-1929

Richard
Henry
Cresswell
1846-1925

m.

Ma
Ro
V
184

Dirk
Cresswell
b.1893
d.infant

Frank
Cresswell
1895-1916

Clarice
Mercedes
Cresswell
1881-1965

A GENEALOGY OF THE CRESSWELLS OF WINCHMORE HILL
AND RELATED FAMILIES, 1666-1965

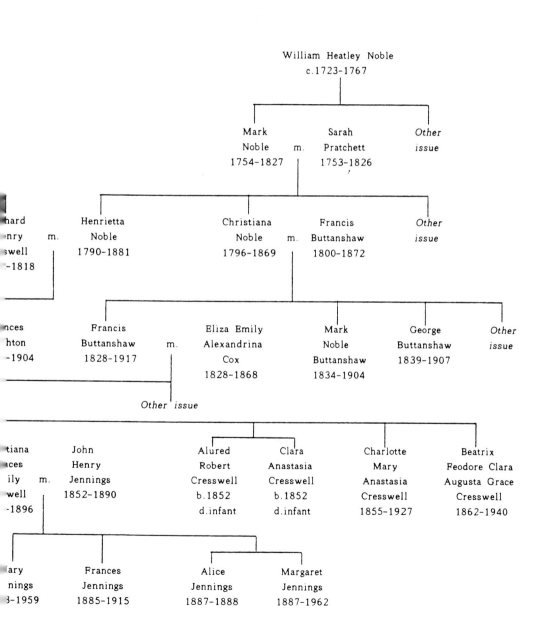